普通高等教育规划教材

物流工程专业英语

（第二版）

李晓霞　主编

人民交通出版社股份有限公司
China Communications Press Co.,Ltd.

内 容 提 要

本书为普通高等教育规划教材,系统地介绍了物流基本概念、供应链重要问题、物流活动、物流经济、客户服务及物流分析方法、物流信息系统基础、电子时代物流、供应链信息模式、企业运作、通信技术、各种运输模式、公铁空海运输、多式联运及港口堆场设施布局与运作、仓库管理、物流搬运、库存管理、调度、采购、业务外包与场站布局、物料搬运装备、提升机械、举升机械、桥式起重机、自动导引车及堆垛机、准时制、精益生产与六西格玛、供应商管理库存、联合管理库存、高效客户响应、协作性计划、预测和补给、敏捷供应链、标杆管理、逆向物流以及全球一体化物流等内容。为读者提供了丰富的现代物流,尤其是物流工程方面的专业英语知识。

本教材可作为物流工程专业本科生的教材,也可作为物流管理、交通运输、汽车服务工程、工业工程、机械工程、市场营销等相关专业的双语教材或教学参考书,同时还可供具有一定英语基础的物流相关行业管理人员、技术人员参阅。

图书在版编目(CIP)数据

物流工程专业英语/李晓霞主编. —2版. —北京:
人民交通出版社股份有限公司,2017.8
ISBN 978-7-114-13987-1

Ⅰ.①物… Ⅱ.①李… Ⅲ.①物流管理—英语 Ⅳ.
①F252

中国版本图书馆 CIP 数据核字(2017)第 183468 号

书　　名:	物流工程专业英语(第二版)
著　作　者:	李晓霞
责任编辑:	曹　静
出版发行:	人民交通出版社股份有限公司
地　　址:	(100011)北京市朝阳区安定门外外馆斜街3号
网　　址:	http://www.ccpress.com.cn
销售电话:	(010)59757973
总 经 销:	人民交通出版社股份有限公司发行部
经　　销:	各地新华书店
印　　刷:	北京市密东印刷有限公司
开　　本:	787×1092　1/16
印　　张:	14.75
字　　数:	349 千
版　　次:	2007 年 9 月　第 1 版 2017 年 8 月　第 2 版
印　　次:	2017 年 8 月　第 2 版　第 1 次印刷　累计第 2 次印刷
书　　号:	ISBN 978-7-114-13987-1
定　　价:	32.00 元

(有印刷、装订质量问题的图书由本公司负责调换)

PREFACE 第二版前言

用飞速发展来描述当今的物流业一点儿都不为过,物流已越来越成为国民经济发展的重要支柱,受到各国政府的普遍重视和支持。

本版博采最新物流领域资料和文献,涉及物流学、物流信息技术、供应链、物流技术装备、运输、仓储、采购、规划布局、物流管理等方面的基础知识及研究焦点,主要突出系统性和工程特点,对学习掌握专业英语以及相关课程知识起到启发和加强作用。

全书共分为6部分:物流基础知识、信息技术、货物运输、其他主要物流活动、物流机械与装备、发展趋势。每部分由4单元组成,每单元分为2节,每节包括正文、生词与词组以及注释。大多数单元、节的内容相互独立,根据教学计划和学时,可适当选择有关单元和章节。为方便使用,书末按照英语字母次序排列了全书生词和词组。

本书由长安大学李晓霞主编,杨京帅、邱兆文、胡卉、高扬、赵娇参编。其中:Unit1~4由胡卉编写,Unit5~8由杨京帅编写,Unit9~11由邱兆文编写,Unit13~16由高扬编写,Unit17~20由李晓霞编写,Unit12及Unit21~24由赵娇编写。全书由李晓霞统稿。

编写过程中,参考引用了国内外大量文献资料,长安大学本科生王安、研究生马冰山、王志祥、许佳瑜、梁娜、高冲、张静波、马海、章云娜、李健民、刘佳浩、张绪祥等同学做了大量的整理工作,对此谨深表谢意。

岁月更迭,推陈出新。然谬误难免,敬请各位批评指正!欢迎联系wlgcx@chd.edu.cn。

编 者
2017年春月于古城西安

CONTENTS 目 录

Part 1 Basic Knowledge

Unit 1 ··· 3
  Passage A Basic Concept ··· 3
  Passage B Major Supply Chain Issues ································· 6
Unit 2 ·· 10
  Passage A What is Logistics ··· 10
  Passage B Logistics Activities ·· 12
Unit 3 ·· 16
  Passage A Logistics in the Economy ································ 16
  Passage B Logistics in the Firm ······································· 18
Unit 4 ·· 22
  Passage A Customer Service ·· 22
  Passage B Techniques of Analysis ··································· 25

Part 2 Information Technology

Unit 5 ·· 31
  Passage A Logistics Information System Functionality ······· 31
  Passage B Logistics in E-Commerce Age ·························· 36
Unit 6 ·· 42
  Passage A Supply Chain Information System Modules (Ⅰ) ··· 42
  Passage B Supply Chain Information System Modules (Ⅱ) ··· 47
Unit 7 ·· 51
  Passage A Enterprise Operations (Ⅰ) ································ 51
  Passage B Enterprise Operations (Ⅱ) ································ 56
Unit 8 ·· 62
  Passage A Communication Technology (Ⅰ) ······················ 62

Passage B	Communication Technology (Ⅱ)	67

Part 3   Freight Transportation

Unit 9			75
Passage A	Modes of Transportation		75
Passage B	Road Transport		79
Unit 10			83
Passage A	Rail Transport		83
Passage B	Air Transport		86
Unit 11			90
Passage A	Ocean Shipping		90
Passage B	Intermodal Transportation		93
Unit 12			97
Passage A	Terminal Structure and Handling Equipment		97
Passage B	Storage and Stacking Logistics		100

Part 4   Other Key Logistics Activities

Unit 13			105
Passage A	Warehouse Management		105
Passage B	Material Handling		108
Unit 14			113
Passage A	Inventory Management (Ⅰ)		113
Passage B	Inventory Management (Ⅱ)		117
Unit 15			123
Passage A	Scheduling		123
Passage B	Procurement		127
Unit 16			132
Passage A	Outsourcing Considerations		132
Passage B	Facility Location		135

Part 5   Logistics Machine and Equipment

Unit 17			141
Passage A	Material Handling Equipment (Ⅰ)		141

Passage B	Material Handling Equipment (Ⅱ)	145

Unit 18 ... 150
Passage A	Hoisting Machines	150
Passage B	Elevating Machines	156

Unit 19 ... 161
Passage A	Up and Away with Overhead Cranes	161
Passage B	Containerization	164

Unit 20 ... 170
Passage A	Automated Guided Vehicle (AGV)	170
Passage B	Palletizers: Man Versus Machine	174

Part 6 Recent Trends

Unit 21 ... 181
Passage A	Just-in-time (JIT)	181
Passage B	Lean Thinking and Six Sigma	183

Unit 22 ... 186
Passage A	Vendor Managed Inventory (VMI) and Joint Managed Inventory (JMI)	186
Passage B	Efficient Consumer Response (ECR) and Collaborative Planning, Forecasting and Replenishment (CPFR)	188

Unit 23 ... 191
Passage A	The Agile Supply Chain	191
Passage B	Benchmarking	193

Unit 24 ... 197
Passage A	Reverse Logistics	197
Passage B	Global Integrated Logistics	200

Vocabulary ... 203

References ... 227

Part 1　Basic Knowledge

Unit 1
Unit 2
Unit 3
Unit 4

Unit 1

Passage A Basic Concept

Supply chain management is not a brand new concept, and it represents the third phase of an evolution that started in the 1960s with the development of the physical distribution concept that focused on the outbound side of a firm's logistics system.[1] A number of studies during the 1950s and 1960s indicated the potential of the systems concept. The focus of physical distribution was on total systems cost and analyzing tradeoff scenarios to arrive at the best or lowest system cost. During the 1980s, the logistics or integrated logistics management concept developed in a growing number of organizations. Logistics, in its simplest form, added inbound logistics to the outbound logistics of physical distribution.

Supply chain management came into vogue during the 1990s and continues to be a focal point for making organizations more competitive in the global marketplace. Supply chain management can be viewed as a pipeline or conduit for the efficient and effective flow of products/materials, services, information, and financials from the supplier's suppliers through the various intermediate organizations/companies out to the customer's customers or the system of connected networks between the original vendors and the ultimate final consumer.[2] The extended enterprise perspective of supply chain management represents a logical extension of the logistics concept providing an opportunity to view the total system of interrelated companies for increased efficiency and effectiveness.[3]

The definition of supply chain management is broad and comprehensive; therefore, demand and value are very relevant as well as synchronization of flows through the pipeline or supply chain.[4] Thus, it could be argued that supply chain, demand chain, value network, value chains, etc., can be used as synonyms. Also, there appears to be a more widespread use and acceptance of the term supply chain management.

Figure 1-1 presents a simplified, linear example of a hypothetical supply chain. Real-world supply chains are usually more complex than this example because they may be nonlinear and/or have more supply chain participants. Also, this supply chain does not adequately portray the importance of transportation in the supply chain.

The three flows enumerated at the bottom of the illustration are very important to the success of supply chain management. The top flow—products and related services—has traditionally been an important focus of logisticians and is still an important element in supply chain management.

Customers expect their orders to be delivered in a timely, reliable, and damage-free manner, and transportation is critical to this outcome. Figure 1-1 also indicates that product flow is a two-way flow in today's environment because of the growing importance of reverse logistics systems for returning products that are unacceptable to the buyer, because they are damaged, obsolete, or worn out.[5]

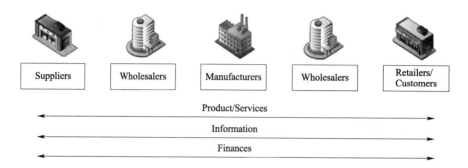

Figure 1-1 Integrated supply chain system

The second flow is the information flow, which has become an extremely important factor for success in supply chain management. Inventory can be eliminated from the supply chain by timely, accurate information about demand. If point-of-sale (POS) data were available from the retail level on a real-time basis, it would help to mitigate the bullwhip effect associated with supply chain inventories and could significantly reduce cost. Note that the illustration also indicates a two-way flow for information.

The third and final flow is financials or, more specifically, cash. Traditionally, financial flow has been viewed as one-directional—backward—in the supply chain. A major impact of supply chain compression and faster order cycle times has been faster cash flow. The faster cash-to-cash cycle or order-to-cash cycle has been a bonanza for companies because of the impact on working capital. Cash flow measures have become an important metric of the financial markets to gauge the viability or vulnerability of companies.

Supply chain management provides organizations with an opportunity to reduce cost (improve efficiency) and improve customer service (effectiveness). However, certain issues or challenges must be addressed before supply chain management will be successful.

New Words and Expressions

1. chain [tʃein]   n. 链,束缚,枷锁
2. outbound ['autbaund]   adj. 开往外地的,开往外国的,出厂的
3. indicate ['indikeit]   vt. 表明,指出,预示,象征
4. tradeoff ['treidˌɔːf]   n. 交换,(公平)交易,折中,权衡,协定
5. scenario [siˈnɑːriəu]   n. 方案,情节,剧本,设想
6. integrate ['intigreit]   vt. 使成整体,使一体化
                           vi. 结合

7. integrated logistics　　　　　　　　一体化物流
8. logistics management　　　　　　　物流管理
9. inbound ['inbaund]　　　　　　　　*adj.* 入境的,回内地的,内部的,入厂的,文中指原料采购物流
10. vogue [vəug]　　　　　　　　　　*n.* 时尚,流行,时髦
　　　　　　　　　　　　　　　　　　adj. 时髦的,流行的
11. marketplace ['mɑːkɪtpleɪs]　　　　　*n.* 市场,商场,市集
12. efficient [ɪ'fɪʃənt]　　　　　　　　*adj.* (直接)生效的,有效率的,能干的
13. effective [ɪ'fektɪv]　　　　　　　　*adj.* 有效的,被实施的
14. material [mə'tɪərɪəl]　　　　　　　*n.* 材料,物料,原料,素材,布,织物,适当人选
15. supplier [sə'plaɪə(r)]　　　　　　*n.* 供应商,供应国,供应者,供给者,补充者
16. perspective [pə'spektɪv]　　　　　*n.* 观点,远景,透视图
　　　　　　　　　　　　　　　　　　adj. 透视的
17. synchronization [ˌsɪŋkrənaɪ'zeɪʃn]　*n.* 同步,同一时刻,使时间互相一致,同时
18. pipeline ['paɪplaɪn]　　　　　　　*n.* 管道,输油管道,渠道,传递途径
　　　　　　　　　　　　　　　　　　v. (通过管道)运输,传递,为……安装管道
19. synonym ['sɪnənɪm]　　　　　　　*n.* 同义词
20. hypothetical [ˌhaɪpəʊ'θetɪkəl]　　　*adj.* 假想,假设的,假定的,有前提的,猜想的
21. reliable [rɪ'laɪəbl]　　　　　　　　*adj.* 可靠的,可信赖的
22. obsolete [ˌɑːbsə'liːt]　　　　　　　*adj.* 过时的,老式的,废弃的
23. inventory ['ɪnvəntɔːri]　　　　　　*n.* 库存,存货清单
24. POS (point-of-sale)　　　　　　　零售点
25. bullwhip effect　　　　　　　　　牛鞭效应
26. reverse [rɪ'vəːs]　　　　　　　　　*n.* 背面,相反,倒退,失败
　　　　　　　　　　　　　　　　　　vt. (使)反转;(使)颠倒;调换,交换;[法]撤销,推翻
　　　　　　　　　　　　　　　　　　vi. 倒退,[桥牌]逆叫
　　　　　　　　　　　　　　　　　　adj. 反面的,颠倒的,反身的
27. reverse logistics　　　　　　　　　逆向物流
28. financial [faɪ'nænʃl]　　　　　　　*adj.* 金融的,财政的,财务的
29. backward ['bækwəd]　　　　　　*adj.* 向后的,反向的,发展迟缓的
　　　　　　　　　　　　　　　　　　adv. 向后地,相反地
30. bonanza [bəʊ'nænzə]　　　　　　*n.* (突然的)财,意想不到的幸运,富矿脉
31. viability [ˌvaɪə'bɪləti]　　　　　　*n.* 生存(存活)能力,发育能力,生活力
32. vulnerability [ˌvʌlnərə'bɪləti]　　　*n.* 易损性,弱点
33. vendor ['vendə]　　　　　　　　*n.* 卖主,小贩,供应商,[贸易] 自动售货机

Notes

[1] Supply chain management is not a brand new concept, and it represents the third phase of an

evolution that started in the 1960s with the development of the physical distribution concept that focused on the outbound side of a firm's logistics system.

供应链管理不是一个全新的概念，它代表始于 20 世纪 60 年代的专注于企业物流系统外部的实物配送概念的发展进化的第三个阶段。

[2] Supply chain management can be viewed as a pipeline or conduit for the efficient and effective flow of products/materials, services, information, and financials from the supplier's suppliers through the various intermediate organizations/companies out to the customer's customers or the system of connected networks between the original vendors and the ultimate final consumer.

供应链管理可以看作是一条管道或通道，该管道或通道将产品流/物料流、服务流、信息流和资金流高效而有效地从供应商的供应商处通过各种中间组织机构/公司传递到客户的客户手中，或被看作是最初的供应商与最终的客户之间的网络连接系统。

[3] The extended enterprise perspective of supply chain management represents a logical extension of the logistics concept providing an opportunity to view the total system of interrelated companies for increased efficiency and effectiveness.

供应链管理所延伸的企业视角代表物流概念上的一种逻辑延伸，该物流概念为高效益和高效率地查看相关公司组成的整个系统提供了机会。

[4] The definition of supply chain management is broad and comprehensive; therefore, demand and value are very relevant as well as synchronization of flows through the pipeline or supply chain.

供应链管理的定义是广泛而全面的；因此，需求和价值以及供应链中各种流的同步都是非常相关的。

[5] Figure 1-1 also indicates that product flow is a two-way flow in today's environment because of the growing importance of reverse logistics systems for returning products that are unacceptable to the buyer, because they are damaged, obsolete, or worn out.

图 1-1 也表明在当今环境下，由于购买者因产品损坏、过期或破损不接受而退换产品所形成的逆向物流日益增长的重要性，产品流是一种双向流。

Passage B Major Supply Chain Issues

The challenge to develop and sustain an efficient and effective supply chain(s) requires organizations to address a number of issues.

The network facilities (plants, distribution centers, terminals, etc.) and the supporting transportation services have long been considered important. Companies and other organizations need a network system that is capable and flexible to respond and change with the dynamics of the marketplace whether in the short run or the long run.[1]

Globalization and consolidation in supply chains have caused an increased complexity for organizations in terms of customer/supplier locations, transportation requirements, trade regulations, taxes, etc.. Companies need to take steps to simplify, as much as possible, the various aspects of their supply chains.

Two interesting characteristics of supply chains are that inventory is often duplicated along the chain and the bullwhip effect arises. Consequently, supply chain management provides an opportunity to reduce inventory levels. Coordination or integration can help reduce inventory levels on horizontal (one firm) and/or vertical (multiple firms) levels in the supply chain. Strategies such as compression and postponement can also have a positive impact. Inventory deployment is a very important issue for supply chains because of the associated cost and related opportunities for increased efficiency.

The technology and communication systems today lead to the collection and storage of vast amounts of data, but interestingly enough, organizations may not be taking advantage of the abundant data to develop information systems to improve decision making.[2] The accumulation and storage of data unless they are shared horizontally and vertically in the supply chain and used to make better decisions about inventory, customer service, transportation, etc., are almost useless. Information can be a powerful tool if it is timely, accurate, managed, and shared. It can be a substitute for inventory because it can reduce uncertainty. The latter is one of the major causes of higher inventory levels because it leads to the accumulation of safety stock.

Frequent reference has been made in this section to efficiency (cost) and effectiveness (value). A challenge for supply chains is the prevention of suboptimization. In today's environment, global supply chains compete against global supply chains, which means that the cost and value at the very end of the supply chain are what is important.

Supply chain management emphasizes a horizontal process orientation that necessitates collaboration with external vendors, customers, transportation companies, third-party logistics (3PLs), and others in the supply chain.[3] In other words, internal collaboration or cooperation with marketing, sales, operations/manufacturing, and accounting/finance are very important as well as collaboration or cooperation with external organizations. Communication is critical to explain the opportunities for system tradeoffs that will make the supply chain more competitive.

Most organizations have measures of performance or metrics in place to analyze and evaluate their efficiency and progress over different time periods. Sometimes, such measures are used for setting baseline performance objectives or expected outcomes, e.g., orders filled and shipped per day.

Technology can be viewed as a change driver, but it is also important as a facilitator of change that will lead to improved efficiency and effectiveness. The challenge is to evaluate and successfully implement the technology to make the improvements desired. The technology available today is almost overwhelming, but analysis and planning are necessary to achieve the expected outcomes.

Transportation can be viewed as the glue that makes the supply chain model function. The critical outcomes of the supply chain are to deliver the right product, at the right time, in the right quantity and quality, at the right cost, and to the right destination.[4] Transportation plays an important role in making these "rights" happen.

Safe, reliable delivery of products to customers is expected of the supply chain. Globalization has obviously increased the risk of interruptions or shutdowns of supply chains. Consequently, organizations must be prepared in case of disruptions. Such risks have changed some of the planning and preparation for supply chains that often include some type of scenario analysis that can consider possible threats, assess probabilities, and plan for alternatives.[5]

New Words and Expressions

1. dynamic [daɪˈnæmɪk]   n. 动态,动力
   adj. 动态的,动力的,动力学的,有活力的
2. consolidation [kənsɒliˈdeɪʃən]   n. 巩固,合并,团结
3. location [loˈkeʃən]   n. 位置,地址,地点,外景拍摄场地
4. coordination [kəʊˈɔːdineiʃən]   n. 协调,调和,对等,同等
5. duplicate [ˈdjuːplɪkət]   vt. 重复,复制,复印
   adj. 复制的,副本的,完全一样的
6. coordinate [kəʊɔːrdneti]   v. 协调,整合
7. integration [ɪntɪˈgreɪʃ(ə)n]   n. 集成,综合,整合,一体化,结合,(不同、种族、宗教信仰等的人的)混合
8. storage [ˈstɔːrɪdʒ]   n. 存储,贮存,储存处
9. horizontal [ˌhɔriˈzɒntəl]   n. 水平线,水平面,水平位置,水平的物体
   adj. 横向的,水平的,卧式的,地平线的
10. vertical [ˈvəːtɪkəl]   n. 垂直线,垂直面,竖杆,垂直位置
    adj. 垂直的,竖立的,头顶的,顶点的
11. postponement [pəˈspəʊnmənt]   n. 延期,推迟,延缓,延期的事
12. deployment [diˈplɔɪmənt]   n. 调度,部署
13. accumulation [əˌkjuːmjuˈleɪʃən]   n. 积聚,累积,堆积物
14. substitute [ˈsʌbstitjuːt]   n. 代用品,代替者
    vi. 替代,代替
15. compete [kəmˈpiːt]   vi. 竞争,比赛,对抗
16. necessitate [niˈsesiteit]   vt. 使……成为必要,需要,强迫,迫使
17. external [ɪkˈstɜːnl]   adj. 外部的,表面的,[药] 外用的,外国的,外面的
    n. 外部,外观,外面
18. manufacturing [ˌmænjuˈfæktʃərɪŋ]   adj. 制造的,制造业的
    n. 制造业,工业,制造
    v. 制造,生产(manufacture 的 ing 形式)
19. facilitator [fəˈsiliteitə]   n. 服务商,促进者,帮助者
20. implement [ˈɪmplɪmənt]   n. 实施,执行

21. overwhelming [ˌəʊvəˈwelmɪŋ]   *adj.* 势不可挡的,压倒一切的,巨大的
22. delivery [dɪˈlɪvəri]   *n.* 递送,交付,分娩,交货,引渡
23. interruption [ˌɪntəˈrʌpʃən]   *n.* 中断,打断,障碍物,打岔的事
24. shutdown [ˈʃʌtdaʊn]   *n.* 关机,停工,关门,停播
25. disruption 英 [dɪsˈrʌpʃn]   *n.* 分裂,瓦解;破裂,毁坏;中断
    美 [dɪsˈrʌpʃn]
26. alternative [ɔːlˈtɜːnətɪv]   *n.* 二中择一,供替代的选择
    adj. 供选择的,选择性的,交替的,替代的,备选的,
          其他的,另类的

Notes

[1] Companies and other organizations need a network system that is capable and flexible to respond and change with the dynamics of the marketplace whether in the short run or the long run.
公司和其他组织机构需要一个网络系统,该(网络)系统能够在短期运营或长期运营中灵活地随着市场的动态性而响应和变化。that is…为定语从句,whether…or…译为:或……或……,不管……还是……。

[2] The technology and communication systems today lead to the collection and storage of vast amounts of data, but interestingly enough, organizations may not be taking advantage of the abundant data to develop information systems to improve decision making.
如今的技术和通信系统导致大量数据被收集和存储,但有趣的是,组织机构却没能利用大量丰富的数据来开发信息系统以改善决策。

[3] Supply chain management emphasizes a horizontal process orientation that necessitates collaboration with external vendors, customers, transportation companies, third part logistics (3PLs), and others in the supply chain.
供应链管理强调与外部供应商、客户、运输公司、第三方物流企业以及供应链中其他成员需要相互协作的横向流程。

[4] The critical outcomes of the supply chain are to deliver the right product, at the right time, in the right quantity and quality, at the right cost, and to the right destination.
供应链的关键结果是在正确的时间、以正确的数量和质量、按合理的成本把正确的产品运送到正确的地点。

[5] Such risks have changed some of the planning and preparation for supply chains that often include some type of scenario analysis that can consider possible threats, assess probabilities, and plan for alternatives.
这样的风险已经改变了供应链的一些规划和准备工作,通常包括能考虑一些可能的威胁、评估概率以及可替代方案的不同类型的远景方案分析。

Unit 2

Passage A What is Logistics

The term logistics has become much more widely recognized by the general public in the last 20 years. However, there is still confusion about its definition. Logistics management is the most widely accepted term and encompasses logistics not only in the private business sector but also in the public/government and nonprofit sectors.[1]

For the purposes of this text, the definition offered by the Council of Supply Chain Management Professionals (formerly the Council of Logistics Management) is utilized. However, it is important to recognize that logistics owes its origins to the military, which has long recognized the importance of logistics activities for national defense.[2] The military definition of logistics encompasses supply items (food, fuel, spare parts) as well as personnel.

The logistics concept began to appear in the business-related literature in the 1960s under the label of physical distribution, which had a focus on the outbound side of the logistics system. The business sector approach to logistics developed into inbound logistics (materials management to support manufacturing) and outbound logistics (physical distribution to support marketing) during the 1970s and 1980s. Then, in the 1990s, the business sector began to view logistics in the context of a supply or demand chain that linked all of the organizations from the supplier's supplier to the customer's customer. Supply chain management requires a collaborative, coordinated flow of materials and goods through the logistics systems of all the organizations in the network.

In the 21st century, logistics should be viewed as a part of management and has four subdivisions.

Business logistics: that part of the supply chain process that plans, implements, and controls the efficient, effective flow and storage of goods, service, and related information from point of use or consumption in order to meet customer requirements.[3]

Military logistics: the design and integration of all aspects of support for the operational capability of the military forces (deployed or in garrison) and their equipment to ensure readiness, reliability, and efficiency.

Event logistics: the network of activities, facilities, and personnel required to organize, schedule, and deploy the resources for an event to take place and to efficiently withdraw after the event.

Service logistics: the acquisition, scheduling, and management of the facilities/assets, personnel, and materials to support and sustain a service operation or business.

All four subdivisions have some common characteristics and requirements such as forecasting, scheduling, and transportation, but they also have some differences in their primary purpose.[4] All four, however, can be viewed in a supply chain context; that is, upstream and downstream other organizations play a role in their overall success and long-run viability.

A general definition of logistics that could be used that appears to encompass all four subdivisions is as follows. Logistics is the process of anticipating customer needs and wants; acquiring the capital, materials, people, technologies, and information necessary to meet those needs and wants; optimizing the good- or service-producing network to fulfill customer requests; and utilizing the network to fulfill customer requests in a timely manner.[5]

Five principal types of economic utility add value to a product or service. Included are form, time, place, quantity, and possession. Generally, production activities are credited with providing form utility; logistics activities with time, place, and quantity utilities; and marketing activities with possession utility.

Form utility refers to the value added to goods through a manufacturing or assembly process. In today's business environment, certain logistics activities can also provide form utility. Logistics provides place utility by moving goods from production surplus points to points where demand exists. Logistics creates place utility primarily through transportation. Logistics creates time utility through proper inventory maintenance, the strategic location of goods and services, and transportation. Logistics creates quantity utility through production forecasting, production scheduling, and inventory control. Possession utility is primarily created through the basic marketing activities related to the promotion of products and services.

New Words and Expressions

1. sector ['sektə]　　　　　　　*n.* 部分,部门,环节,扇形
2. military ['militəri]　　　　　*n.* 军队,军人,军事
　　　　　　　　　　　　　　　adj. 军事的,军人的,战争的
3. confusion [kən'fju:ʒən]　　　*n.* 混乱,混淆,困惑
4. encompass [in'kʌmpəs]　　　*vt.* 围绕,包围,包含或包括某事物,完成
5. literature ['litərətʃə]　　　　*n.* 文学,文献,著作
6. context ['kɔntekst]　　　　　*n.* 语境,上下文,背景,环境
7. subdivision [ˌsʌbdi'viʒən]　　*n.* 分支,细分,一部
8. acquisition [ˌækwi'ziʃ(ə)n]　*n.* 获得物,获得,收购
9. asset ['æset]　　　　　　　　*n.* 资产,财产
10. scheduling ['ʃedju:əliŋ]　　*n.* 行程安排,时序安排,排时间表,调度
11. forecast ['fɔ:kɑ:st]　　　　*vt.* 预报,预测,预示
　　　　　　　　　　　　　　　n. 预测,预报,预想
　　　　　　　　　　　　　　　vi. 进行预报,作预测;forecasting 是动名词或现在分词

12. upstream ['ʌp'striːm]   adv. 逆流地,向上游
                              adj. 向上游的,逆流而上的
                              n. 上游部门
13. utilize ['juːtilaiz]   vt. 利用,适用,运用
14. in a timely manner   及时地
15. location [ləˈkeiʃən]   n. 位置,地址,地点,外景拍摄场地

Notes

[1] Logistics management is the most widely accepted term and encompasses logistics not only in the private business sector but also in the public/government and nonprofit sectors.
物流管理是被最广泛接受的术语,不仅包括私营企业部门的物流,也包括公共/政府和非营利部门的物流。

[2] However, it is important to recognize that logistics owes its origins to the military, which has long recognized the importance of logistics activities for national defense.
然而,重要的是认识到物流起源于军事,长期以来已经认识到物流活动对国防的重要性。It is important to recognize that…是强调句;which 代表前面整个句子。

[3] Business logistics: that part of the supply chain process that plans, implements, and controls the efficient, effective flow and storage of goods, service, and related information from point of use or consumption in order to meet customer requirements.
商业物流:供应链流程中的计划、实施和控制货物高效而有效的流动与存储服务,以及为了满足客户需求的来自使用或消费角度的相关信息。

[4] All four subdivisions have some common characteristics and requirements such as forecasting, scheduling, and transportation, but they also have some differences in their primary purpose.
所有四个不同分支都有一些共同的特点和要求,如预测、调度和运输,但在其主要目的方面也存在一些差异。

[5] Logistics is the process of anticipating customer needs and wants; acquiring the capital, materials, people, technologies, and information necessary to meet those needs and wants; optimizing the good- or service-producing network to fulfill customer requests; and utilizing the network to fulfill customer requests in a timely manner.
物流是预测客户需求和想法的过程;是为了满足这些需求和想法而获取必要资金、物料、人员、技术和信息的过程;是为了满足客户的需求而优化货物生产或服务生产网络的过程;以及利用网络及时地满足客户需求的过程。

Passage B　Logistics Activities

The development of interest in logistics after World War II contributed to the growth in activities associated with logistics. Given the scope of this growth, it is worthwhile to discuss these activities and their relationship to logistics.

Part 1 Basic Knowledge

Transportation is a very important activity in the logistics system and is often the largest variable logistics cost. A major focus in logistics is on the physical movement or flow of goods and on the network that moves the product. The network is composed of transportation organizations that provide service for the shipping firm.

A second area, which has a tradeoff relationship with transportation, is storage. Storage involves two separate, but closely related, activities: inventory management and warehousing. A direct relationship exists between transportation and the level of inventory and number of warehouses required. A number of important decisions are related to storage activities (inventory and warehousing), including how many warehouses, how much inventory, where to locate the warehouses, what size the warehouses should be, and so on.[1]

A third area of interest to logistics is industrial (exterior) packaging. Industrial packaging protects the product during transportation and storage and includes materials such as corrugated (cardboard boxes), stretch wrap, banding, bags, and so on. The type of transportation mode selected affects packaging requirements.

A fourth area to be considered is materials handling. Materials handling is important in warehouse design and efficient warehouse operations. Materials handling is concerned with mechanical equipment used for short-distance movement and includes equipment such as conveyors, forklift trucks, overhead cranes, and automated storage and retrieval systems (ASRS).[2]

A fifth area to examine is that of inventory control. It has two dimensions: assuring adequate inventory levels and certifying inventory accuracy. Assuring adequate inventory levels requires logistics to monitor current inventory levels and either place replenishment orders or schedule production to bring inventory levels up to a predetermined level.[3] Another dimension of inventory control is certifying inventory accuracy, which is essential for assuring that customers' orders are filled complete and on time.

Another activity area that logistics might control is order fulfillment, which generally consists of activities involved with filling and shipping customer orders. Order fulfillment is important to logistics because an important physical distribution factor is the time that elapses from when a customer places an order until the customer receives a satisfactory fulfillment of the order. This is also referred to as lead time.

Another activity important to the logistics area is inventory forecasting. Accurate forecasting is essential to inventory control, manufacturing efficiency, and customer satisfaction. This is particularly true in organizations that use a just-in-time (JIT) or material requirements planning (MRPI, more details see Unit15) approach to controlling inventories.

Another area of growing interest for logistics managers is production planning/scheduling, which is closely related to forecasting in terms of effective inventory control. Once a forecast is developed and the current inventory on hand and usage rate are determined, production managers can calculate the number of units to manufacture to ensure adequate market coverage.[4]

Procurement is another activity that can be included in logistics. Two dimensions of customer service are important to logistics: the process of interacting directly with the customer to influence or take the order and the levels of service an organization offers to its customers.[5]

Other areas might be considered a part of logistics. Areas such as parts and service support, return goods handling, and salvage and scrap disposal indicate the reality of logistics activities managed in organizations producing consumer durables or industrial products.

New Words and Expressions

1. worthwhile[ˌwəːθˈwail]　　　　　　　adj. 有价值的,值得的,值得花时间的
2. warehouse[ˈweəhaʊs]　　　　　　　n. 仓库,货栈,大商店,批发商店,福利库
　　　　　　　　　　　　　　　　　　vt. 储入仓库,以他人名义购进(股票)
3. corrugated[ˈkɔrəgeitid]　　　　　　adj. 波纹的,波纹状的,波纹面的
4. stretch wrap　　　　　　　　　　　拉伸膜,收缩膜
5. conveyor[kənˈveiə(r)]　　　　　　　n. 运送者,传送者,传达者,(财产)转让人,输送机,运输机
6. forklift[ˈfɔːklɪft]　　　　　　　　　n. 叉车,铲车,堆高机,叉式升降机
　　　　　　　　　　　　　　　　　　v. 用铲车搬运
7. crane[krein]　　　　　　　　　　　n. 鹤,吊车,起重机
　　　　　　　　　　　　　　　　　　vt. 伸长,探头
　　　　　　　　　　　　　　　　　　vi. 迟疑,踌躇
8. overhead crane　　　　　　　　　　桥式起重机
9. retrieval[rɪˈtriːvəl]　　　　　　　　v. 检索,收回,挽回
10. ASRS (automated storage and retrieval systems)　　自动存储与分拣系统
11. adequate[ˈædikwit]　　　　　　　adj. 充足的,适当的,胜任的
12. replenishment[riˈpleniʃmənt]　　　n. 补充,补给,库存补充,补货
13. predetermine[ˈpriːdiˈtəːmin]　　　vt. 预先确定,预先决定,预先查明
14. dimension[diˈmenʃən]　　　　　　n. 尺寸,尺度,维度
15. fulfillment[fulˈfilmənt]　　　　　　n. 实现,完成,满足,实施过程
16. lead time　　　　　　　　　　　　前置时间,提前期(即订货至交货的时间)
17. JIT(just-in-time)　　　　　　　　准时制,准时送货
18. MRP(material requirements planning)　物料需求计划
19. coverage[ˈkʌvəridʒ]　　　　　　　n. 保险总额,承保范围
20. procurement[prəʊˈkjuəmənt]　　　n. 采购,获得,取得

Notes

[1] A number of important decisions are related to storage activities (inventory and warehousing), including how many warehouses, how much inventory, where to locate the warehouses, what size the warehouses should be, and so on.

许多重要的决策都与存储活动有关(库存和仓储),包括仓库数量、库存高低、仓库选址、仓库大小等。

[2] Materials handling is concerned with mechanical equipment used for short-distance movement and includes equipment such as conveyors, forklift trucks, overhead cranes, and automated storage and retrieval systems (ASRS).

物料搬运涉及用于短距离移动的机械设备,也包括如输送机、叉车、吊车、自动存储与分拣系统(ASRS)这样的设备。

[3] Assuring adequate inventory levels requires logistics to monitor current inventory levels and either place replenishment orders or schedule production to bring inventory levels up to a predetermined level.

保证足够的库存水平需要物流来监控当前库存水平以及下订单补货或安排生产使库存水平达到预定的水平。

[4] Once a forecast is developed and the current inventory on hand and usage rate are determined, production managers can calculate the number of units to manufacture to ensure adequate market coverage.

一旦进行了预测,且当前库存及其使用率被确定,生产管理者就能够计算出要生产的数量以确保市场覆盖面。

[5] Two dimensions of customer service are important to logistics: the process of interacting directly with the customer to influence or take the order and the levels of service an organization offers to its customers.

客户服务的两个维度对物流是很重要的:直接与客户进行交互的过程以影响或接受订单和组织机构提供给客户的服务水平。

Unit 3

Passage A Logistics in the Economy

The overall, absolute cost of logistics on a macro basis will increase with growth in the economy. In other words, if more goods and services are produced, logistics costs will increase. To determine the efficiency of the logistics system, total logistics costs need to be measured in relationship to gross domestic product (GDP), which is a widely accepted barometer used to gauge the rate of growth in the economy.[1]

Logistics costs as a percent of GDP have declined since 1985 from 12.3% to 9.9% in 2006. In fact, logistics costs were closer to 20% of GDP in the early to mid-1970s. The low point occurred in 2003 with logistics costs being 8.6% of GDP. A modest increase in inventory costs starting in 2004 coupled with a larger increase in transportation costs caused the percentage to increase for 2005 and 2006. The reduction in logistics cost as a percent of GDP has resulted from a significant improvement in the overall logistics systems of the organizations operating in the economy.[2] This reduction in relative cost allows organizations to be more competitive since it directly impacts the cost of producing goods.

Some additional understanding of logistics costs can be gained by examining the three major cost categories included in this cost, including warehousing and inventory costs, transportation costs, and other logistics costs.[3] Warehousing costs are those associated with the assets used to hold inventory. Inventory costs are all the expenses associated with holding goods in storage. Carrying costs include interest expense (or the opportunity cost associated with the investment in inventory), risk-related costs (obsolescence, depreciation), and service-related costs (insurance, taxes). Transportation costs are the total national expenditures for the movement of freight. The third category of logistics costs is the administrative and shipper-related costs associated with managing logistics activities and personnel.

In addition to the managerial focus on managing inventory and transportation more efficiently, the total logistics system has received increased attention. It certainly appears that U.S. managers have realized the power of the message delivered by Peter Drucker in an article written in Fortune in 1962.

Distribution is one of the most sadly neglected but most promising areas of American business. We know little more about distribution today than Napoleon's contemporaries knew about the interior of Africa. We know it is there, and we know it is big; and that is about all. Most of our present concepts focus on production or on the stream of money and credit, rather than on the flow of physical goods and its economic characteristics. To get control of distribution, therefore, it requires seeing and managing it as a distinct dimension of business and as a property of product and process rather than as a collection of technical jobs. The industrial purchaser has to know his own business. He has to know what the product he buys is supposed to contribute to his company's end results. The purpose is to point to distribution as an area where intelligence and hard work can produce substantial results for business. Above all, there is a need for a new orientation — one that gives distribution the importance in business design, business planning, and business policy its costs warrant.

The two largest cost categories in any organization's logistics system are transportation and inventory costs. As indicated, transportation is usually the single largest variable cost in any logistics system. It is worth noting here because logistics management requires examining the total cost of logistics, not just one cost such as transportation.

Also worth noting is that one of the most frequent tradeoffs in logistics systems in an organization is between transportation and inventory costs.[4] For example, an organization might be willing to pay much higher rates for air freight service because of the savings it will experience in inventory costs. In making this tradeoff evaluation, organizations are using a systems approach to arrive at the lowest total cost solution.[5]

New Words and Expressions

1. absolute['æbsəluːt] *adj.* 绝对的,完全的,专制的
   n. 绝对,绝对事物
2. barometer[bə'rɔmitə] *n.* 晴雨表,气压计,显示变化的事物,标记
3. GDP(gross domestic product) 国内生产总值
4. gauge[geidʒ] *vt.* (用仪器)测量,评估,判断,采用
   n. 评估,测量的标准或范围,尺度,标准,测量仪器,铁路轨距,标准尺,规格
5. couple['kʌp(ə)l] *n.* 对,夫妇,数个
   vt. 连接,连合
6. expense[ik'spens] *n.* 损失,代价,消费,开支
   vt. 向……收取费用
7. obsolescence[ɔbsə'lesns] *n.* 废弃,陈旧,过时,[生物]退化,荒废
8. investment[in'vestmənt] *n.* 投资,投资额,(时间、精力的)投入,封锁
9. depreciation[di͵priːʃi'eiʃən] *n.* 折旧,货币贬值,跌价
10. expenditure[iks'penditʃə] *n.* 花费,支出,费用,经费,(金钱的)支出额,(精力、时间、材料等的)耗费
11. category['kætəgɔːri] *n.* 类型,种类,部门,类别
12. substantial[səb'stænʃ(ə)l] *adj.* 大量的,实质的,内容充实的

               n. 本质,重要材料
13. administrative [əd'ministrətiv]   *adj.* 管理的,行政的,行政勤务的

Notes

[1] To determine the efficiency of the logistics system, total logistics costs need to be measured in relationship to gross domestic product (GDP), which is a widely accepted barometer used to gauge the rate of growth in the economy.

为确定物流系统的效率,总物流成本与国内生产总值(GDP)的关系需要被衡量,GDP 是一个被广泛接受的用于衡量经济增长速度的晴雨表。

[2] The reduction in logistics cost as a percent of GDP has resulted from a significant improvement in the overall logistics systems of the organizations operating in the economy.

物流成本占 GDP 百分比的下降已显著改善了整个物流系统中组织机构在经济方面的运营。

[3] Some additional understanding of logistics costs can be gained by examining the three major cost categories included in this cost, including warehousing and inventory costs, transportation costs, and other logistics costs.

通过检查该成本所包括的仓储与库存成本、运输成本以及其他物流成本三种主要成本类型,可以获得一些对物流成本额外的理解。

[4] Also worth noting is that one of the most frequent tradeoffs in logistics systems in an organization is between transportation and inventory costs.

也值得注意的是,在一个组织机构的物流系统中最频繁的权衡之一是运输成本与库存成本之间的权衡。

[5] In making this tradeoff evaluation, organizations are using a systems approach to arrive at the lowest total cost solution.

在进行权衡评估时,组织机构正在使用一种系统方法以达到总成本最低的解决方案。

Passage B Logistics in the Firm

  Another dimension of logistics is the micro perspective, which examines the relationships between logistics and other functional areas in an organization—marketing, manufacturing/operations, finance and accounting, and others.[1] Logistics, by its nature, focuses on processes that cut across traditional functional boundaries, particularly in today's environment with its emphasis on the supply chain. Consequently, logistics interfaces in many important ways with other functional areas.

  A classic interface between logistics and manufacturing relates to the length of the production run. Manufacturing economies are typically associated with long production runs with infrequent manufacturing line setups or changeovers. These long runs, however, easily result in higher inventory levels of certain finished products and limited supplies of others. Thus, the ultimate manufacturing decision requires managers to carefully weight the advantages and disadvantages of long versus short production runs and their impacts on inventories.[2] The trend today is toward "pull" systems, manufacturing/logistics systems where the product is "pulled" in response to demand as opposed to being "pushed" in advance of demand. This practice lowers inventory levels, which can lower total logistics costs.

The interface between logistics and manufacturing is becoming more critical, given recent interest in the procurement of raw materials and components from offshore sources.[3] Also, many organizations today are making arrangements with third-party manufacturers, "co-packers", or contract manufacturers to produce, assemble, or enhance some or all of the organization's finished products.

Logistics is sometimes referred to as the other half of marketing. The physical distribution or outbound side of an organization's logistics system is responsible for the physical movement and storage of products for customers and thus plays an important role in selling a product.[4] In some instances, physical distribution and order fulfillment might be the key variables in selling a product; that is, the ability to provide the product at the right time to the right place in the right quantities might be the critical element in making a sale.

The following briefly discusses the interfaces between logistics and marketing activities in the principal area of the marketing mix. The material is organized according to the four elements of marketing, including price, product, promotion, and place.

From a logistics perspective, adjusting quantity prices to conform to shipment sizes appropriate for transportation organizations might be quite important. Organizations selling products also typically provide a discount schedule for larger purchase quantities. If such discount schedules relate to transportation rate discount schedules in terms of weight, then both the shipper and customer might be able to reduce total transportation cost. Although it is not always possible to adjust prices to meet transportation weight breaks and to have a quantity convenient to manage, organizations should investigate such alternatives. In addition, the logistics manager might be interested in the volume sold under different price schedules because this will affect inventory requirements, replenishment times, and other aspects of customer service.

Another decision frequently made in the marketing area concerns products, particularly their physical attributes. Their size, shape, weight, packaging, and other physical dimensions affect the ability of the logistics system to move and store them. However, keep in mind that collaboration can allow the logistics manager to provide input about the repercussions in these situations. Another marketing area that affects logistics is consumer packaging. The marketing manager often regards consumer packaging as a "silent" salesperson. The physical dimensions and the protection aspects of consumer packages affect the logistics system in the areas of transportation, materials handling, and warehousing.

Promotion is a marketing area that receives much attention in an organization. A further analysis is necessary on the relationship between increasing sales and promotional strategies and their effect on the logistics area. Manufacturers frequently compete to get distribution channels to give their products the sales effort they feel their products deserve. Organizations can attempt to improve their sales by "pulling" their products through the distribution channel with national advertising. The other basic approach is the "push" method. Implied in the push approach is collaboration with the channels of distribution to stimulate customer sales. Arguments can be made both for and against these two approaches. Most organizations combine the two approaches in their promotional efforts.

The place decision refers to the distribution channels decision and thus involves both transactional and physical distribution channel decisions. Marketers typically become more involved in making decisions about marketing transactions and in deciding such things as whether to sell a product to wholesalers or to deal directly with retailers. From the logistics manager's perspective, such decisions might significantly affect logistics system requirements.

Perhaps the most significant trend is that marketers have begun to recognize the strategic value of place in the marketing mix and the increased revenues and customer satisfaction that might result from excellent logistics service. As a result, many organizations have recognized customer service as the interface activity between marketing and logistics and have aggressively and effectively promoted customer service as a key element of the marketing mix.[5]

While manufacturing and marketing are probably the two most important internal, functional interfaces for logistics in a product-oriented organization, there are other important interfaces. The finance area has become increasingly important during the last decade. Increasingly, Chief Financial Offers (CFOs) in organizations have become very knowledgeable about logistics because of the impact that it can have on key financial metrics such as Return on Assets (ROA) or Return on Investment (ROI)[6]. On the other hand, logistics managers have to justify increased investment in logistics-related assets using acceptable financial parameters related to "payback" periods.

Accounting is also an important interface for logistics. Accounting systems are also critical for measuring supply chain tradeoffs and performance.

New Words and Expressions

1. interface ['intəfeis]　　　　　n. 界面,[计算机]接口,交界面
　　　　　　　　　　　　　　　vi. 接合,连接,[计算机]使联系,相互作用,交流,交谈
2. changeover ['tʃeindʒ,əuvə]　　n. 转换,逆转,(方针的)转变
3. weight [weit]　　　　　　　　n. 重量,体重,重担,重任,重要,[统]权,加重值,权重
　　　　　　　　　　　　　　　vt. 加重于,使变重,使负重,使负担或压迫,[统]使加权,
　　　　　　　　　　　　　　　　　附加加重值于
4. versus ['və:səs]　　　　　　　prep. 对,与……相对,对抗
5. component [kəm'pəunənt]　　adj. 组成的,构成的
　　　　　　　　　　　　　　　n. 成分,组件,电子元件,[数]要素,组分,零件
6. offshore ['ɔf'ʃɔ:]　　　　　　 adj. 离岸的,海外的,近海的,吹向海面的
7. be responsible for　　　　　　负责
8. play an important role in　　 在……起着非常重要的作用

9. infrequent [ɪnˈfrikwənt]　　　　　　　n. 罕见的,稀少的
10. appropriate [əˈprəʊprɪət]　　　　　adj. 适当的,恰当的,合适的
　　　　　　　　　　　　　　　　　　　v. 占用,拨出
11. transaction [trænˈzækʃən]　　　　　n. 交易,事务,办理,会报,学报
12. aggressively [əˈgresivli]　　　　　　adv. 积极地,大胆地,侵略地,攻击地
13. revenue [revinjuː]　　　　　　　　　n. 收入,国家的收入,税收
14. cut across　　　　　　　　　　　　 打断,冲破,穿过,跨越,贯穿,与……相抵触
15. ROA（Return on Assets）　　　　　资产回报率
16. ROI（Return on Investment）　　　投资回报率

Notes

[1] Another dimension of logistics is the micro perspective, which examines the relationships between logistics and other functional areas in an organization—marketing, manufacturing/operations, finance and accounting, and others.
物流的另一个维度是微观视角,微观视角考察一个组织机构中物流与其他功能领域——营销、制造/运营、财会及其他——之间的关系。

[2] Thus, the ultimate manufacturing decision requires managers to carefully weight the advantages and disadvantages of long versus short production runs and their impacts on inventories.
因此,最终的生产决策就要求管理者仔细加权长期与短期生产运行之间的优缺点,及其对库存的影响。

[3] The interface between logistics and manufacturing is becoming more critical, given recent interest in the procurement of raw materials and components from offshore sources.
鉴于最近从海外采购原材料和部件的兴起,物流和制造之间的接口变得越来越重要。

[4] The physical distribution or outbound side of an organization's logistics system is responsible for the physical movement and storage of products for customers and thus plays an important role in selling a product.
实物配送或一个组织机构的物流系统出站端是负责客户们的产品的实体移动与存储,因此在产品销售中起着非常重要的作用。

[5] As a result, many organizations have recognized customer service as the interface activity between marketing and logistics and have aggressively and effectively promoted customer service as a key element of the marketing mix.
因此,许多组织机构已经认识到要把客户服务作为市场营销与物流之间的接口活动,并且已经积极并有效地把客户服务作为市场营销组合的一个重要因素得以促进。

[6] Increasingly, Chief Financial Offers (CFOs) in organizations have become very knowledgeable about logistics because of the impact that it can have on key financial metrics such as Return on Assets (ROA) or Return on Investment (ROI).
因为物流会对某些关键财务指标产生影响,如资产回报率(ROA)或投资回报率(ROI),越来越多的组织机构的首席财务官(CFOs)已具备非常渊博的物流知识。

Unit 4

Passage A Customer Service

Customer service is the support you offer your customers — both before and after they buy your product — that helps them have an easy and enjoyable experience with you. It is often said that it is cheaper to keep existing customers than to find new ones. And it is true: bad customer service is a key driver of churn. Prioritizing customer support helps you attract and retain quality customers.

Customer service is critical to competing effectively. In the past, people chose which companies they did business with based on price or brand, but today the overall experience is the driver. Customer support is a major driver of customer experience, but only if you expand the role of your support team beyond the purely reactive role many of them play today.[1] When support agents are empowered to go above-and-beyond with customers, or have a helpdesk solution that makes it easy for them to upsell or cross-sell relevant services, they can create winning experiences that help you stand out from the competition.

Customers are willing to pay more for a better experience. Focusing on the customer experience is not just the latest trend — it is also smart business. Surveys have shown that 86% of consumers would pay more for a better customer experience. You may decide to tier your customer base if some are willing to pay more for premium experiences, including support, early access to features, or other benefits.[2]

The two dimensions of customer service are important to logistics. From an order-taking perspective, logistics is concerned with having adequate inventory levels in the proper locations to meet the customer's order requirements.[3] Also, logistics is concerned with being able to promise the customer, at the time the order is placed, when the order will be delivered. This requires coordination among inventory control, manufacturing, warehousing, and transportation to guarantee that any promises made when the order is taken as to delivery time and product availability will be kept.[4]

The second dimension of customer service relates to the levels of service the organization promises its customers. These service levels might include order fill rates and on-time delivery rates. Decisions about inventories, transportation, and warehousing relate to customer service levels. While the logistics area does not usually completely control customer service decisions, logistics plays an extremely important role in ensuring that the customer gets the right product at the right time in the right quantity.[5] Logistics decisions about product availability and lead time are critical to customer service.

Customer service must be synchronized with evolving customer demands. With changing market dynamics and technology advancements, customer demands have transformed posing a new set of challenges for logistics operators to tackle. The demand for logistics services are likely to increase during sale periods and holiday seasons with the increasing number of orders, especially with 3PL providers.

Many logistics operators cite standard KPIs (on-time delivery and order fill rate) to validate exceptional customer service. Others, however, insist customer service, falls into its own category and deserves its own standards of measurement. These standards of measurements are the actual proof of customer service to review and analyze agent performance. Managers and supervisors can now generate reports on real-time or historical data that implicates strategic decisions, training and coaching.

The role of customer service in logistics supply chain systems will continue to change. Therefore, the need to improve logistics customer service to consumers is greater than ever before. Increasing customer service raises customer satisfaction and increased customer satisfaction improves corporate performance.

The following is the concept of international logistics. The role of international logistics in the global supply chain mirrors that of logistics in the domestic environment. International logistics professionals focus on the tactical aspects of the global supply chain, those activities that are inherent to the movement of goods and paperwork from one country to another, those activities that constitute the basis for export and import activities and operations.

The definition of logistics provided by the Council of Supply Chain Management Professionals can therefore be logically modified to define international logistics by including the elements of the international environment.

International logistics is the process of planning, implementing, and controlling the flow and storage of goods, services, and related information from a point of origin to a point of consumption located in a different country. The emphasis of international logistics is therefore on the creation of internal processes and strategies.

New Words and Expressions

1. churn[tʃəːn]   *n.* 客户流失量,客户更替数
2. empower[im'pauə]   *vt.* 授权,允许,使能够
3. helpdesk['helpdesk]   *n.* 帮助台,技术支持中心,售后服务部门
4. upsell['ʌpsel]   *vi.* 向上促销,增销
5. tier[tiə]   *n.* 等级,阶梯座位等的一排,一行,一层,捆扎装置
                 vt. 层层排列,使层叠,堆积成层,堆叠,堆垛(货)
6. premium['priːmiəm]   *n.* 额外费用,奖金,保险费,溢价

	adj. 高价的,优质的
7. access ['ækses]	*v.* 使用,存取,接近
	n. 进入,使用权,通路
8. order fill rate	订单完成率,订单交付率
9. synchronize ['sɪŋkrənaɪz]	*vi.* 使……合拍,使……同步,同步,同时发生
10. guarantee [ˌgærən'tiː]	*n.* 保证,保证书,担保,抵押品
	vt. 保证,担保
11. mirror ['mɪrə(r)]	*v.* 反射,反映
	n. 镜子,反光镜,真实的写照,反映,借鉴,榜样
12. tactical ['tæktɪkəl]	*adj.* 战术的,策略上的,巧妙设计的,有谋略的,策略(高明)的,善于机变的
13. inherent [ɪn'hɪərənt]	*adj.* 固有的,内在的,与生俱来的

Notes

[1] Customer support is a major driver of customer experience, but only if you expand the role of your support team beyond the purely reactive role many of them play today.

客户支持是客户体验的一个主要驱动力,但是只有超越你的支持团队今天所起着的纯粹反应性的作用,你才能扩展你的支持团队的作用。

[2] You may decide to tier your customer base if some are willing to pay more for premium experiences, including support, early access to features, or other benefits.

如果有人愿意为高级体验支付更多费用,包括支持、提前使用功能、其他益处,你可以决定对你的客户群进行分级。

[3] From an order-taking perspective, logistics is concerned with having adequate inventory levels in the proper locations to meet the customer's order requirements.

从订单奏效的角度来看,物流关注的是在适当的地点有足够的库存水平以满足客户的订单要求。

[4] This requires coordination among inventory control, manufacturing, warehousing, and transportation to guarantee that any promises made when the order is taken as to delivery time and product availability will be kept.

这就需要在库存控制、生产制造、仓储以及运输之间进行协调,以保证在提交订单时给予客户的关于交货时间和产品可用性的所有承诺都将被兑现。

[5] While the logistics area does not usually completely control customer service decisions, logistics plays an extremely important role in ensuring that the customer gets the right product at the right time in the right quantity.

虽然物流领域通常不能完全控制客户服务决策,但物流在确保客户在正确的时间获得正确数量的正确产品上发挥着极其重要的作用。

Passage B Techniques of Analysis

This section mainly analyzes two aspects of logistics technology: on the one hand is the total cost analysis techniques for logistics, while on the other hand is about the location analysis.

Only two basic models are examined. One general approach to total cost analysis for logistics is known as short-run analysis. In a short-run analysis, a specific point in time, or level of production, is chosen and costs are developed for the various logistics cost centers described previously. Multiple short-run analyses would be considered and then the system with the lowest overall cost would be selected, as long as it was consistent with constraints the organization imposed on the logistics area. Some authors refer to this short-run analysis as static analysis. Essentially, they are saying that this method analyzes costs associated with a logistics system's various components at one point in lime or one output level. While short-run analysis concentrates on specific time or level of output, dynamic analysis examines a logistics system over a long lime period or range of output.

A particular organization might consider more than two logistics systems at one time. Many examples show an organization considering three or sometimes four systems. The same basic methodology can be used for graphing and mathematically solving for the points of indifference regardless of how many systems are analyzed.

Mathematical programming methods, which are, classified as optimization techniques, are one of the most widely used strategic and tactical logistics planning tools.[1] Linear programming, one of the most common techniques used for location analysis, selects the optimal supply chain design from a number of available options while considering specific constraints.

An optimization model considers the aggregate set of requirements from the customers, the aggregate set of production possibilities for the producers, the potential intermediary points, the transportation alternatives and develops the optimal system.[2] To solve a problem using linear programming, several conditions must be satisfied. First, two or more activities or locations must be competing for limited resources. Second, all pertinent relationships in the problem structure must be deterministic and capable of linear approximation. While linear programming is frequently used for strategic logistics planning, it is also applied to operating problems such as production assignment and inventory allocation.

One of the most widely used forms of linear programming for logistics problems is network consisting of nodes, which comprises manufacturer, supplier, warehouse, distribution center and wholesalers, and so on. Beyond the basic consideration for all analytical techniques, network optimization has specific advantages and disadvantages that both enhance and reduce its application for logistics analyses. The traditional disadvantages of network optimization have been the size of the problem that can be solved and the inclusion of fixed cost components.

Mixed-integer programming is the other optimization technique successfully applied to logistics problems. The formulation offers considerable flexibility, which enables it to incorporate many of the complexities and idiosyncrasies found in logistics applications.[3] The primary advantage of the mixed-integer format is that fixed as well as different levels of variable cost can be included in the analysis.

These optimization approaches provide effective tools for analysis of location-related issues such as facility location, optimum product flow, and capacity allocation.

A second location analysis method is static simulation. The term simulation can be applied to almost any attempt to replicate a situation.

Static simulation evaluates product flow as if all occurred at a single point during the year. In this sense, the primary difference between static and dynamic simulation is the manner in which time-related events are treated.[4] Whereas dynamic simulations evaluate system performance across time, static simulation makes no attempt to consider the dynamics between time periods. Static simulation seeks to project the outcome of a specified plan or course of future action.

A major benefit of static simulation is the flexibility in the distribution channel alternatives that can be evaluated. Static simulation heuristics can be designed to consider lowest total cost, maximum service, or a combination of the two in the algorithm that assigns markets to distribution centers.[5]

The main advantage of static simulation is that it is simpler, less expensive to operate, and more flexible than most optimization techniques. The replication capabilities of a static simulator create almost unlimited design possibilities. Unlike mathematical programming approaches, simulation does not guarantee an optimum solution. However, static simulation offers a very flexible tool that many be used to evaluate a wide range of complex channel structures.

New Words and Expressions

1. consistent [kən'sɪstənt]　　　　　adj. 一致的,连续的,不矛盾的,坚持的
2. optimal ['ɑːptɪməl]　　　　　　　adj. 最佳的,最优的,最理想的
3. aggregate ['æɡrɪɡət]　　　　　　vt. 集合,聚集,使积聚,合计
　　　　　　　　　　　　　　　　　　n. 合计,聚集体,骨料,集料(可成混凝土或修路等用的)
　　　　　　　　　　　　　　　　　　adj. 总数的,总计的,聚合的,[地]聚成岩的
4. intermediary [ˌɪntə'miːdiəri]　　　adj. 中间的,媒介的,中途的,调解的,居间的
　　　　　　　　　　　　　　　　　　n. 媒介,中间人,调解人,仲裁者,中间阶段
5. pertinent ['pɜːtɪnənt]　　　　　　adj. 有关的,相干的,恰当的,中肯的,切题的
6. deterministic [dɪˌtɜːmɪ'nɪstɪk]　　adj. 确定性的,决定性的,命中注定的
7. approximation [əˌprɒksɪ'meɪʃən]　n. 接近,近似值,粗略估计
8. comprise [kəm'praɪz]　　　　　　v. 包含,由……组成
9. facility [fə'sɪləti]　　　　　　　　n. 设施,设备,容易,灵巧
10. flexibility [ˌfleksə'bɪləti]　　　　n. 弹性,适应性,机动性,灵活性
11. heuristics [hjuə'rɪstɪk]　　　　　n. 启发(法),启发式算法,探索法

12. replication [ˌrepliˈkeiʃən] 　　　　n. 复制,折叠,重复,回答,反响
13. algorithm [ˈælgəriðəm] 　　　　　n. 算法,运算法则
14. expensive [ikˈspensiv] 　　　　　adj. 昂贵的,花钱的
15. linear programming 　　　　　　线性规划

Notes

[1] Mathematical programming methods, which are, classified as optimization techniques, are one of the most widely used strategic and tactical logistics planning tools.
归类为优化技术的数学规划方法,是使用最为广泛的战略战术物流规划工具之一。

[2] An optimization model considers the aggregate set of requirements from the customers, the aggregate set of production possibilities for the producers, the potential intermediary points, the transportation alternatives and develops the optimal system.
一个优化模型考虑到来自客户需求的聚合集以及针对生产者、潜在的中间点、运输备选方案的产品可能性的聚合集,并开发出最优系统。

[3] The formulation offers considerable flexibility, which enables it to incorporate many of the complexities and idiosyncrasies found in logistics applications.
该方法提供了可观的灵活性,使其能够合并在物流应用中所发现的许多复杂性和特质。

[4] Static simulation evaluates product flow as if all occurred at a single point during the year. In this sense, the primary difference between static and dynamic simulation is the manner in which time-related events are treated.
静态仿真评估产品流就好像一年中的产品流都发生在一个单一的时间点上。从这个意义上讲,静态模拟和动态模拟之间的主要区别是对与时间相关的事件的处理方式。

[5] Static simulation heuristics can be designed to consider lowest total cost, maximum service, or a combination of the two in the algorithm that assigns markets to distribution centers.
静态仿真启发式算法可以被设计成考虑总成本最低化、服务最大化,或者把市场营销划归到配送中心的两者(总成本最低化和服务最大化)相结合的算法。

Part 2　Information Technology

Unit 5
Unit 6
Unit 7
Unit 8

Unit 5

Passage A Logistics Information System Functionality

Supply chain information systems initiate activities and track information regarding processes; facilitate information sharing both within the firm and between supply chain partners, and assist in management decision-making.

From its inception, logistics focused on product storage and flow through the distribution channel. Information flow and accuracy was often overlooked because it was not viewed as being critical to customers. In addition, information transfer rates were limited by the speed of paper. There are four reasons why timely and accurate information has become more critical for effective logistics systems design and operations. Firstly, customers perceive information about order status, product availability, delivery schedule, shipment tracking and invoices as necessary elements of total customer service.[1] Customers demand access to real time information. Secondly, with the goal of reducing total supply chain assets, managers realize that information can be used to reduce inventory and human resource requirements. In particular, requirements planning using the most current information can reduce inventory by minimizing demand uncertainty. Thirdly, information increases flexibility with regard to how, when, and where resources may be utilized to gain strategic advantage. Fourthly, enhanced information transfer and exchange capability utilizing the internet is changing relationships between buyers and sellers and redefining channel relationships.

Supply chain information systems (SCIS) are the thread that links logistics activities into an integrated process. The integration builds on four levels of functionality: (1) transaction systems, (2) management control, (3) decision analysis, and (4) strategic planning. Figure 5-1 illustrates logistics activities and decisions at each level of information functionality. As the pyramid shape suggests, management control, decision analysis and strategic planning enhancements require a strong transaction systems foundation.

A transaction system is characterized by formalized rules, procedures, and standardized communications; a large volume of transaction; and an operational, day-to-day focus. The combination of structured processes and large transaction volume places a major emphasis on information system efficiency. At the most basis level, transaction system initiates and records individual logistics activities and their outcomes. Transaction activities include order entry, inventory assignment, order selection, shipping, pricing, invoicing, and customer inquiry.[2] For example, customer order entry represents a transaction that enters a customer request for product into the information system. The order entry transaction initiates a second transaction as inventory is assigned to the order. A third transaction is then generated to direct warehouse operations to select or pick the order from the warehouse storage location. A fourth transaction initiates transport of the order to the customer. The final transaction develops the invoice and records an account receivable. Throughout the process, the firm and customer expect the availability of real time information regarding order status. Thus, the customer order performance cycle is completed through a series of information system transactions.

Figure 5-1　Information functionality

The second SCIS level, management control, focuses on performance measurement and reporting. Performance measurement is necessary to provide management feedback regarding supply chain performance and resource utilization. Common performance measures include cost, customer service, productivity, quality, and asset management measures. As an example, specific performance measures include transaction and warehousing cost per pound, inventory turnover, case fill rate, cases per labor hour, and customer perception.

While it is necessary that SCIS report historical system performance, it is also necessary for the system to identify operational exceptions. Management exception information is useful to highlight potential customer order or operational problems. For example, proactive SCIS should be capable of identifying future inventory shortages based on forecasted requirements and planned inventory. Management exception reporting should also be capable of identifying potential transportation, delivery warehouse, or labor requirements that exceed capacity limitations. While some control measures, such as cost, are well defined; other measures, such as customer service and quality, are less specific. For example, customer service can be measured internally, from the enterprise's perspective, or externally, from the customer's perspective. While internal measures are relatively easy to track; external measures are more difficult to obtain since they require monitoring performance regarding specific customers.

The third SCIS level, decision analysis, focused on software tools to assist managers in identifying, evaluating, comparing supply chain and logistics strategic and tactical alternatives for improved effectiveness. Typical analyses include supply chain design, inventory management, resource allocation, routing, and segmental profitability.[3] Decision analyses SCIS must also include database maintenance, modeling analysis, and reporting over a wide range of potential logistics situations. Similar to management control, decision includes some tactical analysis considerations such as vehicle routing and warehouse planning. Decision analysis applications are also being used to manage customer relationships by determining the trade-offs associated with having satisfied and successful customers. Because the decision analysis is used to guide future operations and needs to be unstructured and flexible to allow consideration of a wide range of alternatives, users require more expertise and training to benefit from its capability.

Strategic planning, the final SCIS level, organizes a synthesized transaction data into a wide range of business planning and decision-making models that assist in evaluating the probabilities and payoffs of various strategies. Essentially, strategic planning focused on information support to develop and refine supply chain and logistics strategy. These decisions are often extensions of decision analyses but are typically more abstract, are even less structured, and have a longer-term focus. Examples of strategic planning decisions include the desirability of strategic alliances, development and refinement of manufacturing capabilities, as well as market opportunities related to customer responsiveness.

Figure 5-2 illustrates relative SCIS development costs and benefits. The left side of the figure illustrates development and maintenance characteristics while the right side reflects benefits. Development and maintenance costs include hardware, software, communications, training, and personnel expenses.

In general, a solid base requires significant SCIS investments for transaction systems. Transaction system costs are high due to the large number of system users, heavy data communications requirements, high transactions volume, and significant software complexity.[4] Transaction systems costs are also relatively well defined and exhibit more certainty and limited payoff with respect to benefits or returns. A comprehensive transaction system does not provide a substantial competitive advantage in today's environment; it is a competitive requirement. Virtually all firms that are still in business have made substantial investments to achieve transaction system efficiency. Therefore, while the investment is substantial, the relative return is often quite small. High level systems, such as management control, decision analysis, and strategic planning typically require fewer hardware and software resources but often involve greater uncertainty and risk with regard to potential system benefits.

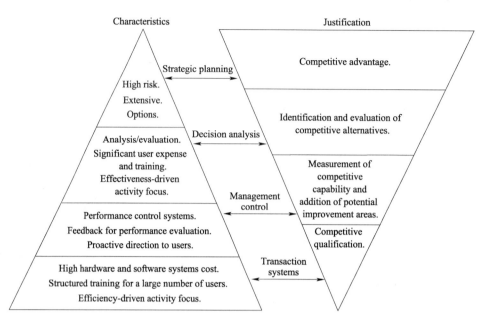

Figure 5-2 SCIS usage, decision characteristics, and justification

Management control and decision analysis systems, on the other hand, focus on providing insight into problem processes and alternatives. For example, benchmarking management control systems can identify processes where a firm lags behind competitors while external customer service audits may identify opportunities for selective, customer-focused programs.[5] Finally, strategic planning systems with the ability to assess supply chain design, customer/profitability, segment contribution, or alliance benefits can have a major impact on enterprise profitability and competitiveness even though they are not particularly hardware or software intensive.[6]

In the past, most systems development focused on improving transaction system efficiency. While these investments offered returns in terms of speed and lower operating costs, anticipated cost reductions have often been elusive. SCIS development and implementation now focus on enhanced supply chain system integration and more effective decision-making.

New Words and Expressions

1. facilitate [fəˈsiliteit]　　　　　　　　vt. 促进，帮助，使容易
2. assist [əˈsist]　　　　　　　　　　　n. 帮助，助攻
　　　　　　　　　　　　　　　　　　v. 参加，出席，帮助，促进
3. inception [inˈcepʃən]　　　　　　　　n. 起初，获得学位
4. real time　　　　　　　　　　　　　实时
5. SCIS (supply chain information systems)　供应链信息系统
6. pyramid [ˈpirəmid]　　　　　　　　　n. 角锥，棱锥，金字塔，叠罗汉
　　　　　　　　　　　　　　　　　　v. (使)成金字塔状，(使)渐增，(使)上涨
7. feedback [ˈfiːdbæk]　　　　　　　　　n. 反馈，反应
8. proactive [prəˈæktiv]　　　　　　　　adj. 前摄的；积极主动的；主动出击的；先发制人的

9. tactical ['tæktikəl] *adj.* 战术的,策略上的,巧妙设计的,有谋略的,策略(高明)的,善于机变的
10. synthesize ['sinθisaiz] *v.* 综合,合成
11. alliance [ə'laiəns] *n.* 联盟,联合
12. comprehensive [ˌkɔmpri'hensiv] *adj.* 综合的,广泛的,有理解力的
13. responsiveness [ris'pɔnsivnis] *n.* 响应,响应性,响应能力
14. hardware ['hɑːdweə] *n.* 计算机硬件,五金器具
15. benchmarking ['bentʃˌmɑːkiŋ] *n.* 基准,定位,标杆管理
16. audit ['ɔːdit] *n.* 会计检查,查账
     v. 检查,查账
17. elusive [i'ljuːsiv] *adj.* 难懂的,难捉摸的
18. perceive…as 把……视为……
19. warehousing cost per pound 每磅仓储成本(成本衡量)
20. inventory turnover 库存周转(资产衡量)
21. case fill rate 供应比率(质量衡量)
22. cases per labor hour 每工时生产量(生产率衡量)
23. customer perception 顾客的满意度(客户服务衡量)
24. database maintenance 数据库维护
25. modeling analysis 建模分析
26. turnover [təːnəuvə] *n.* 营业额,成交量,证券交易额,周转
27. shortage ['ʃɔːrtidʒ] *n.* 缺少,不足,缺点,缺少量
28. internally [in'təːnəli] *adv.* 内部地,国内地,内在地
29. monitoring ['mɔnitəriŋ] *n.* 监视,控制,监测,追踪
30. routing ['ruːtiŋ] *n.* 发送,程序安排,路线选择,轨迹
31. anticipate [æn'tisipeit] *vt.* 预见,预料,先于……行动,预测
32. implementation [implimen'teiʃ(ə)n] *n.* [计]实现,履行,安装启用
33. justification [dʒʌstifi'keiʃən] *n.* 认为有理,认为正当,理由,辩护

Notes

[1] Firstly, customers perceive information about order status, product availability, delivery schedule, shipment tracking and invoices as necessary elements of total customer service.
首先,客户们把关于订单状况、产品可用性、交货时间表、运输路线以及发票的信息视为全部客户服务的要素。

[2] Transaction activities include order entry, inventory assignment, order selection, shipping, pricing, invoicing, and customer inquiry.
交易作业活动包括订单报入、库存管理、订单选择、运输、定价、开具发票以及客户查询。

[3] Typical analyses include supply chain design, inventory management, resource allocation, routing, and segmental profitability.

典型的分析包括供应链设计、库存管理、资源分配、运输路线安排以及各部分的营利性。

[4] Transaction system costs are high due to the large number of system users, heavy data communications requirements, high transactions volume, and significant software complexity.

大量的系统使用者、繁多的数据通信需求、庞大的交易量和重要软件的复杂性使交易系统成本昂贵。

[5] For example, benchmarking management control systems can identify processes where a firm lags behind competitors while external customer service audits may identify opportunities for selective, customer-focused programs.

例如,标杆管理控制系统能识别一个公司落后于竞争对手的流程,而外部的客户服务审查可以确定精心选择的、以客户为中心的计划的良机。

[6] Finally, strategic planning systems with the ability to assess supply chain design, customer/profitability, segment contribution, or alliance benefits can have a major impact on enterprise profitability and competitiveness even though they are not particularly hardware or software intensive.

最后,尽管战略规划系统在硬件或软件上并非特别强,但该系统有能力评估供应链设计、客户/营利性、阶段贡献或联盟利益,会对企业的营利性和竞争能力产生较大影响。

Passage B Logistics in E-Commerce Age

1. Challenges Logistics Faces in E-Commerce Age

Almost within one night, E-Commerce rises up. However, logistics could not change relatively at the same speed. As a result, logistics in E-Commerce is faced up with challenges that have not been witnessed before. To B2C E-Commerce, the online easy, fast ordering of the consumers increase their expectation to the quick and reliable delivery. At the same time, the return goods also become a problem. The vendors could only try to control the inventory and transportation cost to win the market competitive advantages through the reliable and high-effective management to the whole system. To B2B E-Commerce, the focus of vendors' competition has been turned from the products to the service, actually the competition of supply chain. The vendors must use the web-based tools to transfer the information between the partners, establish the integrated supply chain logistics management system, increase the entire supply chain visibility and coordinate the plan and decision support of all participants in the supply chain.[1] In general, E-Commerce creates the customized new business model and sets a high demands on the logistics service, which expresses as follows.

(1) Responsiveness.

The request of E-Commerce customers to distribution is often the JIT. The delivery in the next day or even the same day has been a trend. In the meantime, the delivery of large quantity of goods directly to the consumers reduce the sorting and distribution quantities and increase the times, which requires better responsiveness of the logistics system.

(2) **Flexibility.**

The traditional logistics may fix the optimized facilities and personnel in accordance with the products quantity, peak time and turnover ratio. But E-Commerce business is very difficult to predict. This requires the quick and effective suitableness of the logistics departments.

(3) **Visibility.**

To meet the responsiveness and flexibility requirements of E-Commerce to the logistics, the visibility of the whole supply chain must be increased so that the warehousing and transportation information of the goods could be known in order to guarantee the coordinated operation of the integrated logistics system.

(4) **Optimization.**

To meet the requirement of the customers, enterprises have to set up logistics networks consisting of a lot of small distribution centers in the sales area, which have resulted in the fragmented inventory, higher inventory level, more warehousing facilities and frequent distribution. As a result, the cost is highly increased and the enterprise economic benefit and market competition are affected. Therefore, the supply chain must be optimized in a whole to reduce the logistics cost as soon as possible.

2. Measures That Logistics Industry Takes

(1) **Integrated Logistics Strategy.**

In E-Commerce age, the quick response to the customers in global area has been a big challenge with the continuous expansion of the global market, the development of information technology and speed-up of the commercial steps. The logistics task to deliver the goods and information at right time, in reasonable cost and to the designated place has been more and more complicated. Therefore, it also becomes more and more pressing for working out not only the effective and efficient plans toward the global visibility of the whole supply-chain, but also the accurate and speedy supporting systems for decision-making, which ensure the real-time response toward the changes upon the market and the supply-chain. So, in order to keep competitive in the area, logistics industry has begun to employ the opening, systematical and technical structures, so as to form the consecutive logistics procedures for the enterprise, and then, realize the seamless, multi-placed integration of the full-ranged supply-chain, which not only covering the stock and the on-way inventory, but also including the chain sectors from suppliers to end users.[2] And this integrated logistics strategy holds advantages in solving the problems of fragmentary resources, unnecessary inventory and the lost commercial opportunities.

(2) **Integrated Logistics Information System.**

In E-business times, considering the crucial status of information, the logistics industry must support the continuous, convenient and non-mistaken transfer of data, and the real-time and automatic update of data, via the integrated logistics information system, in order to increase the visibility of the whole logistics procedure; and the final goal is to replace the inventory with information.[3] Thus, first of all, it has to answer two questions. The first is how to build up compatible database. As the basis of the whole information system, database must be of not only the complete compatibility, but also the ability to expand, so as to satisfy the need for business growing. At present, most large-and-middle-sized logistics enterprises use ORACLE system, while the rest of them use the MS SQL. The second is how to choose the best tools for data transfer. The integrated information system inquires the smooth transfer of data and indications between the varying entities, such as buyers, seller and the 3PL providers, etc.. The traditional electronic data interchange(EDI), used by most large companies, is one of the most effective tools to complete the transfer, however, sometimes, EDI is too complicated to achieve. With the prosperity of Internet nowadays, there comes out several new tools, for example, web-based EDI and the Extensible Markup Language(XML). And compared with traditional EDI, the XML is especially of better flexibility. And further more, XML simplifies both the integration process and the data transfer between the databases.

(3) The Development and Application of New Logistics Software.

The new logistics strategy requires the support of the relevant logistics software, for computer provides brand new manners to process the traditional tasks, such as storage and delivery. For instance, the collaborative planning, forecasting, and replenishment(CPFR) strategy makes it possible for both the producers and retailers to compare and contrast separately with the anticipations toward the particular product, and then reach the cooperative agreements upon the production and sales. And besides, the advanced planning and coordinating software supports the dynamic coordination, and the pre-alarming system helps to meet the unfixed market demands and make the in-time inventory adjustment according to orders. And what is more, the Supply-Chain Executing and Planning Software (SCEP) plays the key role in processing in orders collected from the online transactions and market on web, while, correspondingly, the suppliers must have the relevant visual inventory software. The middle-and-small-sized enterprises gain benefits of Warehouse Management System(WMS) and Transportation Management System(TMS) from the new, web-based software models, for they only need to pay monthly or just the transaction costs for the proper solutions from the Application Service Providers (ASP), rather than pay the much larger expense on the software installing and using for further software integration.

(4) Web-Based Virtual Supply-Chain.

To achieve the optimization of the supply-chain, more and more enterprises outsource fourth-party logistics (4PL) service providers, and build up their own virtual supply-chains based on web. Via the web-based information platform, the 4PL service providers, together with other service providers and partners in warehousing, transportation and 3PL, choose the best partners, in accordance with the demands of their clients, at each sector within the cycle, and then, collect and transfer the logistics information via Internet, and finally, build up the customized, integrated, optimized and subjunctive supply-chain[4]. The virtual supply-chain has outstanding advantages in responsiveness, flexibility and visibility. For example, an enterprise can construct its own logistics networks promptly by renting the warehousing space from partners, increase and reduce their space requirements based on demand, and adjust the layout of the sectors in the networks; meanwhile, the enterprise are also able to make use of the computer-aided management system and the material delivery system, and further more, the operating experiences of warehousing partners help to better complete the logistics functions. (e.g., sorting, packaging and delivery) and provide enhanced customer service at relatively low price.

New Words and Expressions

1. witness['witnis]   vt. 目击,为……作证,证明,表明
2. delivery[di'livəri]   n. 递送,交付,分娩,交货,引渡
3. reliable[ri'jaiəbl]   adj. 可靠的,可信赖的
4. sort[sɔːt]   n. 分类,类别;品质,本性;方法;一群
               vt. & vi. 分类;整顿,整理;适合
               vt. 挑选;把……分类;将……排顺序
               vi. 拣选;交往;协调
5. sorting['sɔːtɪŋ]   n. 资料排架
               v. 分类,整理(sort 的现在分词);挑选;[计算机](根据指令的模式)把……分类;把……归类(常与 with, together 连用)
6. optimize['ɔptimaiz]   vt. 使最优化
7. peak[piːk]   n. 山顶,顶点,帽舌,(记录的)最高峰
8. visibility[vizi'biliti]   n. 可见度,可见性,显著,明显度,能见度
9. fragment['frægmənt]   n. 碎片,断片,片段,未完成的部分;(将文件内容)分段
               vt. (使)碎裂,破裂,分裂
               vi. 破碎,碎裂
10. pressing['presiŋ]   adj. 紧迫的
11. consecutive[kən'sekjutiv]   adj. 连续的,连贯的
12. seamless['siːmlis]   adj. 无缝合线的,无伤痕的
13. fragmentary['frægməntəri]   adj. 由碎片组成的,断断续续的,零散的,支离破碎的
14. compatible[kəm'pætəbl]   adj. 兼容的,相容的
15. compatibility[kəmpætə'biliti]   n. [计]兼容性,相容性,适用性
16. indication[indi'keiʃən]   n. 指出,指示,迹象,暗示
17. prosperity[prɔs'periti]   n. 繁荣
18. unfixed['ʌn'fiksd]   adj. 解脱的,放松了的,不固定的,没确定的
19. install[ɪn'stɔːl]   v. 安装,任命,安顿

20. outsource [aut'sɔːs]　　　　　　　v. [商]外部采办,外购,业务外包
21. subjunctive [səb'dʒʌŋktiv]　　　 adj. 虚拟的,持续的,假设的,主观上的
22. layout [lei'aut]　　　　　　　　n. 规划,设计,(书刊等)编排,版面,配线,企划,设计图案
23. multi-placed　　　　　　　　　多个地点的,多点的
24. full-ranged　　　　　　　　　　全方位的,完全的
25. ORACLE system　　　　　　　　大型分布式数据库系统
26. MS SQL　　　　　　　　　　　大型分布式数据库系统
27. EDI (electronic data interchange)　电子数据交换
28. CPFR (collaborative planning,　　协作性计划、预测和补给(是一种软件,也是一种战略)
　　forecasting, and replenishment)
29. WMS (warehouse management　　仓库管理系统
　　system)
30. 4PL (fourth-party logistics)　　　第四方物流

Notes

[1] The vendors must use the web-based tools to transfer the information between the partners, establish the integrated supply chain logistics management system, increase the entire supply chain visibility and coordinate the plan and decision support of all participants in the supply chain.

供货商必须使用基于网络的工具在合作伙伴之间传递信息,建立一体化供应链物流管理系统,增加整个供应链的可视性,并协同供应链中所有参与方的计划和决策。

[2] So, in order to keep competitive in the area, logistics industry has begun to employ the opening, systematical and technical structures, so as to form the consecutive logistics procedures for the enterprise, and then, realize the seamless, multi-placed integration of the full-ranged supply-chain, which not only covering the stock and the on-way inventory, but also including the chain sectors from suppliers to end users.

所以,为了保持在该领域的竞争力,物流业已经开始使用开放的、系统的和技术的结构,以便为企业塑造连贯的物流过程,从而实现全方位供应链的无缝、多点集成,不仅涵盖库存和在途货物,而且包括从供应商到最终客户的链状环节。

[3] In E-business times, considering the crucial status of information, the logistics industry must support the continuous, convenient and non-mistaken transfer of data, and the real-time and automatic update of data, via the integrated logistics information system, in order to increase the visibility of the whole logistics procedure; and the final goal is to replace the inventory with information.

在电子商务时代,考虑到信息至关重要的地位,为了增强整个物流过程的可视性,通过一体化物流信息系统,物流业必须保持连续、方便和无差错的数据传输,以及实时和自动的数据更新;其最终目标是用信息来代替库存。

[4] Via the web-based information platform, the 4PL service providers, together with other service providers and partners in warehousing, transportation and 3PL, choose the best partners, in accordance with the demands of their clients, at each sector within the cycle; then, collect and transfer the logistics information via Internet; and finally, build up the customized, integrated, optimized and subjunctive supply-chain.

利用基于网络的信息平台,第四方物流服务提供商,与仓储、运输和第三方物流等方面的其他服务提供商和合作伙伴一起,根据其客户的需要,选择循环中每一个环节的最佳合作伙伴;然后,通过因特网收集和传递物流信息;最后,建立客户定制的、一体化的、最优的虚拟供应链。

Unit 6

Passage A Supply Chain Information System Modules (Ⅰ)

A comprehensive SCIS initiates, monitors, assists in decision making, and reports on activities required for completion of logistics operations and planning. The major system modules and their interfaces as illustrated in Figure 6-1 are: (1) Enterprise Resource Planning (ERP), (2) communication systems, (3) execution systems, and (4) planning systems. While Figure 6-1 provides a software-oriented perspective, Figure 6-2 illustrates a more application-oriented perspective. This application perspective is used to discuss each module's specific characteristics and functionality.

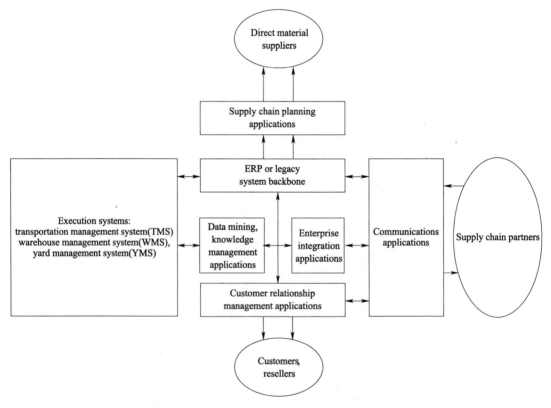

Figure 6-1 SCIS: integrated modules

The ERP systems in Figure 6-2 are the backbone of most firms' logistics information system. This backbone maintains current and historical data and processes to initiate and monitor performance.[1] During the 1990s, many firms began to replace legacy systems with ERP systems designed as integrated transaction modules and processes with a common and consistent database. The database includes information storage capability for both operations (i.e., product and activity based) and financial (i.e., monetary based) transactions. ERP systems facilitate integrated operations and reporting to initiate, monitor, and track critical activities such as order fulfillment and replenishment. ERP systems also incorporate an integrated corporate-wide database, sometimes referred to as a data warehouse, along with appropriate transactions to facilitate logistics and supply chain planning and operations. Supply chain transactions facilitated by ERP systems include order entry and management, inventory assignment, and shipping. Beyond these supply chain applications, ERP systems typically include financial, accounting, and human resource capability. Table 6-1 lists the traditional and emerging capabilities of ERP systems. Data mining, knowledge management, and other enterprise integration applications operate using the ERP backbone to develop and organize insight regarding customers, products, and operations.

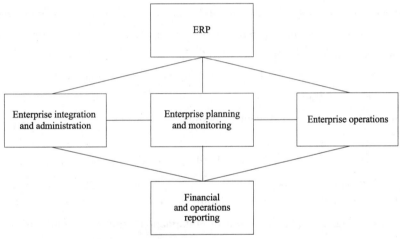

Figure 6-2   Application-Oriented SCIS Framework

ERP system capability   Table 6-1

Typical	Advanced
Accounts payable and receivable	Collaborative planning, forecasting, and replenishment
General ledger	Customer relationship management
Human resource management	Supply chain event management
Bill of materials	Web-enabled applications
Inventory control	Advanced planning and scheduling
Routings	
Order management	
Project requirements planning	
Execution systems	

The application-oriented modules include: (1) ERP data warehouse, (2) enterprise integration and administration, (3) enterprise operations, (4) enterprise planning and monitoring, and (5) communications technology.[2]

The following in this Passage is about data warehouse, while other four in next Passage.

The core of an ERP system is the central database or information warehouse where all information is maintained to facilitate access to common and consistent data by all modules. Surrounding the database are the functional modules that initiate and coordinate business activities. Although total ERP benefits can best be achieved when all functions are integrated into a common application, many firms select to implement systems using a modular approach to spread resource requirements and minimize risk, so a limited number of firm functions are in transition at any time.

The central database is the relational information repository for the entire ERP system. The central database is described as relational because it relates or links information regarding operational entities so that there is minimal information redundancy.[3] Over time, information redundancy usually leads to inaccuracy because one reference to a data item is eventually changed without a comparable change in the other reference. For example, if a customer address is contained in two different locations in the database, it is likely that eventually one reference will be changed if the customer moves but the second reference may be forgotten. At that point, the database would no longer be consistent and all references to the second address would be incorrect. Although the central database is extensive and can contain millions of data items in numerous files, eight major data files are critical to logistics operations: (1) customer file, (2) product-price file, (3) supplier file, (4) order file, (5) bill-of-materials file, (6) purchase order file, (7) inventory file, and (8) history file.

The customer file contains information describing the firm's customers. Each entry defines one customer, including name, address, billing information, ship-to location, company contact, price list, terms of sale, and special instructions. A common customer file is helpful particularly when multiple divisions of the firm serve the same customer.

The product-price file contains the information describing the products and services offered by the firm. Specific entries include product number, description, physical characteristics, purchase source or manufacturing location, references to equivalent or updates, and standard cost data.[4] The product-price file or related file information regarding prices and quantity breaks. Product-price file maintenance is increasingly challenging because of shorter product life cycles and more frequent price changes.

The supplier file lists the firm's suppliers for materials and services.[5] Specific entries include supplier number, supplier name, address, transportation and receiving information, and payables instructions. A common supplier file is critical to achieve purchasing economies through supplier rationalization and consolidation.

The order file contains the information regarding all open orders in some stage of processing or fulfillment by the firm.[6] Each order represents a current or potential request by a customer to ship product. The order file contains the customer number and name, requested receipt date, and the list of products and quantities that are being ordered. The order file is increasingly being required to include special shipping and packaging requests for unique customers. The system must also increasingly accept orders from multiple sources, including EDI and the Internet, as well as by internal order entry.

The bill-of-materials file describes how raw materials are combined for finished products. For example, a simple bill-of-materials for an automobile would indicate that it requires a body, a chassis, four seats, an engine, a transaxle, and four tires. Although these product relationships are typically used in manufacturing, it is becoming increasingly important for logistics as well. Logistics operations are beginning to use bills of materials to facilitate packaging, customization, and kitting in distribution center operations.

The purchase order (PO) file is similar to the order file except that it contains the records of purchase orders that have been placed on suppliers.[7] The purchase order may be for raw material to support product or for MRO (Maintenance, Repair, and Operating) supplies necessary to support operations and administration. MRO items are not directly included as finished products sold by the firm. Specific purchase order file information includes purchase order number, supplier number and name, request date, ship to location, transportation mode and carrier, and a list of the items to be purchased and the corresponding quantity. Other critical requirements of the PO file are the product specifications, delivery requirements, and contracted price.

The inventory file records the physical inventory or quantity of product that the firm has available or may be available in the future according to current production schedules. The file also tracks the physical location of the product within the material storage system and facility; the product status in terms of available to ship, damaged, quality hold, or on-hold for a key customer; and lot numbers for products that must be tracked. Specific inventory file information includes product number, facility location, storage location, and inventory quantity for each product status.

The history file documents the firm's order and purchase order history to facilitate management reporting, budget and decision analyses, and forecasting.[8] In essence, this file contains summaries of the customer orders that have been filled and the purchase orders that have been received.

New Words and Expressions

1. backbone [ˈbækbəʊn]   n. 支柱,主干网,决心,毅力,脊椎
2. legacy [ˈlegəsɪ]   n. 遗赠,遗产
3. execution [ˌeksɪˈkjuːʃ(ə)n]   n. 执行,实行,完成
4. APS (Advanced Planning and Scheduling)   高级计划与排程
5. modular [ˈmɒdjʊlə]   adj. 模块化的,模数的,有标准组件的
6. redundancy [rɪˈdʌnd(ə)nsɪ]   n. [计数]冗余,裁员
7. bill-of-materials file   物料清单文档

8. instruction [ɪnˈstrʌkʃ(ə)n]   n. 指令,命令,指示,教导,用法说明
9. equivalent [ɪˈkwɪvələnt]   adj. 相等的,对等的,相当的
                                     n. 对等物,当量
10. transaxle [trænzˈsæksəl]   n. 变速驱动桥,变速差速器
11. specification [spesɪfɪˈkeɪʃ(ə)n]   n. 规格,说明书,详述
12. ERP (Enterprise Resource Planning)   企业资源计划
13. application-oriented modules   面向应用模块
14. central database   中央(心)数据库
15. over time   随着时间的过去
16. PO (purchase order)   采购订单
17. except…that   除了……之外
18. MRO (Maintenance, Repair, and Operating)   维护修理及操作

Notes

[1] This backbone maintains current and historical data and processes to initiate and monitor performance.

该主要成分维护当前数据和历史数据,并处理这些数据以启动并监测绩效。

[2] The application-oriented modules include: (1) ERP data warehouse, (2) enterprise integration and administration, (3) enterprise operations, (4) enterprise planning and monitoring, and (5) communications technology.

面向应用的模块包括:(1)ERP 数据仓库;(2)企业一体化及管理;(3)企业运作;(4)企业计划与监测;(5)通信技术。

[3] The central database is described as relational because it relates or links information regarding operational entities so that there is minimal information redundancy.

中央数据库之所以被描述为具有相关性,是因为它关联或连接与营运企业有关的信息,从而信息冗余最小。

[4] Specific entries include product number, description, physical characteristics, purchase source or manufacturing location, references to equivalent or updates, and standard cost data.

具体条目包括产品序号、产品说明书、产品的物理特性、采购地或生产地、可参照的同等产品或最新产品以及标准成本数据。

[5] The supplier file lists the firm's suppliers for materials and services.

供应商文档列明了公司的物料和服务供应商。

[6] The order file contains the information regarding all open orders in some stage of processing or fulfillment by the firm.

订单文档包含公司处于某运作或实现阶段时所有开放式订单的有关信息。

[7] The purchase order (PO) file is similar to the order file except that it contains the records of purchase orders that have been placed on suppliers.

除了采购订单文档包含供应商已签订的采购订单记录之外,采购订单(PO)文档与订单文档相同。

[8] The history file documents the firm's order and purchase order history to facilitate management reporting, budget and decision analyses, and forecasting.

历史文档记录了公司的历史产品订单和历史采购订单,以便于管理报告、预算与决策分析以及预测。

Passage B　Supply Chain Information System Modules(Ⅱ)

1. Enterprise Integration and Administration

Enterprise integration and administration applications are the ERP modules that are not specifically supply chain applications but do have substantial interactions.[1] Figure 6-3 illustrates the major enterprise integration and administration components. The specific components include (1) general administration, (2) accounts receivable and payable, (3) financial inventory accounting, (4) general ledger, and (5) human resources.

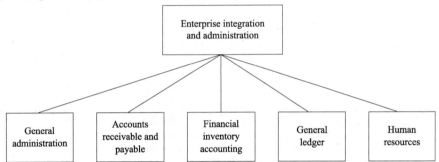

Figure 6-3　Enterprise integration and administration components

General administration includes the various transactions to structure the firm and define firm process flows. Supply chain operations use these modules to define reporting, functional, and organizational structures as well as to define process flows such as customer and replenishment order fulfillment. Accounts receivable and payable represent the functions for invoice collection from customers and invoice payment to suppliers. While these are typically acknowledged as accounting functions, there is a significant interaction with supply chain operations since accounts payable is influenced by materials and services acquisition and accounts receivable is influenced by delivery and invoicing of complete orders.[2] Financial inventory accounting relates to the tracking of value-added processes through the supply chain to facilitate financial and tax reporting. The timing and location of supply chain value-added processes (e.g., production, inventory control, and packaging) can have a significant influence regarding what can be reported to the treasury (for taxation purposes) and the financial markets (for stock valuation purposes). General ledger relates to the structure of the detailed accounts for monitoring and reporting revenues and accounts. Since supply chain involves substantial interaction with firm and external processes, the structure of the general ledger accounts significantly influences the supply chain's ability to measure, monitor, and report cost related to delivering product or serving customers. The human resource module of the ERP systems tracks personnel profiles and their activity levels. Since most firms have a large number of individuals involved in supply chain operations (e.g., manufacturing, distribution, and purchasing) and often in different global environments, the ability to track pay scales and activity levels is critical to make effective supply chain personnel decisions.[3]

2. Enterprise Operations

Enterprise operations include the SCIS modules required to support day-to-day supply chain operations. Figure 6-4 illustrates the specific modules including: (1) customer accommodation, (2) logistics, (3) manufacturing, (4) purchasing, and (5) inventory deployment. Enterprise operations systems work in conjunction with the firm's ERP system to provide specific functionality to support supply chain operations. While some ERP systems support required supply chain functionality, others lack some functionality such as that required to support warehouse and transportation operations.

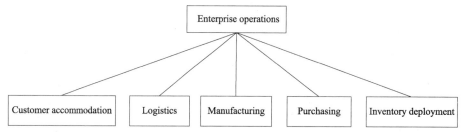

Figure 6-4 Enterprise operations modules

Customer accommodation systems, also known as customer relationship management (CRM) systems, are relatively new applications designed to facilitate information sharing during customers, sales force, and operations management. The logistics module directs and monitors logistics activities including finished goods inventory management, warehouse management, transportation management, and yard management. The manufacturing module schedules and allocates production resources and determines component requirements. The purchasing module initiates and tracks procurement activities including purchase order initiation, expediting, and supplier management. The inventory deployment system module schedules and monitors material flows to meet production and deployment requirements.

3. Enterprise Planning and Monitoring

Enterprise planning and monitoring are the processes and technologies that facilitate exchange of planning and coordinating information both within the firm and between supply chain partners.[4] Figure 6-5 illustrates the major enterprise planning and monitoring components. The specific modules include (1) sales and operations planning, (2) supply chain visibility and event management, and (3) supply chain compliance. Since many of these activities involve interaction with other members of the supply chain, effective applications require substantial standardization with other firm functions and supply chain partners.

Figure 6-5 Enterprise planning and monitoring modules

Sales and operations planning (S&OP) describes the process used to balance demand requirements and supply capabilities of the firm and its supply chain partners. While S&OP itself is a process requiring functional coordination and integration, it requires information technology to evaluate the demand, supply, and resource trade-offs. This technology is generally characterized as planning and scheduling applications. Supply chain visibility and event management tracks shipments while they are in-transit and are increasingly capable of proactively suggesting changes in supply chain flows to minimize the potential of manufacturing shutdowns or service failures. Supply chain compliance systems monitor component and product flow information to make sure they comply with government and regulatory requirements for label, taxation, and security restrictions.

4. Communication Technology

Communication technology is the hardware and technical software that facilitates information exchange between the systems and physical infrastructure within the firm and between supply chain partners. The real-time information interchange between functions and supply chain partners facilitate coordination of inbound material, production, inventory, customer orders, and customer shipment. From a supply chain perspective, the availability of common and consistent requirements, activity, and performance information between supply chain partners enhances both effectiveness and efficiency.[5] These technologies include electronic bar coding and scanning, exchange portals, product codes, radio frequency, and XML.

New Words and Expressions

1. acquisition [ˌækwɪˈzɪʃ(ə)n] 　　　　　n. 获得物,获得,收购
2. conjunction [kənˈdʒʌŋ(k)ʃ(ə)n] 　　n. 结合,连接词,同时发生
3. CRM (customer relationship management) 客户关系管理
4. S&OP (sales and operations planning) 销售和运作计划
5. infrastructure [ˈɪnfrəstrʌktʃə] 　　　n. 基础设施,公共建设,下部构造

6. interchange [ˌɪntəˈtʃeɪn(d)ʒ]　　　　　　　n. 互换，立体交叉道
　　　　　　　　　　　　　　　　　　　　v. 交换，互换
7. finished goods　　　　　　　　　　　　产成品

Notes

[1] Enterprise integration and administration applications are the ERP modules that are not specifically supply chain applications but do have substantial interactions.

企业的一体化管理应用就是 ERP 模块，这些 ERP 模块并不是专门的供应链应用但却有真正的互动。do 用于加强语气。

[2] While these are typically acknowledged as accounting functions, there is a significant interaction with supply chain operations since accounts payable is influenced by materials and services acquisition and accounts receivable is influenced by delivery and invoicing of complete orders.

虽然这些通常被公认为是会计职能，但因为应付账款受物料和服务取得的影响，而且应收账款受交货和完整订单发票的影响，因此它们与供应链运作有着重要的互动。

[3] Since most firms have a large number of individuals involved in supply chain operations (e.g., manufacturing, distribution, and purchasing) and often in different global environments, the ability to track pay scales and activity levels is critical to make effective supply chain personnel decisions.

由于大多数公司都有大量参与供应链运作的个体（例如制造、配送和采购），并且经常处于不同的全球环境中，跟踪薪级和活动水平的能力就是做出有效的供应链人事决策的关键。

[4] Enterprise planning and monitoring are the processes and technologies that facilitate exchange of planning and coordinating information both within the firm and between supply chain partners.

企业规划和监控是促进公司内部和供应链合作伙伴之间的规划及协调信息交换的过程和技术。

[5] From a supply chain perspective, the availability of common and consistent requirements, activity, and performance information between supply chain partners enhances both effectiveness and efficiency.

从供应链的角度来看，供应链合作伙伴之间共同一致的要求、活动及绩效信息提高了有效性和效率。

Unit 7

Passage A Enterprise Operations (I)

Enterprise operations include customer accommodation module, logistics module, manufacturing module, purchasing module, and inventory deployment module. Figure 7-1 lists the major elements of each module, which are discussed in detail below.

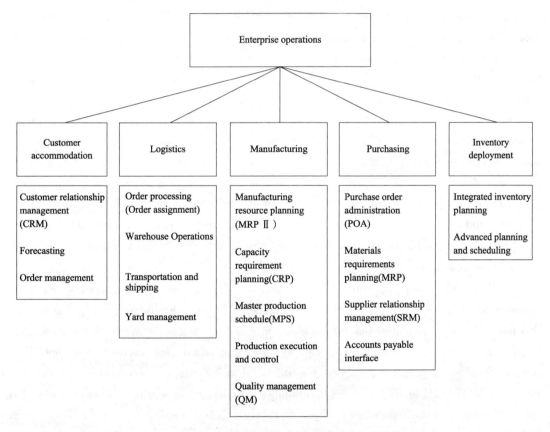

Figure 7-1 Enterprise operations modules

1. Customer Accommodation

Customer accommodation systems facilitate the synthesis and exchange of relevant and accurate information regarding order history, status, and demand generation information between a firm and its customers. The major system components include (1) customer relationship management

(CRM), (2) forecasting, and (3) order management.

(1) CRM.

CRM is designed to extend the functionality of the ERP sales and delivery applications.[1] CRM provides sales representatives and customers with current information regarding sales history, shipment history, order status, promotional summaries, and shipment information. The history and current status information, combined with product development, pricing, and promotion information, allow firms to better create and manage customer orders. Such timely and accurate information exchange between a firm and its customers increases the likelihood that the product sales and promotion plans will be supported with required product.

While traditional ERP applications focus on efficiently taking customer orders, firms are finding it necessary to transition from treating customers as income sources to be exploited to treating customers as assets to be nurtured. While the traditional sales and delivery technology is configured to accept customer orders in a wide range of formats and allow those orders to be managed throughout the fulfillment process, a broader range of capabilities is necessary to manage the overall customer relationship. An integrated CRM system includes a combination of a server-based common database, remote personal computers (PCs) carried by sales representatives, and a global synchronization process to ensure that both corporate and sales representative data are timely and consistent. Beyond this base functionality, CRM today requires sales tracking, sales history analysis, pricing management, promotion management, product mix management, and category management. In some cases, customers expect their supplier's sales force to manage the entire category of products at the customer's facility. For example, it is becoming more common for grocers to expect their suppliers to manage both the product mix and shelf quantities for major product categories such as beverages and specialty products. This practice, termed category management, requires substantial information support from the manufacturer but also facilitates information sharing.

(2) Forecasting.

While the CRM system facilitates collaboration between the firm and its customers, the other customer accommodation modules focus on synthesizing the available information into a forecast that best reflects the combined information of the firm and its customers. While all these elements generate forecasts to drive supply chain activity, they represent increasing degrees of sophistication. Demand management systems use the historical data but also work proactively with the customer to shift demand timing or product requirements to develop a plan that is achievable within the firm's constraints. Collaborative Planning, Forecasting and Replenshment (CPFR) is even more interactive and proactive as the firm and its key customers develop a joint plan that meets their combined objectives within their operating constraints.

(3) Order Management.

Once the individual or joint forecast is developed and the planned orders are created, an order management system (OMS) places the orders in the ERP system and allows for their maintenance, processing, and tracking. The effective OMS allows both the firm and its customers to have the most up-to-date status of current orders.

2. Logistics

Coordinated, integrated logistics operations are essential for supply chain competitiveness. Coordination and integration facilitate smooth and consistent customer and replenishment order information flow throughout the firm and offer current order status visibility. Integrated information sharing reduces delays, errors, and resource requirements. The logistics processes required for customer order fulfillment and to coordinate receipt of purchase orders are (1) order processing, (2) order assignment, (3) warehouse operations, (4) transportation and shipping, and (5) yard management.

(1) Order Processing.

Order processing is the entry point for customer orders and inquiries. It allows entry and maintenance of customer orders by using communication technologies such as mail, phone, fax, EDI, and the Internet. As orders or inquiries are received, order processing enters and retrieves required information, edits for appropriate values, and retains acceptable orders for assignment. Order processing can also offer information regarding inventory availability and delivery dates to establish and confirm customer expectations. Order processing, in conjunction with customer service representatives, forms the primary interface between the customer and the ERP or legacy system.

(2) Order Assignment.

Order assignment allocates available inventory to open customer and replenishment orders. Assignment may take place in real time, as orders are received, or in a batch mode. Batch mode means that orders are grouped for periodic processing such as by day or shift. While real-time allocation is more responsive, a batch process provides the firm with more control over situations when inventory is low. For example, in a batch process, order assignment can be designed to allocate stock from current inventory only or from scheduled production capacity. The operational system is more responsive if it allows inventory assignment from scheduled production quantities or capacity. However, there is a trade-off, since assigning scheduled production capacity reduces the firm's ability to reschedule production. The best order assignment applications operate interactively in conjunction with order processing to generate an order solution that satisfies customer requirements within enterprise resource constraints. In this type of operational environment, the customer service representative and the customer interact to determine the combination of products, quantities, and performance cycle length that is acceptable for both parties. Possible solutions when there is conflict in order assignment include delivery date adjustments, product substitutions, or shipment from an alternative source.

(3) Warehouse Operations.

Warehouse operations, also known as WMS, incorporate processes to guide physical activities, including product receipt, material movement and storage, and order selection. For this reason, they are often termed inventory control or warehouse management systems and sometimes warehouse locator systems, referring to the capability to track inventory storage locations in warehouses. Warehouse operations direct all material handling activities using a combination of batch and real-time assignments.[2] In a batch environment, the warehouse operations system develops a "to do" list of instructions or tasks to guide each material handler in the warehouse. Material handlers are the individuals who operate equipment such as forklifts. In a real-time environment, information-directed technologies such as bar coding, radio-frequency communication, and automated handling equipment operate interactively to reduce the elapsed time between decision and action. The real-time information-directed materials handling technologies, also must interface directly with the warehouse operations process to provide operational flexibility and reduce internal performance cycle time requirements.

(4) **Transportation and Shipping.**

A transportation management system (TMS) plans, executes, and manages transport and movement functions. The TMS includes shipment planning and scheduling, shipment consolidation, shipment notification, transport documentation generation, and carrier management.[3] These processes facilitate efficient transport resource utilization as well as effective carrier management.

A unique characteristic of the TMS is that it often involves three parties—shipper, carrier, and consignee (recipient).[4] To effectively manage the process, a basic level of information integration must exist. Information sharing requires standardized data formats for transport documents.

(5) **Yard Management.**

A yard management system (YMS) manages full and empty trailers in the parking lot or yard at manufacturing plants and distribution centers. In many operations, there may be hundreds or more trailers in the yard and they move in and out daily. The trailers and containers may represent inbound receipts, outbound orders, or may be empty. For the trailers that are full, the contents may represent a single shipment or a combination of orders. It is clear that the accuracy of a manual system would quickly decline, resulting in lost trailers and inventory.

3. Manufacturing

Manufacturing systems form the information system foundation to plan and control manufacturing planning and operation. These components define core activities that guide enterprise resource allocation and performance from procurement to product delivery. The manufacturing module includes (1) manufacturing resource planning (MRP II, more details see Unit15), (2) capacity requirement planning(CRP), (3) master production scheduling (MPS), (4) production execution and control, and (5) quality management(QM).

4. Purchasing

Purchasing manages purchase order (PO) preparation, modification, and release and tracks vendor performance and compliance.[5] The specific elements of the purchasing system include administering purchase orders, sharing materials requirements with suppliers, and managing the overall supplier relationship. Although purchasing systems have not traditionally been considered as a part of logistics systems, the importance of integrating purchasing with logistics schedules is critical to facilitate the coordination of material receipt, facility capacity, and transportation backhaul.

New Words and Expressions

1. synthesis [ˈsɪnθɪsɪs] n. 综合, [化学]合成, 综合体
2. likelihood [ˈlaɪklɪhʊd] n. 可能性, 可能, 似然
3. configure [kənˈfɪgə] v. 安装, 使成形
4. sophistication [sə,fɪstɪˈkeɪʃn] n. 复杂, 诡辩, 老于世故, 有教养
5. retrieve [rɪˈtriːv] v. 重新得到
   n. 找回
6. conjunction [kənˈdʒʌŋ(k)ʃ(ə)n] n. 结合, 连接词, 同时发生
7. batch [bætʃ] n. 一批, 一次所制之量
   v. 分批处理
8. responsive [rɪˈspɔːnsɪv] adj. 应答的, 响应的, 反应灵敏的, 共鸣的, 易反应的
9. material handling 物料搬运, 原材料处理
10. handler [ˈhændlə] n. 处理者, 管理者, 训练者
11. notification [nəʊtɪfɪˈkeɪʃn] n. 通知, 通告, [法]告示
12. consignee [kɔnsaɪˈniː] n. 受托者, 收件人, 代销人
13. trailer [ˈtreɪlə(r)] n. 拖车
    v. 用拖车运
14. backhaul [ˈbækhɔːl] n. 回程, 载货反航
15. TMS (Transportation Management System) 运输管理系统
16. CRP (capacity requirement planning) 能力需求计划
17. MPS (master production schedule) 主生产计划
18. modification [mɔdifiˈkeiʃən] n. 更改, 修改, 修正

Notes

[1] CRM is designed to extend the functionality of the ERP sales and delivery applications.
客户关系管理(CRM)的设计用来拓展企业资源计划(ERP)在销售和送货应用方面的功能。

[2] Warehouse operations direct all material handling activities using a combination of batch and real-time assignments.
仓储运作采取分批与实时分配的组合方式指导所有物料的搬运活动。

[3] The TMS includes shipment planning and scheduling, shipment consolidation, shipment notification, transport documentation generation, and carrier management.
运输管理系统(TMS)包括装运计划与进度安排、装运确认、装运通知、运输单据生成以

及承运人管理。

[4] A unique characteristic of the TMS is that it often involves three parties-shipper, carrier, and consignee (recipient).

运输管理系统(TMS)的一个独特之处在于它通常涵盖运输环节中的三方当事人——发货人、承运人和收货人。

[5] Purchasing manages purchase order (PO) preparation, modification, and release and tracks vendor performance and compliance.

采购模块对采购订单(PO)的准备、修改、发送等活动进行管理,同时对供应商的绩效和合同遵守情况进行跟踪。

Passage B　Enterprise Operations (Ⅱ)

This Passage will illustrate inventory depolyment, which involves integrated inventory planning and advanced planning and scheduling.

Inventory deployment represents one of the major enterprise integrators of sales, marketing, and financial goals. The inventory deployment activity can be completed independently by individual supply chain functions, in an integrated manner by supply chain overall, or in a coordinated manner by the entire firm.[1] When it is done in a coordinated manner by the entire firm, it is often referred to as S&OP.

These strategic objectives are typically developed for a multiyear planning horizon that often includes quarterly updates. Sales and marketing's strategic objectives define target markets, product development, promotions, other marketing mix plans, and the role of logistics value-added activities such as service levels or capabilities. The objectives include customer scope, breadth of products and services, planned promotions, and desired performance levels. Sales and marketing goals are the customer service policies and objectives that define logistics and supply chain activity and performance targets. The performance targets include service availability, capability, and quality elements discussed earlier. Financial strategic objectives define revenue, financial and activity levels, and corresponding expenses, as well as capital and human resource constraints.

The combination of sales, marketing, and financial objectives defines the scope of markets, products, services, and activity levels that logistics and supply chain managers must accommodate during the planning horizon. Specific goals include projected annual or quarterly activity levels such as revenue, shipments, and case volume. Events that must be considered include product promotions, new product introductions, market rollouts, and acquisitions. Ideally, the marketing and financial plans should be integrated and consistent, as inconsistencies result in poor service, excess inventory, or failure to meet financial goals.

The inventory deployment process must include both long- and short-term elements. The long-term element focuses on annual and quarterly plans with the objective of coordinating the marketing and financial plans to achieve enterprise goals. While supply chain and logistics operations are not the major focus, they do merit some consideration, as planners must ensure that there is enough aggregate production, storage, and movement capacity available. The short-term element focuses on weekly and daily plans with the objective of coordinating supply chain and logistics resources to ensure that specific customer requests can be satisfied. The key objective of an inventory deployment system is an integrated inventory plan through what is increasingly being termed an Advanced Planning and Scheduling (APS) system.[2]

(1) **APS System Overview.**

To correspond with the planning and execution of effective logistics and supply chain strategies, supply chain planning systems incorporate both spatial and temporal considerations.[3] The spatial considerations include movement between raw material providers, manufacturing plants, warehouses, distributors, retailers, and the end customer. The temporal considerations include moving timing and scheduling.

(2) **APS System Components.**

While there are many conceptual approaches to designing supply chain planning application like APS, the major components are fundamentally the same: demand management, resource management, resource optimization, and resource allocation.

(3) **Supply Chain Planning Benefits.**

While some supply chain planning system benefits were discussed earlier, there are three broad benefits that accrue from planning system utilization. These are responsiveness to changes, comprehensive perspective, and resource utilization.

First, logistics and supply chain managers have used extended lead times and schedule freezes to plan for future supply chain activity.[4] For example, production would be schedule three to four weeks into the future and then frozen to minimize uncertainty and allow for effective resource utilization. Long lead times and freeze periods were necessary since the planning process was complex and required substantial analyses. While this approach reduced uncertainty, it also substantially reduced flexibility and responsiveness. Today's customer requires more responsiveness to market needs, and demand for lower inventory levels rules out long cycle times. Marketplace and firm changes can be quickly made in the demand management and resource management modules, allowing for the planning process to use the most current and accurate information. The requirements optimization module then solves the allocation, allowing daily and single week planning cycles rather than multiple weeks or months. Supply chain planning thus results in a process that can be much more responsive to marketplace or firm changes.

Second, effective supply chain management requires planning and coordination across firm functions and between supply chain partners.[5] The process must consider the trade-offs associated with shifting activities and resources across functions and organizations. Such a comprehensive perspective increases planning process complexity substantially. The complexity follows from the number of organizations, facilities, products, and assets that must be considered when coordinating activities and resources across an entire supply chain. Supply chain planning systems offer the capability to consider the extended supply chain and make the appropriate trade-offs to achieve optimal performance.

Third, supply chain planning typically results in substantial performance improvements. While more comprehensive planning and reduced uncertainty usually result in improved customer service, another major planning system benefit is enhanced resource utilization.

More effective and responsive planning allows a more level assignment of resources for existing sourcing, production, storage, and transportation capacity. The result is that existing capacity is used more effectively. Firms also report that supply chain planning systems have significantly reduced asset requirements by smoothing resource demands. The decreases include estimates of 20%~25% reductions in plant, equipment, facilities, and inventory.

(4) Supply Chain Planning Considerations.

While comprehensive supply chain planning is a relatively new capability, the future outlook is bright as the technology and capacity to effectively evaluate and manage integrated supply chains are developed. Supply chain planning can take a comprehensive and dynamic perspective of the entire supply chain and focus on reducing the supply chain asset requirements as demanded by financial markets. Prior to the actual implementation, there are many considerations for supply chain planning system adoption. Managers cite their major considerations to be (1) integrated versus bolt-on application, (2) data integrity, and (3) application education.

The first consideration concerns the level of integration with other supply chain applications. Technically, there are three options for acquiring and implementing planning applications. The first is development using internal firm resources. This is not very common, as planning system development requires substantial expertise and most firms without substantial software competency could not effectively design, develop, or maintain such complex planning systems. In addition, the planning process of individual industries or firms is not usually different enough to be able to achieve any significant competitive advantage. Options two and three are to use a supply chain planning application that is integrated with the firm's ERP or one from a third-party that bolts on to the firm's ERP system. Some ERP providers, such as SAP, offer an APS that is designed to be closely integrated with their ERP system. The obvious benefits of such integration include data consistency and integrity, as well as reduced need to transfer data between applications, which results in delays and potential errors. The alternative is to use a bolt-on or best-of-breed approach that seeks to identify the best supply chain planning system for the firm on the basis of features and functionality and then attach it to the firm's ERP system. The result is a planning system that better meets the firm's specific requirements or offers improved performance but at a probable cost of reduced integration. While providers of both integrated and bolt-on supply chain planning applications are attempting to enhance their integration with ERP system providers, operational integration between execution and planning systems remains a challenge.

Data integrity is a second major consideration for supply chain planning system implementation. Planning systems rely on absolute data integrity for effective decision making. While data integrity has always been important, it is more critical for planning systems since missing and inaccurate data can dramatically impact decision reliability and stability. One often-cited data integrity problem concerns product level detail such as cube and weight. While this is basic data, accuracy is not easy to maintain when there are large number of products with constant changes and new product introductions. Managers cite that in the process of implementing supply chain planning applications, it is not uncommon to find a few hundreds of products with incorrect or missing physical characteristics. While it may not be a large percentage of products in number, the inaccuracy can substantially impact planning system decision making. For example, missing or inaccurate cube can result in transportation planning system making a recommendation to overload a transportation vehicle. Specifically, the planning system will think that a large amount of product can be loaded into a truck when the product data contains an incorrect or zero cube. While the decision errors resulting from data integrity problems can be significant, the larger problem is that such errors substantially reduce the credibility of planning systems in general. A few highly visible errors such as overloading transportation vehicles or storage facilities cause management and planners to question the integrity of the entire planning system and process. The result is that management and operations personnel don't trust the results and prefer to return to the old tried and true methods of planning and scheduling. Thus, the potential for improved planning is reduced until the trust can be redeveloped. A strong focus on developing and maintaining data integrity is critical to effective planning system implementation.

Education regarding planning system application is a third major consideration. User training for supply chain execution and planning systems has usually focused on the mechanics to initiate the transactions. So, the user would be trained in data or parameter entry where the system would provide quick feedback regarding the acceptability of the entry. Supply chain planning systems are relatively more complex, as the feedback is not immediate and the impact may be extensive. For example, changing the requirements or forecast for one item in a time period may shift production schedules for related items on the other side of the world. Understanding planning system dynamics is critical to successful application. Such understanding requires thorough knowledge of APS system mechanics and system interactions. Although such knowledge can be initiated through training, it must be refined and extended through education and experience. Planning system education must focus on the characteristics and relationships between supply chain management activities and processes both internal and external to the firm. The education process must be much broader than existing training approaches. Planning system experience can be developed by using job shadowing experience and simulations. The shadowing environment provides actual on-the-job experience in a real-time environment. The simulated environment provides a laboratory where inexperienced planners can see or observe the results of their planning environment at low risk to the firm. The combination of these two educational experiences provides a solid foundation for implementing successful supply chain planning applications.

(5) Supply Chain Planning Summary.

The major objective of an integrated inventory deployment or APS system is integrated and co-ordinated capacity management of relevant supply chain resources including manufacturing plants, distribution centers, and transportation resources.[6] Capacity management planning balances the market demands with the production resources. On the basis of activity levels defined by the forecasting system, these constraints determine material bottlenecks and guide resource allocation to meet market demands. For each product, capacity constraints influence the where, when, and how much for production, storage, and movement. The constraints consider aggregate limitations such as periodic production, movement, and storage capacities.

Capacity problems can be resolved by resource acquisition or speculation/postponement of production or delivery. Capacity adjustments can be made by acquisition or alliances such as contract manufacturing or facility leasing. Speculation reduces bottlenecks by anticipating production capacity requirements through prior scheduling or contract manufacturing. Postponement delays production and shipment until specific requirements are known and capacity can be allocated. It may be necessary to offer customer incentives such as discounts or allowances to postpone customer delivery. The capacity limitations time-phase the enterprise's S&OP by taking into account facility, financial, and human resource limitations. These constraints have a major influence on logistics, manufacturing, and procurement schedules.

New Words and Expressions

1. breadth [bredθ]   n. 宽度,幅度,宽宏
2. spatial ['speiʃl]   adj. 空间的,存在于空间的,受空间条件限制的,占大篇幅的
3. dynamic [daɪ'næmɪk]   n. 动态,动力
   adj 动态的,动力的,动力学的,有活力的
4. consistency [kən'sɪst(ə)nsɪ]   n. 一致性
5. overload [əʊvə'ləʊd]   v. 使负担太重(overload 的现在分词),使超载,使过载,给……增加负荷,超过负荷
   n. 超载,负荷过多,过载,过负载
6. parameter [pə'ræmɪtə]   n. 参数,参量,限制因素,决定因素
7. bottleneck ['bɒt(ə)lnek]   n. 瓶颈,障碍物
8. incentive [in'sentivz]   n. 动机,诱因,刺激,鼓励

Notes

[1] The inventory deployment activity can be completed independently by individual supply chain functions, in an integrated manner by supply chain overall, or in a coordinated manner by the entire firm.
库存调度活动可以以整体供应链一体化的方式或以整个公司协调的方式,由供应链的个别功能独立完成。

[2] The key objective of an inventory deployment system is an integrated inventory plan through what is increasingly being termed an Advanced Planning and Scheduling (APS) system.

一个库存配置系统的关键目标就是通过一个高级计划与排程系统(APS)(正在被越来越多的这样称之为)形成一个整合库存计划。

[3] To correspond with the planning and execution of effective logistics and supply chain strategies, supply chain planning systems incorporate both spatial and temporal considerations.

为了与有效的物流和供应链战略的规划及实施相符,供应链规划系统必须将空间和时间相结合。

[4] First, logistics and supply chain managers have used extended lead times and schedule freezes to plan for future supply chain activity.

首先,物流和供应链管理者通过延长提前期和进度冻结期以计划未来的供应链活动。

[5] Second, effective supply chain management requires planning and coordination across firm functions and between supply chain partners.

第二,有效的供应链管理要求在横贯公司各种职能部门和供应链合作伙伴之间进行计划和协调。

[6] The major objective of an integrated inventory deployment or APS system is integrated and coordinated capacity management of relevant supply chain resources including manufacturing plants, distribution centers, and transportation resources.

一体化库存调度系统或高级计划与排程系统(APS)的主要目的是相关供应链资源一体化和协调能力管理,其资源包括制造工厂、配送中心、运输资源。

Unit 8

Passage A Communication Technology (I)

Information-sharing technology is critical to facilitate logistics and supply chain planning and operations. Historically, logistics coordination has been difficult since essential work and is typically performed at locations remote from information technology hardware. As a result, information was not available at the work location in terms of both time and content. The past decade has witnessed remarkable advances in logistical communication systems capability, including bar code and scanning, global data synchronization, the Internet, extensible markup language, satellite technology, and image processing.

1. Bar Code and Scanning

Auto identification (ID) systems such as bar coding and electronic scanning were developed to facilitate logistics information collection and exchange. Typical applications include tracking warehouse receipts and retail sales. Those ID systems require significant capital investment but replace error-prone and time-consuming paper-based information collection and exchange processes. In fact, increased domestic and international competition is driving shippers, carriers, warehouses, wholesalers, and retailers to develop and utilize auto ID capability to compete in today's marketplace.

Auto ID allows supply chain members to quickly track and communicate movement details with high accuracy and timeliness, so it is fast becoming a fundamental service requirement for freight tracking by carriers. Both consumers and B2B customers expect to be able to track the progress of their shipment using the Web-based system offered by carriers such as S. F. Express, United Parcel Service and FedEx.

Bar coding is the placement of computer-readable codes on items, cartons, containers, pallets, and even rail cars.[1] Bar code development and applications are increasing at a very rapid rate. Table 8-1 summarizes the benefits of auto ID technologies. While the benefits are obvious, it is not clear which symbologies will be adopted as industry standards. Standardization and flexibility are desirable to accommodate the needs of a wide range of industries, but they also increase cost, making it more difficult for small- and medium-size shippers, carriers, and receivers to implement standardized technologies. Finally, while continued convergence to common standards is likely, surveys indicate that select industries and major shippers will continue to use proprietary codes to maximize their competitive position.

Part 2　Information Technology

Benefits of automatic identification technologies　　　　　　　　Table 8-1

Shippers	Warehousing
Improve order preparation and processing	Improved order preparation, processing, and shipment
Eliminate shipping errors	Provide accurate inventory control
Reduce labor time	Customer access to real-time information
Improve record keeping	Access considerations of information security
Reduce physical inventory time	Reduced labor costs
Carriers	**Wholesalers/Retailers**
Freight bill information integrity	Unit inventory precision
Customer access to real-time information	Price accuracy at point-of-sale
Improved record keeping of customer shipment activity	Improved register checkout productivity
Shipment traceability	Reduced physical inventory time
Simplified container processing	Increased system flexibility
Monitor incompatible products in vehicles	
Reduced information transfer time	

　　Another key component of auto ID technology is the scanning process, which represents the eyes of a bar code system. A scanner optically collects bar code data and converts it to usable information. There are two types of scanners: handheld and fixed position. Each type can utilize contact or noncontact technology. Handheld scanners are either laser guns (noncontact) or wands (contact). Fixed-position scanners are either automatic scanners (noncontact) or card readers (contact). Contact technologies require the reading device to actually touch the bar code. A contact technology reduces scanning errors but decreases flexibility. Laser gun technology is the most popular scanner technology currently in use, outpacing wands as the most widely installed technology.

　　Scanner technology has two major applications in logistics.

　　The first is point-of-sale (POS) in retail stores. In additions to ringing up receipts for consumers, retail POS applications provide accurate inventory control at the store level. POS allows precise tracking of each stock keeping unit (SKU) sold and can be used to facilitate inventory replenishment. In addition to providing accurate resupply and marketing research data, POS can provide more timely strategic benefits to all channel members.

　　The second logistics scanner application is for materials handling, vehicle identification, and tracking. Through the use of scanner guns, materials handlers and gate operators can track product and vehicle movement, storage location, shipments, and receipts. While this information can be tracked manually, it is very time-consuming and subject to error. Wider usage of scanners in logistical applications will increase productivity and reduce errors. The demand for faster and less-error-prone scanning technology drives rapid changes in the marketplace for applications and technology.

2. Global Data Synchronization

　　While the phone, fax, and direct computer connection have enabled information exchange in the past, EDI and the Internet are quickly becoming the standards for effective, accurate, and low-cost information exchange.[2] EDI is defined as direct computer-to-computer exchange of business documents in standard formats to facilitate high-volume transactions. It involves both the capability and practice of communicating information between two organizations electronically instead of via the traditional forms of mail, courier, or even fax.

Communication and information standards are essential for EDI. Communication standards specify technical characteristics necessary for the computer hardware to correctly accomplish the interchange. Communication standards deal with character sets, transmission priority, and speed. Information standards dictate the structure and content of the message. Standards organizations have developed and refined two general standards as well as numerous industry-specific standards in an effort to standardize both communication and information interchange.

(1) EDI Transaction Sets.

Communication standards are implemented using transaction sets. A transaction set provides a common standard to facilitate information interchange between partners in a specific industry and country. Table 8-2 lists the common logistics-related industry transaction standards. For each industry, the transaction set defines the documents that can be transmitted. Documents typically cover common logistics activities such as ordering, warehouse operations, and transportation.

Primary logistics industry EDI standards   Table 8-2

UCS (Uniform Communication Standards)	Grocery
VICS (Voluntary Interindustry Communication Standards Committee)	Mass merchandisers
WINS (Warehouse Information Network Standards)	Warehouse operators
TDCC (Transportation Data Coordinating Committee)	Transportation operators
ALAG (Automotive Industry Action Group)	Automotive industry

(2) Electronic Product Code (EPC).

EPC is an emerging form of product identification. The Auto-ID Center at Massachusetts Institute of Technology, with support from both manufacturers and retailers, collaborated to develop an "intelligent tracking infrastructure" for supply chains. The two standards organizations EAN (European Article Number) and UCC (Uniform Code Council), which were developers of previous bar code standards, formed an organization called EPC global Inc., which is driving the adoption and implementation of the "EPC global Network".

(3) Radio Frequency Exchange.

Radio-frequency data communication (RFDC) technology is used within relatively small areas, such as distribution center, to facilitate two-way information exchange.[3] A major application is real-time communication with mobile operators such as forklift drivers and order selectors. RFDC technology allows drivers to have instructions and priorities updated on a real time basis instead of using a hard copy of instructions printed hours earlier. Real-time or Wi-Fi transmissions guide work flow, offer increased flexibility and responsiveness, and can improve service using fewer resources. Logistics RFDC technology applications also include two-way communication for warehouse picking, cycle counts, verification, and label printing.[4]

Advanced RFDC capabilities in the form of two-way voice communication are finding their way into logistics warehouse applications. Instead of requiring warehouse operations personnel to interface with a mobile or handheld computer, voice RFDC prompts operators through tasks with audible commands and waits for verbal responses or requests. United Parcel Service uses speed-based RFDC to read zip codes from incoming packages and print routing tickets to guide packages through their sortation facilities. The voice recognition systems are based on keywords and voice patterns of each operator. The primary benefit of voice-based RFDC is an easier operator interface; since keyboard data entry is not required, two hands are available for order picking.

Radio frequency identification (RFID) is a second form of radio-frequency technology. RFID can be used to identify a container or its contents as it moves through facilities or on transportation equipment. RFID places a coded electronic chip in the container or box. RFID chips can be either active or passive. Active chips continuously emanate radio waves so that product can be located in a warehouse or a retail store, using receivers located throughout the store. Active chips technology is good for locating product in a facility as well as for identifying when it is moving in and out of the facility. Passive chips respond only when they are electronically stimulated by having the product pass through a relatively small gateway for or portal that has scanners built in. Since the product must be passed through a gateway for passive chips to operate, these can be used only for tracking product movement in, out, and around a facility. With current technology, the cost of active chips is approximately ten times that of passive chips because of the need for a battery and larger antenna. As the container or box moves through the supply chain, it can be scanned for an identifying code or even for the list of contents. Retailers are beginning to use RFID to allow entire cartloads of merchandise to be scanned simultaneously. WalMart and other major retailers began initiatives to require their major suppliers place RFID tags on their cases to facilitate processing in distribution warehouses, receipt at stores, and shelf restocking. While the benefits were apparent for the retailers, they were not so evident for the manufactures, particularly since the retailers were not generally willing to pay for the chip and the technologies to employ it. While the initiatives to use RFID to track activity for consumer products have declined, there is significant activity investigating the use of RFID to enhance security and minimize counterfeiting. For example, there is increasing use of RFID for pharmaceuticals and expensive technology to reduce counterfeiting and enhance security. It is anticipated that the lessons learned through these applications will reduce the price of RFID and will lead to future logistics applications.

Typically, information on a bar code is captured via a fixed or handheld scanner device. The EPC-based identification system, on the other hand, can use RFID tags in conjunction with readers in orders to collect more extensive product information. The RFID tags are miniature circuits that contain the EPC code. A reader can transmit a request for product identification that will stimulate the tag on a responding item to transmit the identification number on the tag back to the reader. The identification number on the reader can then be transmitted to a computer, which can identify both the unique item (SKU number as well as unique serial number) as well as physical location. Information about a product in a warehouse, store, or any place within transmission range can then be shared and updated in real time across a network. EPC read speed and lack of requiring line-of-sight reading are major advantages over bar code scanners.

New Words and Expressions

1. markup [ˈmɑːkʌp]   *n.* 涨价,利润,审定
2. ID (identification)   *n.* 鉴定,识别;验明;身份证明;认同
3. carton [ˈkɑːtən]   *n.* 硬纸盒,纸板箱
4. pallet [ˈpælɪt]   *n.* 托盘,平台,运货板,扁平工具,[机]棘爪,货盘
5. proprietary [prəˈpraɪət(ə)rɪ]   *n.* 所有权,所有人
   adj. 所有的,专利的,私人拥有的
6. precision [prɪˈsɪʒən]   *n.* 精确,精密度,精度
7. optically [ˈɒptɪkəlɪ]   *adv.* 眼睛地,视力地
8. dictate [dɪkˈteɪt]   *v.* 命令,支配,指定
9. transmit [trænzˈmɪt]   *vt.* 传输,传播,发射,传达,发射信号
   vi. 传输,发射信号
10. merchandiser [ˈmɜːtʃənˌdaɪzə]   *n.* 商人
11. EPC (electronic product code)   电子产品码
12. radio-frequency data communication (RFDC)   无线电频数据通信技术
13. collaborate [kəˈlæbəreɪt]   *v.* 合作
14. audible [ˈɔːdɪb(ə)l]   *adj.* 听得见的
15. sortation [sɔːˈteɪʃən]   *n.* 分类
16. RFID (radio frequency identification)   无线射频识别
17. chip [tʃɪp]   *n.* [电子]芯片,筹码,碎片
    v. 削,凿,削成碎片
18. gateway [ˈgeɪtweɪ]   *n.* 门,网关,方法,通道,途径
19. antenna [ænˈtenə]   *n.* [电讯]天线
20. counterfeit [ˈkaʊntəfɪt]   *n.* 赝品,冒牌货,伪造品
    v. 伪造,仿造,假装,伪装
    adj. 假冒的,伪造的,虚伪的

21. circuit [ˈsɜːkɪt]　　　　　　　　　　n. [电子]电路,回路,巡回,一圈,环道
　　　　　　　　　　　　　　　　　　v. 环行,绕回……环行
22. SKU (stock keeping unit)　　　　　货物储存单元

Notes

[1] Bar coding is the placement of computer-readable codes on items, cartons, containers, pallets, and even rail cars.
条形码技术是在商品、纸盒、集装箱、托盘甚至是机动轨道车上安置了一个计算机可读取的代码。

[2] While the phone, fax, and direct computer connection have enabled information exchange in the past, EDI and the Internet are quickly becoming the standards for effective, accurate, and low-cost information exchange.
虽然电话、传真和计算机直接互联在过去已实现信息交换,但电子数据交换(EDI)和互联网正在迅速成为高效、准确以及低成本信息交换的标准。

[3] Radio-frequency data communication (RFDC) technology is used within relatively small areas, such as distribution center, to facilitate two-way information exchange.
无线电频数据通信(RFDC)技术被用于相对较小的区域内,如配送中心,以实现双向信息交流。

[4] Logistics RFDC technology applications also include two-way communication for warehouse picking, cycle counts, verification, and label printing.
无线电频数据通信技术物流应用还包括仓库拣选、循环计数、盘点以及标签打印的双向通信。

Passage B　Communication Technology (Ⅱ)

1. Internet

Widespread availability of the Internet and standardized communication interfaces offered through browsers such as Internet Explorer have substantially expanded the opportunities capability to exchange information between firms of all sizes. The Internet is quickly becoming the supply chain information transmission device of choice for exchanging forecasts, orders, inventory status, product updates, and shipment information.[1] In conjunction with a server and a browser, the Internet offers a standard approach for order entry, order status inquiry, and shipment tracking.

The availability of the Internet has also enabled the development of the exchange portal, a communication medium that has significant supply chain implications. An exchange portal is an infomediary that facilitates horizontal and vertical information exchange between supply chain partners. Figure 8-1 illustrates an exchange portal designed to facilitate communication between supply chain participants. The facilitating firm can provide information regarding raw material requirements, product availability, and price changes and allow the marketplace to react by placing bids or orders.

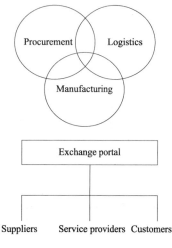

Figure 8-1 Single-firm exchange portal

A second type of exchange portal is industry based. It facilitates communication between all participants within an industry and can substantially reduce transaction costs. Figure 8-2 illustrates the exchange portal that the electronics industry has developed to facilitate communication between the original equipment manufacturers and their multiple tiers of suppliers. This portal offers a common framework for exchanging information, including design information, proposal requests, commodity availability, bids, and schedules.[2] While the information can be made available to all interested parties, it is also possible to restrict information availability. There is increasing fear that industry portal collaborations might increase the potential for monopolistic practices and trade restraints.

A third type of exchange portal is cross-industry-based and is designed to facilitate communication between firms that have common interests in commodities and services.[3] Figure 8-3 illustrates a cross-industry exchange portal for manufacturers, suppliers, service providers, and customers. When one of the member firms has a need for raw material, product, or service, it can access the exchange portal to determine availability and potential price. Similarly, when one of the member firms has excess product or service capacity, such availability can be posted on the portal to solicit interest or a possible bid by one of the exchange members. Reverse auctions can be used most effectively with cross-industry-based portals.

The Internet and the exchange portal have advanced supply chain communication from one-to-one or limited capability to a one-to-many environment capable of being extended to a many-to-many capability. The result is that extended Internet communication is a reality that offers substantial challenge in terms of exploiting widely available information.

One of the major challenges to the wide adoption of exchange portals is the definition and acceptance of online catalogs. Much like the paper version, an online catalog contains a listing of the products and services offered along with their descriptions and specifications. A catalog that is consistent across firms is critical to facilitate effective comparison of products and services across firms. For example, a firm desiring to purchase a simple T-shirt from a portal would like all the T-shirt suppliers on that portal to have a similarly formatted entry describing the shirt, its coloring, its content, as well as other minute details so that the customer can make an effective comparison. While customers prefer consistent catalogs, suppliers prefer to use a catalog as a differentiator and are thus reluctant to deviate from their proprietary format. To facilitate information sharing and exchange, the Voluntary Interindustry Commerce Standards (VICS) and CPFR are actively promoting common and consistent catalog definitions and standards.

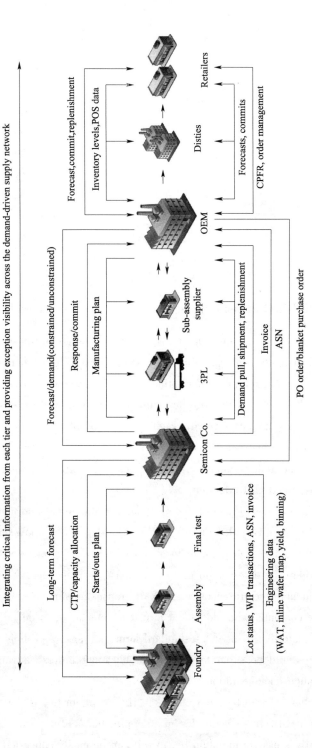

Figure 8-2 Electronics industry exchange portal

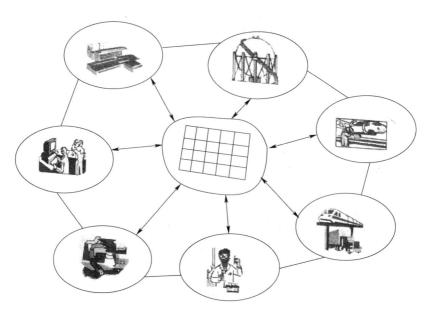

Figure 8-3 Cross-industry exchange portal

2. Extensible Markup Language

XML is a flexible computer language that facilitates information transfer between a wide range of applications and is readily interpretable by humans. It was published in 1998 by the World Wide Web Consortium to facilitate information transfer between systems, databases, and Web browsers. Since EDI is very structured, the setup cost and required expertise are relatively high, limiting applications to situations involving high transaction volumes. XML is emerging as the information transfer medium between firms and service providers that do not have transaction volumes to justify EDI. XML facilitates communication by breaking down many information technology barriers that have constrained EDI adoption.

A basic XML message consists of three components: the actual information being transmitted, data tags, and a document type definition (DTD). The data tag is a key feature, as it defines the data being transmitted. The tags indicate to all computer applications what the data between the brackets are and where the date should go in a database or Web page. The use of common terms and the lack of sequencing requirements make XML transactions much easier to use than EDI. The XML DTD tells the computer what document format to refer to when decoding a message. A DTD is essentially a template that maps out a standard form, its tags, and their relation in a database. For example, there would be separate schema for customer orders, advanced shipping notifications, or transportation documentation.

In situations characterized by low volume, XML is superior to EDI for three reasons. First, it is not expensive to install. It is easy to design an application and requires much less time to implement. Second, XML is easy to maintain because it can be easily converted to Hyper Text Markup Language (HTML), the language of Web browsers. This makes it much easier to modify and share data between applications. Finally, XML is more flexible, allowing for broad applications and quick definition and extension of standards.

3. Satellite

Satellite technology allows communication across an expansive geographic area such as a region or even the world. The technology is similar to that of microwave dishes used for home television in areas outside the reach of cable.

Satellite communication provides a fast and high-volume channel for information movement. Schneider National, a nationwide truckload carrier, uses communication dishes mounted on its trucks to enable two-way communication between drivers and their dispatchers. Such real-time interaction provides up-to-date information regarding location and delivery information, allowing dispatchers to redirect trucks according to need or congestion. Retail chains also use satellite communication to quickly transmit sales information back to headquarters.

4. Image Processing

Image processing utilizes facsimile (fax) and optical-scanning technology to transmit and store freight bill information, as well as other supporting documents such as proof of delivery receipts (POD) or bills of lading (BOL).[4] The rationale for this service is that timely customer shipment information is almost as important as delivering the goods on time. As freight is delivered to customers, support documentation is sent to image processing locations, electronically scanned, and logged into the system.

Electronic images of the documents are then transmitted to a central database where they are stored. By the next day, customers can access the documents through computer linkage or a phone call to their service representative. Customer requests for a hard copy of a document can be filled within minutes by a facsimile transmission. Customer benefits include more accurate billing, faster response from carrier personnel, and easy access to documentation. The carrier also benefits because the system eliminates the need to file paper documents, reduces the chance of loss, and provides improved credibility with customers.

Satellite technology, radio frequency(RF), and image processing require substantial capital investment prior to achieving significant returns. Experience has shown, however, the primary benefit of those communication technologies is not always lower cost but improved customer service. Improved service is provided in the form of more timely and accurate order entry, quicker shipment tracing, and faster transfer of sales and inventory information. There will be increased demand for these communication technology applications as customers observe the competitive benefits of real-time information transfer.

New Words and Expressions

1. commodity[kəˈmɒdɪtɪ]   n. 商品,货物,日用品

2. monopolistic [mə,nɒpə'lɪstɪk]　　　　　adj. 垄断的,独占性的,专利的
3. auction ['ɔːkʃ(ə)n]　　　　　　　　　n. 拍卖
　　　　　　　　　　　　　　　　　　v. 拍卖,竞卖
4. differentiator [difə'renʃieitə]　　　　　n. [自]微分器,微分电路,区分者
5. interpretable [in'tə:prətəbl]　　　　　adj. 可说明的,可判断的,可翻译的
6. bracket ['brækɪt]　　　　　　　　　　n. 支架,括号
　　　　　　　　　　　　　　　　　　v. 括在一起,把……归入同一类,排除
7. mount [maunt]　　　　　　　　　　　vt. 装上,设置,安放
8. truckload ['trʌkloud]　　　　　　　　n. 一货车的容量;整车货;通常缩写为TL
9. dispatcher [dɪs'pætʃə]　　　　　　　n. 调度员,[计]调度程序,[计]分配器
10. congestion [kən'dʒestʃən]　　　　　n. 拥挤,堵车,阻塞
11. headquarter ['hedkwɔːtə]　　　　　v. 设立总部;在……设总部
12. optical ['ɔptɪkəl]　　　　　　　　　adj. 光学的;视觉的;视力的;眼睛的
13. rationale [ræʃə'nɑːli]　　　　　　　n. 基本理论
14. facsimile [fæk'sɪmɪli]　　　　　　　n. 传真,复写
　　　　　　　　　　　　　　　　　　adj. 复制的
　　　　　　　　　　　　　　　　　　v. 传真,临摹
15. POD (proof of delivery receipts)　　交货收据证明

Notes

[1] The Internet is quickly becoming the supply chain information transmission device of choice for exchanging forecasts, orders, inventory status, product updates, and shipment information.
互联网已经迅速成为供应链信息传送所选工具,用于预测、订单、库存状态、产品更新以及运输信息的交换。

[2] This portal offers a common framework for exchanging information, including design information, proposal requests, commodity availability, bids, and schedules.
这种接口为信息交换提供了一个通用框架,包括设计信息、需求建议、商品可用性、投标和日程安排。

[3] A third type of exchange portal is cross-industry-based and is designed to facilitate communication between firms that have common interests in commodities and services.
第三种类型的交换接口是基于跨行业的,并且被设计成方便在商品及服务方面有着共同利益的公司之间沟通。

[4] Image processing utilizes facsimile (fax) and optical-scanning technology to transmit and store freight bill information, as well as other supporting documents such as proof of delivery receipts (POD) or bills of lading (BOL).
图像处理利用传真和光学扫描技术来传送和储存运货单信息以及其他支撑文件,例如交货收据证明和提货单。

Part 3   Freight Transportation

Unit 9
Unit 10
Unit 11
Unit 12

Part 3 Freight Transportation

Unit 9

Passage A Modes of Transportation

There are five major modes of freight transportation: airlines, motor carriers, pipelines, railroads, and water carriers. Each of these modes has distinct characteristics that give them advantages over the others. Which mode is best depends on the freight hauled, cost, speed, reliability, capability, capacity, length of haul, and flexibility (see Table 9-1).[1]

U. S. domestic freight modal comparisons modes of transportation   Table 9-1

Comparison factors	Airlines	Motor carriers	Pipelines	Railroads	Water carriers	Other
Freight hauled (ton-miles)	0.2%	27.9%	17.6%	26.7%	20.4%	7.2%
Revenue generated	2.7%	69.4%	4.2%	4.8%	2.5%	17.4%
Cost①	1	2	4	3	5	
Speed②	1	2	5	3	4	
Reliability③	3	2	1	4	5	
Capability④	4	3	5	2	1	
Flexibility⑤	3	1	5	2	4	
Capacity⑥	4	5	1	3	2	
Tons	Up to 125t	Up to 25t	Up to 2,500,000t	Up to 12,000t	Up to 60,000t	
Average value per pound of freight shipped	$21.14	$0.35	$0.09	$0.12	$0.06	

①1 = most costly, ②1 = fastest, ③1 = most reliable in terms of meeting schedules on time, ④1 = best ability to transport various products, ⑤1 = most flexible in terms of door-to-door delivery and number of geographic points served, ⑥1 = ability to carry highest amount of tons in one trip.

1. Airlines

Airlines are the fastest terminal-to-terminal mode of transportation. This is their primary advantage. They specialize in the time-sensitive movement of documents, perishable items, technical instruments, medical supplies, and high-valued products. Also, air transportation has the highest percentage of revenues coming from passenger travel. While airlines are important for some freight movement, their primary business has traditionally been passenger travel. Airfreight services cost more than other modes, primarily due to their speed. Air carriers provide terminal-to-terminal service, meaning that direct delivery to a consumer's door is the rarest of exceptions. Airlines are reasonably reliable. While weather-related flight delays might disrupt service, the disrupted service is often still faster than the next fastest mode, the motor carrier. The airlines' speed advantage is most apparent for hauls over 500 miles. For trips less than 500 miles, motor carriers often outperform airlines door-to-door.

Airlines transport small volumes shipments rather than large volumes, and packaged products rather than heavy, bulk commodities. The physical configuration and cost of air service also limit the variety of products shipped by air. Measured by weight, airlines transport very little freight. The percentage of total freight dollars shipped by air is relatively small, although the revenue growth rate is promising. As customer service expectations increase, so does the demand for shorter transit times. As a result, many shippers have turned to air transportation.

Most airline costs change over a short period of time and depend on output, making airlines predominantly variable cost carriers.[2] While the initial cost of the air fleet is significant, these fixed costs are spread over the long useful life of the aircraft. Terminals represent a major fixed cost in other modes, but airline terminals are publicly owned facilities for which the airlines pay user fees. The significant start-up costs associated with an airline limit the number of competitors, creating an oligopolistic market structure, with only a few large carriers.

2. Motor Carriers

Motor carriers are the most flexible major mode of transportation. This means better direct access to motor carriage for more shippers and final consumers. Motor carriers compete with airlines for higher-valued products, as well as time-sensitive products (electronics, perishables, etc.) within a 500-mile radius. Motor carriers also compete with rail transportation for some higher-valued freight, such as automobiles. Motor carriage ranks as the second fastest mode of transportation, with the additional advantages of door-to-door flexibility and broad geographic coverage. Because trailers vary in length, temperature control, and form, motor carriers can carry a variety of products. In fact, they can carry almost anything. An industry saying "If it got there, a truck brought it" rings very nearly true. Motor carrier rates are high compared with all other modes but air. They also face gross weight and length restrictions, as well as other legal limits. Motor carriers are susceptible to delays because of bad weather or traffic congestion. Also, motor carriers are not well suited to handle extremely heavy, bulky products because the trailer is not properly constructed to ship such significant weight efficiently—even when permits allow the legal restrictions to be lifted.[3]

Motor carriers are often classified as less-than-truckload (LTL) or truckload (TL) carriers. LTL carriers accept less-than-load amounts, while TL carriers ship full truckloads. LTL operations are more costly to establish. These entities accept small packages, transport them to a consolidation facility, consolidate the small packages of freight into one large shipment, move the large shipment to another facility, and break it back down into small packages for delivery. This type of operation is more asset-intensive than a truckload operation because LTL carriers require more motor carrier equipment, an extensive information network, and consolidation facilities.

3. Pipelines

Pipelines are a unique mode of transportation. They are fixed in place, and the product moves through them. This limits the types of products they can transport, but within these limits they can move more tons in a single shipment than any other mode of transportation (30,000t to 2,500,000). They can transport product only in a liquid or gaseous state. Petroleum is the number one product moved by pipelines. Slurry pipelines, which move solid materials such as coal that is suspended in a liquid, do exist, but they have met with considerable opposition from railroads and water carriers. Pipelines are cost-effective where large quantities of liquid products need to be transported. Pipelines offer an advantage that none of the other modes can offer: a pipeline is a continuous flow mode. When the pipeline is full, the product flows to the destination immediately and continues to do so, almost without fail. Pipelines are the most dependable mode of delivery, unaffected by external factors like weather. However, pipeline transportation is slow, rigid in terms of routes and product types, and limited to terminal-to-terminal service. A pipeline's average speed is usually between two and five miles per hour. Pipelines can rarely deliver the product to the consumer's door, and the origin and destination of the mode are fixed — unless household water and gas lines are taken into account.

Pipeline costs are predominantly fixed. Pipelines must build their own right-of-way, an extremely expensive undertaking. Pipelines most often move large quantities of liquid products from a fixed origin to a fixed destination. The construction of a pipeline becomes cost-effective only when the high initial fixed cost can be spread over enough volume to keep the unit transportation cost competitive with other modes.

4. Railroads

Railroads transport a significant amount of domestic freight. Railroads haul high-density, low-valued freight over long distances at rates lower than trucking and air, but higher than water and pipeline. Products hauled include coal, stone, sand, metals, grain, and automobiles. Their primary competitors include domestic water carriers for large, bulk products and motor carriers for higher-valued goods. Railroads can handle a wide variety of goods, but generally have not. They lack flexibility and high-speed delivery in their standard operation.

Recently, rail has regained some freight lost to motor carriers through increases in intermodal operations — trailer on flatcar (TOFC) or piggyback and container on flatcar (COFC). The use of standardized containers that can be removed from a ship and placed directly on a railcar for surface transportation has helped rail carriers regain market share. Railcars have also been adapted to meet intermodal needs. Double-stack railcars allow for two containers to be stacked onto a specialized railcar, effectively doubling the capacity of the car.

5. Water Carriers

Water carriers dominate international transportation because of their cost structure and ability to transport large volumes. Their significant modal market share is derived from these international operations. Advantages of water transport include long-haul capabilities — particularly for low-valued products such as coal, stone, grain, and ores — at low rates. They can and do haul a broad range of products, from ores and grains to Christmas toys.

Water carriers compete heavily with railroads along certain routes, and with pipelines for the movement of some products, particularly petroleum.[4] Water carriers' cost structure and volume levels are such that they can charge very low rates. Water carriers are relatively slow, unreliable, and inflexible compared with other modes. They depend on other modes for door-to-door delivery and suffer from a high degree of variability in delivery schedules.

New Words and Expressions

1. perishable ['periʃəbl]　　　　　　 adj. 容易腐烂的
2. disrupt [dis'rʌpt]　　　　　　　　 v. 使中断,使分裂,使瓦解,使陷于混乱,破坏
3. outperform [autpə'fɔ:m]　　　　　vt. 做得比……好,胜过
4. bulk [bʌlk]　　　　　　　　　　　n. 体积,容量,大多数,大部分,大块
　　　　　　　　　　　　　　　　　　vt. 使扩大,使形成大量,使显得重要
5. configuration [kən,figə'reiʃn]　　 n. 配置,布局,构造,结构,外形
6. predominantly [pri'ɔmineit]　　　vt. 掌握,控制,支配
　　　　　　　　　　　　　　　　　　vi. 统治,成为主流,支配,占优
7. oligopolistic　　　　　　　　　　　市场供应垄断者
8. susceptible [sə'septəbl]　　　　　 adj. 易受影响的,易受感染的
9. LTL(less-than-truckload)　　　　零担货
10. TL(truckload) ['trʌkləud]　　　　n. 整车货
11. consolidate [kən'sɑ:lideit]　　　　v. 统一,把……合成一体,合并,巩固,加强,合计金额
12. intermodal [ˌɪntə,məʊdl]　　　　adj. 联合运输的,多式联运
13. railcar [reil'kɑ:]　　　　　　　　　n. (单节)机动有轨车
14. stack [stæk]　　　　　　　　　　n. 堆,一堆,堆栈
　　　　　　　　　　　　　　　　　　v. 堆叠
15. ore [ɔ:(r)]　　　　　　　　　　　 n. 矿,矿石,矿砂
16. TOFC(trailer on flatcar)(铁路)　 平板车装运载有集装箱的拖车
17. COFC(container on flatcar)　　 集装箱平车
18. variability [veəriə'biləti]　　　　　n. 可变性,变化性,[生物][数]变异性

Notes

[1] Which mode is best depends on the freight hauled, cost, speed, reliability, capability, ca-

pacity, length of haul, and flexibility(see Table 9-1).

哪种运输方式最好取决于货运量、成本、运输速度、可靠性、运输能力、运输容量、运输长度和机动性(见表 9-1)。which 引导的从句为主语从句。

[2] Most airline costs change over a short period of time and depend on output, making airlines predominantly variable cost carriers.

多数航线成本不仅在短期内会变化,且取决于运输量,这就使航空运输成为成本变化最大的运输方式。making …… 表示结果。

[3] Also, motor carriers are not well suited to handle extremely heavy, bulky products because the trailer is not properly constructed to ship such significant weight efficiently — even when permits allow the legal restrictions to be lifted.

同样,汽车运输不太适合运输重量极重、体积庞大的货物,因为挂车没有适合的空间来有效地运载相当重的货物——即便是法律允许。even when…… 为假设条件,译成 "即便是……"。

[4] Water carriers compete heavily with railroads along certain routes, and with pipelines for the movement of some products, particularly petroleum.

水路运输在某些线路上与铁路运输竞争激烈,并且在一些货物运输上与管道运输竞争激烈,特别是石油运输。

Passage B Road Transport

1. Road Transport in General

Road transport is capable of providing a door-to-door service without any break in the journey to change from one vehicle to another; so it can, unlike any other means of transport, move a product from anywhere to anywhere else. Road vehicles, being relatively small, can also be transported by other means of transport such as ships and aircraft, hence providing the ability to offer direct delivery in the same vehicle even when other means of transport become a necessity. In most countries, the road system is perceived by the authorities as being a part of the national infrastructure and is funded out of taxation, effectively providing a subsidy to road transport. As a result, it can frequently offer competitive prices relative to other forms of transport, an advantage that is enhanced further by the fact that the road haulage industry comprises many independent operators fighting for their share of the market, making it highly competitive. Road transport is also, for most companies, the only mode of transport for which an in-house operation is a realistic option.

Although there has been significant investment in road in most developed countries over the past decades, this has been matched by a corresponding increase in road traffic, leading to serious congestion in many cities and urban areas. Estimating delivery times and maintaining schedules becomes difficult with resultant risks to meeting on-time delivery targets.[1]

Road transportation has expanded rapidly since the end of World War II. To a significant degree the rapid growth of the motor carrier industry has resulted from speed and ability to operate door-to-door.

Motor carriers have flexibility because they are able to operate on all types of roadways. Nearly one million miles of road are available to motor carriers, which is more mileage than all other modes combined. The fleet of over-the-road trucks exceeds 1.5 million tractors and 4.4 million trailers.

In comparison to railroads, motor carriers have relatively small fixed investment in terminal facilities and operate using publicly financed and maintained roads. Although the cost of license fees, user fees, and tolls is considerable, these expenses are directly related to the number of trucks and miles operated. The variable cost per mile for motor carriers is high because a separate power unit and driver are required for each trailer or combination of tandem trailers. Labor requirements are also high due to driver safety restrictions and need for substantial dock labor. Motor carrier operations are characterized by low fixed and high variable costs. In comparison to railroads, motor carriers more efficiently handle small shipments moving short distances.

Motor carrier characteristics favor manufacturing and distributive trades, at distances up to 500 miles for high-value products. Motor carriers have made significant inroads into rail traffic for medium and light manufacturing. Due to delivery flexibility, motor carriers dominate freight moving from wholesalers or warehouses to retail stores. The prospect for maintaining stable market share in road transport remains.

2. Convention on the Contract for International Carriage of Goods by Road

The Convention on the Contract for International Carriage of Goods by Road of 19 May 1956 (CMR) has for its purpose to uniformly regulate the contract of international carriage of goods by road with particular attention to the consignment note and to the liability of the carrier.

On 5 July 1978, a Protocol amending the CMR was adopted. While introducing a new monetary system featuring the Special Drawing Right (S. D. R.), the Protocol also brought about changes to the section concerning the liability of the carrier.

The application of the Convention is limited to a situation where the point of departure and the point of destination of the goods are located in different countries of which at least one is a member of the Convention.

Since the consignment note was being used extensively in conjunction with the contract of carriage of goods, certain formalities regarding this document were adopted in order to regulate and uniform the trade. First of all, the consignment note is not a document of title but it does constitute evidence of the making of the contract and the receipt of the goods by the carrier from the consignor. In turn, the carrier is also entitled to a receipt from the consignee once delivery of the goods is completed.

Since it is sufficient that only one of the States crossed during the transport be a member to the Convention, a notification to the other non-member State of the applicability of the present

Convention is required in the consignment note.

Successive transport by different carriers, whether or not done by road, is possible under this Convention when it is all covered by a single contract of carriage. The first carrier, the last carrier and the actual carrier under whom the damage happened, may be held liable for damage, loss or delay of the goods.[2]

Other provisions relating to the consignment note include an obligation to make the document in three copies so that the consignor, the consignee and the carrier each receive a copy. The interest of having a copy of the consignment note is so that it will be used as proof of receipt or delivery of the goods to the subsequent party.

When filling the consignment note, the consignor must specify certain particulars relating to the goods such as their nature and weight, and any inaccuracy of information resulting in damage to the carrier will engage the consignor's liability.

All necessary conditions respected, the ensuing applicability of the CMR is mandatory to the contract of carriage of goods by road.

One of the Convention's main attributes is the liability regime imposed on the carrier.[3] The proof that a damage, loss or delay of the goods took place while in transit will conclude the claimant's burden of proof.[4] Ensuing will be a legal presumption that the carrier is responsible for the incident unless he can prove that it was impossible for him to prevent such consequences. Exceptionally, when damage is either caused by the claimant or by an inherent vice of the goods, the latter will be required to prove the carrier's fault.[5] Fortunately, provisions limiting financially the amount of compensation payable to the shipper attenuate the effect of such strict presumptions of fault.

The institution of proceedings against the carrier is restricted by provisions of formality requiring written notices of damage to goods within a specific number of days. Action is also limited by a one-year period with a possibility of extension to three years in the case of willful misconduct of the carrier.[6]

New Words and Expressions

1. subsidy['sʌbsidi]   n. 津贴,补助金
2. haulage[hɔːlidʒ]   n. 拖运,运输
3. in-house   adj. &adv. 内部的,室内的
4. resultant[ri'zʌltənt]   adj. 作为结果而发生的,合成的
5. tandem['tændəm]   n. 前后双座车,一前一后排列,串联
6. tandem trailer   串列拖车
7. dock 英[dɒk]   n. 船坞,码头,(供汽车或火车装卸货物的)月台,
   美[dɒk]   港区
8. departure[dɪ'pɑrtʃə]   n. 离开,出发,违背
9. subsequent['sʌbsɪkw(ə)nt]   adj. 后来的,随后的

10. presumption[pri'zʌmpʃən]	n. 假定
11. attenuate[ətenjueit]	v. 变(稀)薄,变细(小),减弱
12. CMR(Convention relating to the International Road Consignment Note)	国际道路托运票据协定
13. consignment[kən'sainmənt]	n. 交货,托运物,送货
14. S.D.R.(the Special Drawing Right)	特别提取权
15. consignor[kən'sainə]	n. 委托者,发货人,货主
16. delay[dilei]	vi. 延期,耽搁
	vt. 延期,耽搁
	n. 延期,耽搁,被耽搁或推迟的时间
	v. (使)船停靠码头(dock 的第三人称单数),(使宇宙飞船在外层空间)对接,减少,扣除

Notes

[1] Estimating delivery times and maintaining schedules becomes difficult with resultant risks to meeting on-time delivery targets.

由于满足按时交货的目标有一定风险,估计交货时间和保持工作进度变得很难实现。

[2] The first carrier, the last carrier and the actual carrier under whom the damage happened, may be held liable for damage, loss or delay of the goods.

首承运人、最后承运人和造成货损的实际承运人,应该对货损、货差或迟延交付负责。under whom the damage happened 为定语从句,修饰 the actual carrier。

[3] One of the Convention's main attributes is the liability regime imposed on the carrier.

协定的主要特征之一是承运人承担的责任范围。

[4] The proof that a damage, loss or delay of the goods took place while in transit will conclude the claimant's burden of proof.

在运输途中发生货损、货差或货物延误的证明将断定索赔人的举证责任。that 引导的从句为同位语从句。

[5] Exceptionally, when damage is either caused by the claimant or by an inherent vice of the goods, the latter will be required to prove the carrier's fault.

例外地,如果货损是由于索赔人的过失或是由于货物本身的缺陷所致,后者将被要求证明承运人过失。the latter 是指 by an inherent vice of the goods。

[6] Action is also limited by a one-year period with a possibility of extension to three years in the case of willful misconduct of the carrier.

诉讼行动也限定为一年,在承运人故意拖延的情况下可以延长至三年。Action 指上一句中的"proceeding"诉讼"。

Part 3 Freight Transportation

Unit 10

Passage A Rail Transport

1. General Introduction

Rail transport is one of the most energy efficient means of mechanized land transport. Environmental and safe considerations also favor rail over road transport. Railways can be built with different distances between the two rails, the distance between the two rails is known as the rail gauge. Railways use signaling (usually color lights) to prevent trains from colliding. Railroads may or may not be electrified. If they are not, they can only be used by non-electric trains, mainly diesel trains. To be electrified, a means of supplying electricity to the train is needed. This can be done with overhead wires or with a third rail system. The former is the most common method. High speed rail, with speeds up to 350 km/h, are achieved by a specially built railroad and special trains. For short, steep stretches funiculars or cable car railways and cog railways provide railway functionality.

Depending on how much traffic they carry, railways can be built with a varying number of tracks. Rail lines that carry little traffic are often built with a single track which is used by trains traveling in both directions; on rail lines like these, "passing loops" or "passing sidings", which consist of short stretches of double track, are provided at certain points along the line to allow trains to pass each other, and travel in different directions. Alternatively, there may be larger sections of the line that are double track-effective timetabling can allow train travel up and down the partially double track line equivalent to travel on fully double tracks.

A train consists of a combination of a locomotive and attached carriage (also known as coaches or cars) or wagons, or a self-propelled multiple units (or occasionally a single powered coach, called a railcar). Special kinds of trains running on corresponding special "railways" are atmospheric railways, monorails, high speed railways, maglev, rubber-tired underground, funicular and cog railways.[1] Freight trains comprise wagons or trucks rather than carriages, though some parcel and mail trains (especially Traveling Post Offices) are outwardly more like passenger trains. A train hauled by two locomotives is said to be "double headed". Mixed trains, hauling both passengers and freight, have become rare in many countries. A light one- or two-car rail vehicle running through the streets is not called a train but a tram or streetcar, but the distinction is not strict. The term "light rail" is sometimes used for a modern tram, but it may also mean an intermediate form between a tram and a train, similar to metro except that it may have level crossings.[2] Maglev trains and monorails represent minor technologies in the train field. The term "rapid transit" is used for public transport such as commuter trains, metro and light-rail.

There are many different types of freight train, which are used to carry many different kinds of freight, with many different types of wagon. One of the most common types on modern railways are container trains, whereby the containers can be lifted on and off the train by cranes and loaded off or onto trucks or ships. This type of freight train has largely superseded the traditional "box wagon" type of freight train, whereby the cargo had to be loaded or unloaded manually. In some countries "piggy back" trains are used whereby trucks can drive straight onto the train and drive off again when the end destination is reached. A system like this is used on the Channel Tunnel between England and France. There are also some "inter-modal" vehicles, which have two sets of wheels, for use in a train, or as the trailer of a road vehicle. There are also many other types of wagon, such as "low loader" wagons for transporting road vehicles. There are refrigerator wagons for transporting food. There are simple types of open-topped wagons for transporting minerals and bulk material such as coal and tankers for transporting liquids and gases.

2. The Challenge of the Rail Transport

Rail transport has once been boomed. But in recent twenty years, its importance in the transportation has been declining. The rail transport is challenged by radical change. Radical change in the railway industry is being driven by:

(1) the evolution in the transport market resulting from the globalization of the economy;

(2) the increasing deregulation of the market;

(3) competition based on customer service;

(4) the increasing need for harmonization to permit a trans-countries rail network;

(5) the need to ensure long-term operational profitability.

Managing the future has become an imperative for the railway industry at large. To pursue business strategies based on past traditions will be to live on borrowed time, structural and cultural changes are therefore required within the railway sector. These changes demand innovative approaches to business and services, consistent with a competitive, market-driven posture in the overall transport market.

Nowadays, sustained business success demands continuous customer orientation. Survival in the evolving and highly competitive transport market implies a continuous search for excellence. This will enable railway operators and their suppliers to achieve a world-class profile. Success requires efficient, accessible and competitive rail transport systems. These systems must fulfill economic and social expectations whilst ensuring wider environmental, resource efficiency and safety objectives.[3] Moreover, rail development should allow for maximum synergy with other transport modes, thus responding to modern, door-to-door requirements for transport and mobility.

The quest for excellence has to cover the entire range of business activity, beginning with market demand and ending with customer satisfaction. It entails the integrated development and timely deployment of adequate organizational, technological and skill infrastructures, which enable companies to transform them into bodies that solve customers' problems.

The growing interdependence between the main players in the sector points to the need for a concept of "innovation through cooperation".[4] Under-investment in the railway industry, and an increasing technological gap as compared with competing modes, reinforce this view. A competitive and business-driven railway sector is the required outcome. But it must be achieved within a context which allows best use to be made of country's significant physical and intellectual assets.

New Words and Expressions

1. funicular[fju'nikjulə]　　　　　*n.* 索道
2. self-propelled　　　　　　　　*adj.* 自力推进的,自行驱动的
3. monorail['mɔnəureil]　　　　　*n.* 单轨铁路
4. supersede[sju:pə'si:d]　　　　*v.* 代替,接替
5. imperative[im'perətiv]　　　　*adj.* 紧急的,必要的
6. locomotive[ləukə'məutiv]　　　*n.* 机车,火车头
7. self-propelled　　　　　　　　*adj.* 自力推进的,自行驱动的
8. rail car[reil'kɑ:]　　　　　　*n.* (单节)机动有轨车
9. maglev['mæglev]　　　　　　　　*n.* & *adj.* 磁力悬浮火车(的);磁浮列车
10. diesel train　　　　　　　　　柴油机车
11. cable car(美)　　　　　　　　缆车
12. cog rail way　　　　　　　　　齿轮铁路
13. rubber-tired under ground　　胶轮地下轨道列车
14. point to　　　　　　　　　　　对准,瞄准,指向
15. whilst[wailst]　　　　　　　　*conj.* 同时
16. synergy['sinədʒi]　　　　　　*n.* 协同,配合,企业合并后的协力优势或协同作用

Notes

[1] Special kinds of trains running on corresponding special "railways" are atmospheric railways, monorails, high speed railways, maglev, rubber-tired underground, funicular and cog railways.
特种火车运行在相应的特殊"轨道"上,有高架铁路、单轨铁路、高速铁路、磁浮铁路、胶轮地下轨道、索道和齿轨。

[2] The term of "light rail" is sometimes used for a modern tram, but it may also mean an intermediate form between a tram and a train, similar to metro except that it may have level crossings.
术语"轻轨"有时用来指现代有轨电车,但是也可用来指一种介于有轨电车和火车之间的交通工具,除了有平面岔道之外,它(轻轨)与地铁很相像。

[3] These systems must fulfill economic and social expectations whilst ensuring wider environmental, resource efficiency and safety objectives.

这些(铁路运输)系统必须满足经济和社会的期望,同时还要达到保护较宽阔的环境、有效利用资源和安全的目的。

[4] The growing interdependence between the main players in the sector points to the need for a concept of "innovation through cooperation".

该领域内主要参与者之间日益增长的互相依存瞄准"以合作促创新"此概念的需要。

Passage B Air Transport

With the rapid development of aeronautic science and technology, air traffic has been increasing tremendously and become the most recent form of transportation in international trade and plays a more important role than ever before. Notwithstanding the fact that it still accounts for a very small percentage of world total imports and exports, its growth rate in recent years is the highest among modes of transport.[1]

Air freight has many advantages over other modes of transport. It is generally most practical for goods which have a high unit values, i.e. a high ratio of price to weight. Commodities of low value such as ordinary furniture, newsprint, cotton, rice, potato, washing machine, rubber shoes, and etc. cannot afford to bear the air freight rates; but precious art goods, fur garments, high-class instruments, computers, cameras, watches, and etc. can bear the high cost of transportation without any dampening effect on their marketability. Merchants are more inclined to have their goods of these kinds shipped by air.

Above all, quick delivery is the most obvious advantage of air freight service, which means a saving of time spent on transit. For instance, if silk piece goods are shipped from shanghai to Hamburg or Paris, it may take 4 to 5 weeks to reach the port of destination. Now if they are transported by air, the length of time may be reduced to a period of 3 or 4 days. To tie up a large amount of capital, say USD100,000, for one month at 1% interest per month would cost USD1000. For high-priced commodities the time value which a shipper is able to gain usually outweighs the high cost of air transport. For this reason, many exporters prefer air freight, especially when they may not be able to afford having their capital tied up for one month while a ship completes her voyage.

Furthermore, exporters can benefit from quick delivery in that they can achieve quick turnover and maintain a relatively small inventory of raw materials or finished products, particularly in the export market. The advantage is even more conspicuous where the market is demanding and the commodities are highly competitive. There are instances where the buyers in overseas markets required immediate delivery and those who promise fast delivery are in a better position to win the orders in competition.[2]

Air transportation proves to be almost indispensable to perishable goods, which are liable to deteriorate or become useless if the voyage takes a longer time, say more than a week. During the winter of 1974 and the spring of 1975 a consignment of small eels was exported from Fujian to Japan by sea route, the death rate was as high as 50%. Soon afterwards, the exporter made a change in the mode of transport and switched to air transport. It proved to be a more desirable method of transportation as the death rate of eels declined to 5% or less in spite of the fact that the eels were trans-shipped at Hong Kong where the temperature is usually around 32℃. Another striking example is that exporting lichee from South China to Singapore by sea was a losing business because the fruit, though stored in refrigeration installations, mostly became rotten or turned dark when it arrived at the port of destination; but if shipped by air, lichee remains fresh and thus can find a ready market.[3] Crabs exported from Shanghai, mango from Kunming, grapes and melons from XinJiang are known to people living in Hong Kong, who willingly pay a price much higher than that obtainable on the home market.

For goods of high unit value, shippers usually pay extra charges to the shipping line at the ad valorem rate on FOB value, in addition to the freight charge, which is higher than that on a weight basis; while shipping by air, no extra charge at the ad valorem rate is collected by airline, unless there is a declared value of the cargo and valuation charge is paid for it, in order to protect against possible loss or damage.[4] The latter is not a freight charge.

In ocean transport, freight is charged on a weight ton or a measurement ton, whichever is greater, the ratio being 40 cu ft against one metric ton. In air transport, bulky commodities, i.e. low density cargo, are also charged by cubic measurement, but the ratio is 7000 cu cm against 1kg. Obviously airlines allow a lot more cubic space for one measurement ton than shipping lines. In view of this difference, to ship quite a few kinds of bulky cargo by air will, in certain cases, be more economical than by sea. Fresh flowers are a typical example of perishable goods which must be shipped by air; otherwise they are liable to deteriorate and become rubbish. Airlines charge less freight for flowers than they would otherwise be charged if the same ratio (40 cu ft for 1 mt) used by shipping lines were adopted in air freight. All this contributes to the development of the flower export trade between countries which are thousands of miles apart.

The insurance company charges the shipper a lower premium for the same kind of coverage if goods are shipped by air rather than by sea on account of gentler handling of air freight, smoother ride, less jostling in transit and hence less probability of damage to the cargo.[5] Air cargo is relatively well taken care of as compared with the rough handling which often occurs at the docks and terminals, and is less susceptible to theft and pilferage. When the insurance premium is taken into consideration, the cost of air freight is not as high as it appears to be. This advantage is conspicuous especially when goods of high unit value are consigned.

Air freight packing is less expensive than that of consignment by sea. Normally domestic packing is often sufficient; therefore, no extra export packing is required. Lighter packing can be a big advantage in those export transactions for countries where custom duties are based on the total weight of the consignment. Sometimes the saving in this connection is considerable. For example, an exporter ships ceramic heating tubes made up in consignment of 24 tubes of different diameters with an average weight of 300g each. The total net weight is 7.2 kg. If the consignment is shipped by sea, he has to pack the consignment in five smaller wooden cases, which in turn go into a big wooden case. The packing together with the strappings weighs 64.5 kg, nine times as much as the net weight. After consultation with an air freight forwarder he decides to devise a new packing and ship the goods by air. It consists of a corrugated cardboard box, expanded polystyrene and foam rubber for cushioning and two wooden boards for stiffening. The total weight of this new packing is 6.9 kg, hence a saving of 57.6 kg. What a difference it makes!

Air transport is all the more preferable to the other modes of transport under the following circumstances:

(1) when a certain consignment of goods must be rushed and arrive at destination before the expiration date of the import license;

(2) when some seasonal goods must be put on the market before holidays;

(3) when some commodities are exported for publicity purposes, such as newspaper and magazine and any delay would make them valueless.

Last but not least, air transport has a vast network of airlines, which can reach remote places in the interior across high mountains, which are hardly accessible by rail or road transport, to say nothing of sea transport. Desirable as it is, air transport has its limitations. There are a number of commodities which are unsuited to carriage by air, including bulky commodities of low value, raw materials, etc., where the high cost of air, freight outweighs the other advantages. Besides, owing to technical reasons, hazardous cargoes and commodities of awkward sizes are out of the question. Government regulations forbid the transportation of hazardous goods by air.

It is essential for a dispatch clerk or a manager in charge of foreign trade transportation to strike a balance between the advantages and disadvantages of air transport so as to get the most economical results.

New Words and Expressions

1. notwithstanding ［英］［ˌnɔtwiθˈstændiŋ］ *prep.* 尽管,还是,虽然
   ［美］［ˌnɑtwiθˈstændiŋ,-wið-］ *adv.* 尽管如此,仍然,还是
   conj. 虽然,尽管
2. dampen［ˈdæmpən］ *v.* 弄湿,消沉,抑制;
3. indispensable 英［ˌindiˈspensəbl］ *adj.* 不可缺少的,绝对必要的,责无旁贷
   美［ˌindiˈspɛnsəbəl］ 的,不可避开的
   n. 不可缺少的人或物
4. refrigeration［riˌfridʒəˈreiʃn］ *n.* 冷藏,冷冻
5. susceptible［səˈseptəbl］ *adj.* 易受影响的,易受感染的
6. pilferage［ˈpilfəridʒ］ *n.* 小偷小摸,赃物

7. be in a position to　　　　　　　　　　　能够
8. 40 cu ft for 1 mt　　　　　　　　　　　　40 立方英尺为 1 公吨
9. polystyrene[ˌpɔliˈstaiəriːn]　　　　　　　n. 聚苯乙烯
10. cushion[ˈkuʃən]　　　　　　　　　　　n. 垫子，起保护作用的东西
　　　　　　　　　　　　　　　　　　　　v. 起缓冲作用（cushioning 为动名词）
11. FOB（Free On Board）　　　　　　　　离岸价
12. on account of　　　　　　　　　　　　由于
13. circumstance[ˈsɜːkəmstənsɪz]　　　　 n. 境遇，境况（由其指经济情况）
14. hazardous[ˈhæzədəz]　　　　　　　　 adj. 危险的，冒险的，危害的

Notes

［1］ Notwithstanding the fact that it still accounts for a very small percentage of world total imports and exports, its growth rate in recent years is the highest among modes of transport.
尽管它（空运）占世界总进出口量的比例仍然很小，但近年来其增长率是运输方式中最高的。

［2］ There are instances where the buyers in overseas markets required immediate delivery and those who promise fast delivery are in a better position to win the orders in competition.
在海外市场上存在买方需要立即交货的实例，那些承诺快速交货者在竞争中更能赢得订单。

［3］ Another striking example is that exporting lichee from South China to Singapore by sea was a losing business because the fruit, though stored in refrigeration installations, mostly became rotten or turned dark when it arrived at the port of destination; but if shipped by air, lichee remains fresh and thus can find a ready market.
一个引人注目的例子是，从中国南方地区海运荔枝出口到新加坡是一桩赔本生意，因为水果虽然存储在冷藏设施内，到达目的港时大多变得腐烂或暗黑了；但如果采取空运，荔枝保持新鲜，因此能找到一个大好市场。

［4］ For goods of high unit value, shippers usually pay extra charges to the shipping line at the ad valorem rate on FOB value, in addition to the freight charges, which is higher than that on a weight basis; while shipping by air, no extra charge at the ad valorem rate is collected by airline, unless there is a declared value of the cargo and valuation charge is paid for it, in order to protect against possible loss or damage.
对于单位价值很高的货物，通常除按照 FOB 价（离岸价）给运输公司支付运费外，托运人还须支付高于比按重计费的额外运费；而空运则不收价格之外的额外付费，除非为了免遭丢失和损坏，托运人申报了货物的价值并支付了保值费用。

［5］ The insurance company charges the shipper a lower premium for the same kind of coverage if goods are shipped by air rather than by sea on account of gentler handling of air freight, smoother ride, less jostling in transit and hence less probability of damage to the cargo.
对于同样的货物保险范围，如果采用空运而非海运，保险公司对托运人收取的保费就比海运低，因为空运对货物的搬运更小心、飞行过程更平稳、运输途中颠簸更少，因而货物损坏的可能性较小。

Unit 11

Passage A Ocean Shipping

It is well-known that an immense area of the earth, over two-thirds in fact, is covered by water, and land masses or continents, as they are often called, are surrounded by water, as are also islands scattered throughout the earth.

With only rare exceptions, continents are separated by great expanses of water. Asia, for instance, is separated from North America by the Pacific Ocean over a span of several thousand miles.

Even within the confines of a continent there are waters here and there, with distances sometimes of hundreds or thousands of kilometers which cut the land apart.

Such natural peculiarities of the earth pointed to the need, even in the distant past, to devise means of water transportation which would provide access to places otherwise difficult to reach. As a matter of fact, primitive means of transport were already made use of in times dating back a thousand years as handy conveyors of whatever was desired to places along or across the waters. This helped to facilitate the exchange of necessities among the inhabitants at a time when life was simple and agriculture was still anything but prolific.

With the passage of time and in the face of increased population, coupled with growing agricultural production and the development of commerce, maritime transport was much sought after and became more important. This was reflected in the overgrowing demand for movement, within the boundaries of a country, of agricultural produce and other merchandise from places of origin to places where low productivity made it difficult or even impossible to satisfy local demands. This was quite logical, as maritime transport is ideal for carrying weighty and bulky loads and is a medium which can be used more economically than land conveyance.

Following the renovation of maritime transport with the attendant advantages of large carrying capacity, speedier movement and fewer hands required, the saving achieved in both labor and time was apparent.[1] This resulted in much more reliance on transport by water to convey agricultural produce and commodities to and from various places, which was instrumental in meeting the needs of the people on the one hand and expanding commerce on the other.[2]

Increased production called for expansion of markets, and to achieve this, transportation became all the more important. Land transport was, of course, useful in distributing manufactured products or raw materials to places for sale or processing, but maritime transport could, in most cases, perform better and was more economical, especially when inland water or coastal transit was involved.

It can thus be seen that even at an early stage maritime transport, albeit rudimentary and far from efficient, played an important part in the distribution of agricultural and industrial products and proved indispensable to the development of the economy of a country.

As the economy develops and the needs of domestic markets are well met, there is, perforce, the question of disposal of surpluses of products and materials. To this question the ideal solution is to seek foreign markets.

Free movement of merchandise to places beyond the border of a country presupposes convenient and economical transit routes. Where there are common border on land, it is always possible to rely on highways or railways, but land transport can hardly do its part when the destination lies far beyond the continent. Whilst air passage can be relied upon to carry commodities abroad by planes to any distance at greater speed, the exorbitant air freight makes the cost prohibitive, particularly in the case of heavy and bulky lifts. This, in turn, diminishes the chance of a successful sale in overseas markets where keen competition is almost the rule.

Therefore, whether it is possible to dispose of commodities in overseas markets on favorable terms depends, to a large extent, on the feasibility of acquiring the most economical means of transportation. In this respect, maritime transport is, without doubt, the best medium.

To seek oversea markets is only one aspect of the problem. Oftentimes, raw materials or manufacture products have to be procured from other countries to meet domestic requirements. In certain cases, production is impossible without taking in raw materials from abroad. This likewise necessitates the services of maritime transport for the same reason that it is less expensive than if the services of other types of transport are made use of. Thus, the advantage to be derived from the use of maritime transport is enormous.

Fully conscious of the usefulness of maritime transport and the necessity to develop shipping, most maritime countries attach great importance to the building up of a merchant fleet. And since the earlier part of the 20th century there has been a tremendous growth of the world fleet, and the different types of vessels have been made available to cater for the requirements for the carriage of diversified categories of commodities.[3] Even the improved railway system and expansion of highways as well as the rapid development that has been registered lately in air transport have failed to abate the growth of the merchant fleet, which serves to testify that, as the principal means of transport, ships can hardly be replaced by any other conveyance. This is not surprising because they are not only indispensable for the carriage of commodities across seas and oceans to all the remote corners of the world but also a prerequisite to the building up of the shipping industry, which is becoming increasingly important to the modern world as a ramification of invisible trade.

It can be predicted that the world's merchant fleet will continue to increase in size in the time to come.

China's merchant fleet remains moderate in size, although a marked growth has been registered in recent years. China is expanding her foreign trade at a tempo much faster than before. Therefore, a corresponding growth in her merchant fleet is envisaged.

Marine transport is being used in trade in two principal types of shipping services: one is as liners; the other being as trampers.[4]

Liners offer shipping space, as common carriers, on ships playing along fixed routes on regular schedule, principally engaged in carrying general cargo in relatively small shipments and limited volumes, such as metals, textile products, bagged foodstuffs, artware, daily utensils, and other manufactured products along predetermined routes. These consignments are not full cargoes and do not usually call for the entire shipping space of a ship hold as required by bulky commodities. Such shipments are entrusted to the carriers as needed whereupon bills of lading covering the shipments are issued by the carriers against payment of freight according to tariff rates either in advance or on delivery of the shipments at destination.[5]

Trampers refer to ships playing on waterways without pre-set schedule or fixed routes and sailings normally depend on an availability of cargoes entrusted for carriage.

In point of fact, most trampers are engaged in chartering trade for the carriage of a full shipload of cargoes or cargoes in bulk, such as grains, oils, mineral ores, ect.. When under charter, all sailings of the ship are subject to charterers' requrements.

Trampers may be chartered on a time or voyage basis. They may also be hired on a demise charter basis which implies that, to all intents and purposes, the ownership changes hand for the period of hire. The charterer takes a lease of the entire vessel for an agreed time. The management of the ship is in his hand and he provides his own master and crew.

New Words and Expressions

1. be instrumental in　　　　　　　　有助于,助长
2. cater for　　　　　　　　　　　　　供应伙食;迎合;为……提供必要条件
3. albeit [ɔːlˈbiːit]　　　　　　　　　conj. 尽管,假使
4. rudimentary [ruːdiˈmentəri]　　adj. 初步的,未发展完善的
5. perforce [pəˈfɔːs]　　　　　　　adv. 必然,一定
6. abate [əˈbeit]　　　　　　　　　v. 减少,减轻
7. prerequisite 英 [ˌpriːˈrekwəzit]　n. 先决条件,前提,必要条件
   　　　　　　　美 [priˈrɛkwɪzɪt]　adj. 必须先具备的,必要的,先决条件的,
8. ramification 英 [ˌræmɪfɪˈkeɪʃn]　n. 衍生物,结果,分叉,分支,支流,
   　　　　　　　美 [ˌræməfɪˈkeʃən]
9. tramper [ˈtræmpə]　　　　　　　n. 不定期货船

Notes

[1] Following the renovation of maritime transport with the attendant advantages of large carrying capacity, speedier movement and fewer hands required, the saving achieved in both labor and time was apparent.

海洋运输革新之后运输能力大大提高，运输速度加快并且需用人力减少，其劳动力和劳动时间上得到的节省是显而易见的。

[2] This resulted in much more reliance on transport by water to convey agricultural produce and commodities to and from various places, which was instrumental in meeting the needs of the people on the one hand and expanding commerce on the other.

这就导致了更加依赖水路把农产品和商品运抵和运出各地，这一方面有助于满足人们的需求，另一方面有助于扩大贸易。

[3] And since the earlier part of the 20th century there has been a tremendous growth of the world fleet, and the different types of vessels have been made available to cater for the requirements for the carriage of diversified categories of commodities.

从20世纪早期世界船队就已经有了急速成长，并且已经制造了各种类型的轮船为满足多种多样的货舱需求提供必要的条件。

[4] Marine transport is being used in trade in two principal types of shipping services: one is as liners; the other being as trampers.

在海洋运输以两种基本运输服务型式用于贸易：一种是定期班轮；另一种则是不定期船运。

[5] Such shipments are entrusted to the carriers as needed whereupon bills of lading covering the shipments are issued by the carriers against payment of freight according to tariff rates either in advance or on delivery of the shipments at destination.

像需要的那样，把这样的运输委托给承运人，在有关运输的提单上由承运人按照税率开立运费，可以是提前支付运费或是于目的地交货时支付。

Passage B Intermodal Transportation

While the five primary modes give supply chain managers numerous transportation options, another group of alternatives exist. Intermodal transportation service refers to the use of two or more carriers of different modes in the origin-to-destination movement of freight. Shifting freight between modes may seem inefficient and time consuming, but the improved reach and combined service advantages created by intermodal transportation offset these issues. These primary benefits of intermodalism include the following.

(1) Greater accessibility is created by linking the individual modes. The road infrastructure allows trucks to reach locations that are inaccessible to other modes, especially air transportation, water transportation, and pipelines. For example, air transportation can only move freight between airport facilities. Trucks provide the flow between the origin and departure airport as well as the arrival airport and the customer destination. Railroads can also facilitate the use of domestic river transportation and international ocean transportation. Getting low sulfur coal from a Wyoming mine to a utility company in Japan would be best accomplished through a combination of rail and water transportation.

(2) Overall cost efficiency can be achieved without sacrificing service quality or accessibility.[1] In other words, intermodal transportation allows supply chains to utilize the inherent capabilities of multiple modes to control cost and fulfill customer requirements. If a furniture manufacturer needed to move 20 loads of furniture from North Carolina to California, a combination of truck and rail transportation would improve upon truck-only service. The speed and accessibility of trucks would be used for the initial pickup and final delivery, while the cross-country transportation would be handled by the cost-efficient railroads.[2]

(3) Intermodal transportation facilitates global trade. The capacity and efficiency of ocean transportation allow large-volume shipments to be transported between continents at relatively low per-unit costs. The speed of air transportation allows perishable goods to flow quickly between countries. The final domestic leg of the delivery can take place via truck. The ocean-truck combination makes product competitive across global markets by keeping the landed cost in check. The air-truck combination facilitates expedited distribution of "hot commodities" like fashion and rapid replenishment of products that are in high demand.[3]

Although no universal statistics are kept on intermodal transportation, there is strong evidence that intermodal transportation is growing in importance and volume.

Much of this intermodal growth can be attributed to the development of standardized containers that are compatible with multiple modes. A standard dry box container looks much like a truck trailer without the chassis; can be lifted, stacked, and moved from one piece of equipment to another; and is built to standard dimensional height and width specifications in a variety of lengths (10-, 20-, and 40-foot marine containers for international transportation and 40-, 48-, and 53-foot containers for domestic truck/rail transportation). Specialized containers are also available for handing temperature-sensitive goods (refrigerated containers), commodities (tank and dry bulk cargo containers), and other unique cargoes.

Other factors have contributed to the growth of intermodal transportation. They include better information systems to track freight as it moves through the supply chain and the development of intermodal terminals to facilitate efficient freight transfers between modes.[4] In addition, new generations of ocean vessels, railcars, and truck trailers are being built specifically to handle intermodal freight in greater quantity and with greater ease.

Ocean carriers are continually developing larger containerships to handle international intermodal traffic. These vessels have evolved from first generation ships, capable of handling less than 1000 TEUs (pre-1960), to fourth generation Post-Panamax ships that can hold more than 4000 TEUs. These ships are relatively fast (speeds of up to 25 knots), serve Pacific or Atlantic routes only (as they cannot pass through the Panama Canal), and can only serve deep-water ports. Future construction will focus on even larger containerships. Roll-on-roll-off (RO-RO) ships and combination vessels can also handle intermodal freight.

The rail industry also offers a variety of equipment for moving intermodal shipments. Initial efforts focused on moving standard truck trailers on flatbed rail cars. This was called "piggy-back" service or TOFC service. This type of service is shrinking in favor of COFC service and double-stack container services. These methods allow rail companies to carry a wider variety of containers—everything from 10ft ocean containers to 53ft domestic freight containers—in nearly any combination. Double-stack service is especially efficient.

The freight services provided by intermodal transportation can be viewed in terms of product-handling characteristics as follows.

(1) Containerized freight is loaded into/onto storage equipment (a container or pallet) at the origin and delivered to the destination in/on that same piece of equipment with no additional handling. For example, if a load of DVD players needed to be shipped from the factory to the market, the players would be loaded into a 40ft container at the factory in Taiwan, transferred to the port via truck, and then loaded on a containership bound for Los Angeles. Upon arrival, the container would be moved from the ship onto another truck and delivered to the retailer's distribution center.

(2) Transload freight involves goods that are handled and transferred between transportation equipment multiple times. Transload freight primarily consists or bulk-oriented raw materials that must be scooped, pumped, lifted, or conveyed from one container to another when transferred from one mode to another. For example, orange juice concentrate may be picked up using a rail tank car, pumped into the hold of a cargo ship for the line haul move, and then pumped into a tank truck for final delivery.

Another way to look at the intermodal option is based on the type of service used. The most prevalent forms of intermodal transportation are truck-rail, truck-air, and truck-water, although other combinations are also used. In the majority of cases, the carrier makes the determination of what mode or modal combinations to use.[5] After all, when customers drop overnight letters in the express delivery box, they are not concerned about the combination of modes used as long as the letters arrive on time!

The most pressing issue in the intermodal transportation market is congestion.[6] While the ocean carriers are adding capacity to meet the growing demand levels, transfer points can quickly get clogged with freight. The U.S. seaport facilities along the Pacific coast have struggled to keep product flowing through their facilities in a timely fashion during peak shipping seasons. Intermodal capacity problems in the rail industry have also surfaced. Equipment shortages, transfer facility congestion, and labor issues create delivery delays and supply chain disruptions. Significant infrastructure investment, equipment purchases, and operator hiring will be needed to overcome existing challenges and prepare for the anticipated growth of intermodal transportation.

New Words and Expressions

1. offset ['ɒfset]   *n.* 抵消,补偿,平版印刷,支管
   vt. 抵消,弥补,用平版印刷术印刷
   vi. 装支管
2. TEU(twenty foot equivalent unit)   标准箱(系集装箱运量统计单位,以长20英尺的集装箱

3. evolve [i'vɔlv]　　　　　　　　　为标准)
　　　　　　　　　　　　　　　　vt. 发展,进化,制订出,发出,散发
4. containerized [kən'teɪnəraɪzd]　v. 用集装箱装运(货物),使……集装箱化
5. pump [pʌmp]　　　　　　　　　n. 泵
　　　　　　　　　　　　　　　　v. 用泵抽
6. clog 英 [klɒg]　　　　　　　　　n. 木底鞋,障碍
　　　美 [klɑg]　　　　　　　　　v. 阻碍;堵塞
7. RO-RO (roll-on-roll-off)　　　　滚上滚下(滚装)
8. piggy-back　　　　　　　　　　背驮式

Notes

[1] Overall cost efficiency can be achieved without sacrificing service quality or accessibility.
总成本效率可以在不牺牲服务质量或可达性的情况下实现。

[2] The speed and accessibility of trucks would be used for the initial pickup and final delivery, while the cross-country transportation would be handled by the cost-efficient railroads.
货车的速度和可达性应该用于最初的提货和最后的送货,而横跨全国的运输应该用具有成本效益的铁路运输。

[3] The air-truck combination facilitates expedited distribution of "hot commodities" like fashion and rapid replenishment of products that are in high demand.
飞机-汽车(航空-公路)组合促使"热销品"的配送迅速完成,比如急需的时尚品和快速补货的产品。

[4] They include better information systems to track freight as it moves through the supply chain and the development of intermodal terminals to facilitate efficient freight transfers between modes.
它们(其他因素)包括货物通过供应链移动时追踪货物的更好的信息系统和促进货运模式之间有效运输的多式联运场站的发展。

[5] In the majority of cases, the carrier makes the determination of what mode or modal combinations to use.
在大多数情况下,承运人决定采用什么样的模式或组合。

[6] The most pressing issue in the intermodal transportation market is congestion.
多式联运市场最紧迫的问题是拥堵。

Unit 12

Passage A Terminal Structure and Handling Equipment

In general terms, container terminals can be described as open systems of material flow with two external interfaces.[1] These interfaces are the quayside with loading and unloading of ships, and the landside where containers are loaded and unloaded on/off trucks and trains.[2] Containers are stored in stacks thus facilitating the decoupling of quayside and landside operation.

After arrival at the port, a container vessel is assigned to a berth equipped with cranes to load and unload containers.[3] Unloaded import containers are transported to yard positions near to the place where they will be transshipped next. Containers arriving by road or railway at the terminal are handled within the truck and train operation areas. They are picked up by the internal equipment and distributed to the respective stocks in the yard. Additional moves are performed if sheds and/or empty depots exist within a terminal; these moves encompass the transports between empty stock, packing center, and import and export container stocks (Figure 12-1).

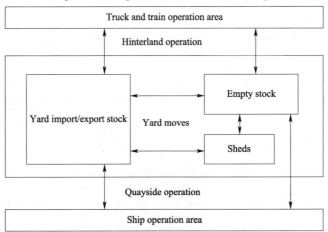

Figure 12-1 Operation areas of a seaport container terminal and flow of transports

It should be noted that the quayside operation or container transshipment as well as the container movement to and from the wharf is sometimes also referred to as waterside transshipment process.[4] Correspondingly, one may find the terms hinterland transshipment processes and landside transshipment processes.

Different types of ships have to be served at the quayside. The most important ones are deep-sea vessels with a loading capacity of up to 8000 container units (TEU) which serve the main ports of different countries and continents. Such vessels are about 320m long with a breadth of 43m and a draught of 13m; on deck containers can be stowed 8 tiers high and 17 rows wide, in the hold 9 high and 15 wide. The ships' data call for respective dimensions of the cranes' height and jib length. Loading of about 2000 boxes is common in large ports; the same is valid for unloading. Feeder vessels with a capacity of 100 to 1200 TEU link smaller regional ports with the oversea ports delivering containers for deep-sea vessels. Inland barges are used to transport containers into the hinterland on rivers and channels. Functionally, barges are means of hinterland transportation (like trucks and trains), operationally they are ships which are served by quay cranes.

Trucks have a capacity of up to 3 TEU. At container terminals they are directed to transfer points where they are loaded and unloaded. To serve trains, railway stations with several tracks may be part of container terminals. The capacity of one train is about 120 TEU. Shuttle trains connecting a terminal with one specific hinterland destination obtain increased importance. The modal split of hinterland transportation is very specific for different ports, which has a direct impact on the terminals' layout and type of equipment.

The container storage area is usually separated into different stacks (or blocks) which are differentiated into rows, bays and tiers.[5] Some stack areas are reserved for special containers like reefers which need electrical connection, dangerous goods, or overheight/overwidth containers which do not allow for normal stacking. Often stacks are separated into areas for export, import, special, and empty containers.

Besides in these general functions some terminals differ also in their operational units.[6] For example, if railway stations do not exist inside the terminal, containers have to be transported by trucks or other landside transportation means between the external station and the terminal. This results in additional logistic demands.

Other differences occur if sheds exist within the terminal area. At sheds containers are stuffed and stripped, and goods are stored. Additional movements have to be performed connecting the yard stacks with the sheds. The same applies to empty depots where empty containers are stored according to the needs of shipping lines.

New Words and Expressions

1. berth[bə:θ]   *n.* (车、船、飞机等的)铺位,停泊处,泊位
2. wharf[wɔ:f]   *vt.* 使靠码头,为……建码头,把货卸在码头上
         vi. 靠码头
         n. 码头,停泊处
3. transshipment[træns'ʃɪpmənt]   *n.* 转运,转载
4. hinterland['hɪntəlænd]   *n.* 内地,穷乡僻壤,靠港口供应的内地贸易区
5. draught[drɑ:ft]   *n.* 吃水
6. deck[dek]   *n.* 甲板,行李仓,露天平台
7. stow[stəʊ]   *v.* 装;载装收藏;使暂停;堆装

8. reefer [ˈriːfə(r)]　　　　　　　　　　　　　*n.* 冷藏车,收帆的人,双排扣水手上衣
9. overheight 英 [əʊvəhaɪt]　　　　　　　　　*adj.* 超高的
　　　　　　　美 [əʊvə haɪt]
10. overwidth [英] [əʊvəwidθ]　　　　　　　 *adj.* 超宽的,超广的
　　　　　　　　[美] [əʊvəθ, əʊvə, əʊvəwitθ]
11. shed [ʃed]　　　　　　　　　　　　　　　*vt.* 流出,摆脱,散发,倾吐
　　　　　　　　　　　　　　　　　　　　　　 vi. 流出,脱落,散布
　　　　　　　　　　　　　　　　　　　　　　 n. 小屋,棚,分水岭
12. stuffed [stʌft]　　　　　　　　　　　　　 *n.* 东西,材料,填充物,素材资料
　　　　　　　　　　　　　　　　　　　　　　 vt. 塞满,填塞,让吃饱
　　　　　　　　　　　　　　　　　　　　　　 vi. 吃得过多
13. strip [strip]　　　　　　　　　　　　　　　*vt.* 剥夺,剥去,脱去衣服
　　　　　　　　　　　　　　　　　　　　　　 n. 带,条状,脱衣舞
　　　　　　　　　　　　　　　　　　　　　　 vi. 脱去衣服

Notes

[1] In general terms, container terminals can be described as open systems of material flow with two external interfaces.
一般情况下,集装箱港口会被描述成具有两个外部接口的物料流的开放系统。

[2] These interfaces are the quayside with loading and unloading of ships, and the landside where containers are loaded and unloaded on/off trucks and trains.
这些接口是船舶装载和卸载的码头前沿,也是集装箱被装载到卡车和火车上/从卡车和火车上卸载下来的场所。

[3] After arrival at the port, a container vessel is assigned to a berth equipped with cranes to load and unload containers.
到达港口以后,集装箱船被分配到安装着用于装卸集装箱的起重机的泊位上。

[4] It should be noted that the quayside operation or container transshipment as well as the container movement to and from the wharf is sometimes also referred to as waterside transshipment process.
应该注意的是,岸边作业或集装箱转运以及集装箱抵达或离开码头有时也被称为水侧转运作业。

[5] The container storage area is usually separated into different stacks (or blocks) which are differentiated into rows, bays and tiers.
集装箱存储区域通常被分成不同的堆垛区域(或条块区域),这些区域被分为不同的行、贝位和层。

[6] Besides in these general functions some terminals differ also in their operational units.
除了这些一般功能之外,一些港口(场站)在操作单元方面也不同。

Passage B Storage and Stacking Logistics

Stacking logistics has become a field of increasing importance because more and more containers have to be stored in ports as container traffic grows continuously and space is becoming a scarce resource. Generally containers are stacked on the ground in several levels or tiers and the whole storage area is separated into blocks.[1] A container's position in the storage area (or yard) is then addressed by the block, the bay, the row and the tier. The maximum number of tiers depends on the stacking equipment, either straddle carriers or gantry cranes. According to operational needs the storage area is commonly separated into different areas. There are different areas for import and export containers, special areas for reefer, dangerous goods or damaged containers. The average daily yard utilization of large container terminals in Europe is about 15,000 ~ 20,000 containers resulting in about 15,000 movements per day. The dwell time of containers in the yard is in the range of 3 ~ 5 days at an average.

A storage planning or stacking decision system has to decide which block and slot has to be selected for a container to be stored.[2] Because containers are piled up, not everyone is in direct access to the stacking equipment. Containers that are placed on top of the required one have to be removed first. Reshuffles (or rehandles) may occur due to several reasons; the most important ones result if data of containers to be stacked are wrong or incomplete. At European terminals 30% ~ 40% of the export containers arrive at the terminal lacking accurate data for the respective vessel, the discharge port, or container weight-data which are necessary to make a good storage decision. Even after arrival, vessel and discharge port can be changed by the shipping line. For import containers unloaded from ships the situation is even worse: the landside transport mode is known in at most 10% ~ 15% of all cases at the time of unloading a ship, e.g., when a location has to be selected in the yard.

To ease the situation and to ensure a high performance of ship, train and truck operation, containers sometimes are pre-stowed near to the loading place and in such an order that it fits the loading sequence. This is done after the stowage plan is finished and before ship loading starts. Because pre-stowage needs extra transportation, it is cost extensive and terminals normally try to avoid it by optimizing the yard stacking, but it is executed when ship loading has to be as fast as possible. Storage and stacking logistics are becoming more complex and sophisticated; they play an important role for the terminals' overall performance.

Two classes of storage logistics can be distinguished. In storage or yard planning systems, stack areas and storage capacities are allocated to a ship's arrival in advance according to the number of import and export containers expected. An appropriate number of slots in blocks and rows are reserved for a special ship. Depending on the planning strategy, the reservation for export containers can be split for discharge port, container type/length, and container weight. A common strategy for export planning is to reserve slots within a row for containers of the same type and discharge port while heavier containers are stacked on lighter ones assuming that they are loaded first because of the ship stability. For import containers only a reservation of yard capacity of respective size is done without further differentiation. This is because data and transport means of delivery generally are unknown at the time of discharge. If the transport mode is known, import areas can be subdivided according to them. Common strategies for import containers are either selecting any location in the import area or piling containers of the same storage date.

Yard or storage planning seldom matches the real delivery because container delivery is a stochastic process not exactly to be foreseen. The quality of this yard concept mainly depends on the strategy how to determine a good stack configuration and a good forecast of the container delivery distribution. Both factors are hard to solve, the result is a comparatively high amount of yard reshuffles. In addition, the reservation of yard locations occupies stack capacity.

Because of these disadvantages some terminals installed an alternative stacking concept, called scattered stacking. In scattered stacking, yard areas are no longer assigned to a specific ship's arrival but only once to a berthing place.[3] On arrival of a container the computer system selects the berthing place of the ship from the ships schedule and automatically searches for a good stack location within the area assigned to the berth.[4] A stack position is selected in real-time and containers with the same categories — ship, type/length, discharge port, and weight — are piled up one on top of the other. Containers for one ship are stochastically scattered over the respective stack area; reservation of yard slots is no longer necessary. This concept results in a higher yard utilization (because no slots are reserved) and a remarkable lower amount of reshuffles (because the stacking criteria merge the ship's stowage criteria).

Although the container attributes play a major role in yard stacking concepts, additional parameters have to be taken into account for improving logistic processes. Evidently, containers have to be stacked near to the future loading place, e.g., the transport distance should be minimal to ensure a high performance of the future operation. The performance of quay cranes is a multitude higher than the performance of stacking and transport equipment.[5] Therefore, containers with the same categories have to be distributed over several blocks and rows to avoid congestions and unnecessary waiting times of vehicles. The actual workload of a gantry crane or other stacking equipment also has to be considered because allocating additional jobs to highly utilized equipment provokes waiting times. All these factors can be integrated into an algorithm while the weight of each factor is measured by parameters. The objective of yard optimization is to minimize the number of reshuffles and to maximize the storage utilization.[6]

New Words and Expressions

1. straddle['strædl]   n. 跨坐,观望
                        v. 跨坐,叉开腿,不表明态度
2. straddle carrier   集装箱吊车,轮胎吊
3. gantry['gæntri]   n. 构台,桶架,门式起重机

4. utilization [juːtɪlaɪˈzeɪʃən]   n. 利用,使用
5. crane [kreɪn]   n. 鹤,吊车,起重机
                                            vt. 伸长,探头
                                            vi. 迟疑,踌躇
6. reshuffle [ˌriːˈʃʌfl]   n. 重新洗牌,改组(尤指政治组织),倒垛
                                            vt. 改组,重新洗牌,重作安排
7. stochastic [stəˈkæstik]   adj. [数]随机的,猜测的
8. discharge [disˈtʃɑːdʒ]   vt. 解雇,卸下,放出,免除,放出
                                            vi. 排放,卸货,流出,流注
                                            n. 排放,卸货,解雇
9. storage planning   存储计划
10. reservation [rezəˈveɪʃ(ə)n]   n. 预约,预订,保留
11. stowage [ˈstəʊidʒ]   n. 装载,装载物,装载方法,堆装物,积载
12. criteria [kraiˈtiəriə]   n. 标准
13. provoke [prəˈvəʊk]   vt. 驱使,激怒,煽动,惹起
14. berthing place   泊位

Notes

[1] Generally containers are stacked on the ground in several levels or tiers and the whole storage area is separated into blocks.
通常,集装箱在地面上被堆叠成若干行或层,并且整个存储区域被分成不同的条块区域。

[2] A storage planning or stacking decision system has to decide which block and slot has to be selected for a container to be stored.
存储计划或堆垛决策系统必须决定出哪一个条块和堆层必须被选择以存放某一个集装箱。

[3] In scattered stacking, yard areas are no longer assigned to a specific ship's arrival but only once to a berthing place.
在分散堆放模式中,堆场区域不再为到达的某艘具体船舶分配存储空间,而是仅仅为停靠在泊位上的船舶一次分配存储区域。

[4] On arrival of a container the computer system selects the berthing place of the ship from the ships schedule and automatically searches for a good stack location within the area assigned to the berth.
在集装箱到达时,计算机系统从船舶时刻表中选择船舶的停靠泊位,并且在已分配的停靠区域内自动寻找合适的堆放位置。

[5] The performance of quay cranes is a multitude higher than the performance of stacking and transport equipment.
岸边吊的性能比堆垛设备和运输设备的性能好得多。

[6] The objective of yard optimization is to minimize the number of reshuffles and to maximize the storage utilization.
堆场优化目标是使倒垛次数最少且存储空间利用率最大。

Part 4 Other Key Logistics Activities

Unit 13
Unit 14
Unit 15
Unit 16

Part 4 Other Key Logistics Activities

Unit 13

Passage A Warehouse Management

1. Purpose of Warehouses

Stocks occur at any point in the supply chain where the flow of materials is interrupted. Traditionally, it is kept in warehouses—and this gives a convenient label for any storage areas.[1]

In practice, there are many arrangements for storage, and warehouse might be open areas where raw materials like coal, ores or vegetables are heaped; or sophisticated facilities that give the right conditions for frozen or delicate materials; or databases that hold stocks of information; or people who have a stock of skills; or tanks that store bulk liquids like oil; or almost any other that you can think of. Reflecting the different physical arrangements, people use different names for the stores, with the most common being distribution centres and logistics centres.[2] Often distribution centres are described as storing finished goods on their way to final customers, while logistics centres store a wider mix of products at different points in a chain. Other names, such as depot and transit centre, suggest that they not only store materials but do some other jobs. To make things easy, the general term will be used to cover all kinds of places where materials are stored.

From an organisation's point of view, there are two main types of warehouse: (1) those linked to upstream suppliers and dealing with the raw materials that are collected before operations; (2) those linked to downstream customers and dealing with finished goods during distribution to customers.

So a typical configuration has materials arriving from suppliers and put into araw materials warehouse, moving through operations, and then put into a finished goods warehouse before being sent to customers.[3] In addition, there are smaller stores of spare parts, consumables and work in progress (formed by products that are between operations).

2. Activities within a Warehouse

The purpose of a warehouse is to support the broader logistics function by storing materials until they are needed, with a combination of low costs and high customer service. Specific aims might include:

(1) providing safe and secure storage at key points in a supply chain, and keeping materials in good condition and with minimal damage;

(2) efficiently doing the associated handling, moving, sorting and checking of materials;

(3) keeping accurate records, processing information and transferring this as by suppliers and customers;

(4) adding value by doing other tasks that may be best performed in the warehouse, such as packing of finishing for postponement;

(5) being flexible enough to deal with uncertainty, variations, special requirements, ect..

These aims say what a warehouse might want to do emphasising its core function as a store of goods and now we can see how it achieves these. All warehouses do similar activities, essentially receiving deliveries from upstream suppliers, storing them until they are needed, and passing them on to downstream customers. We can add some details and get the following list of activities that are generally included in warehousing. You can imagine these as a sequence of jobs that are done as materials move through the warehouse operations. We are clearly giving a general picture here, and while some warehouses do not do all of the following activities, others do many more:

(1) meeting delivery vehicles from upstream suppliers and directing them to arrival bays;

(2) unloading materials from vehicles, and checking their condition, quantity and quality;

(3) sorting goods and forming convenient units for storage;

(4) labelling storage units so they can be identified (generally with bar upstream strips or RFID devices);

(5) moving storage units to a bulk storage area;

(6) holding them in stock until needed;

(7) when necessary, removing storage units from bulk storage, breaking them into smaller parts and transferring them to a picking store.

(8) when requested by customer orders, picking materials from this store, checking them and consolidating them into orders.

3. Moving Beyond Storage

Organisations are increasingly trying to move materials quickly though supply chains, without interrupting the flow or having them sit in stock. So the focus of warehouses has changed, moving away from long-term storage and towards giving convenient locations for a range of associated activities. For example, warehouses can be the best places for inspecting and sorting materials, packing and consolidating deliveries. They might also be used for finishing products, labelling, packaging, making products "store read" for retailers, other aspects of postponement, servicing vendor managed inventories, collection points for reverse logistics, and so on. The trend is clearly for warehouses to do more jobs, positively adding value. This is an important point, as warehouses have traditionally been seen as pure cost centres. By looking at their ability to reduce overall costs, add value (and generally increase utility), managers can see warehouses as an asset rather than a necessary overhead.[4]

The broader role of warehouses has developed from their traditional jobs. For instance, they have always been the places where organisations do most sorting of materials[5]. Transport is often divided into full-load and part-load operations, and you might hear of TL and LTL operators. Here part-loads are amounts that do not fill the transport used, so a part-load might be part of a container, some of a tanker of liquid, or less than a full van load[6]. Managers prefer full-load operations because they are a lot easier to organise and give cheaper unit costs. This is the approach of containers, where the whole container moves on its journey through intermodal operators. Unfortunately, not all customers want full loads, and you can imagine them wanting several part-loads of different materials from different suppliers. The best way of organising this is to consolidate the part-loads into fewer full-loads. The practicalities are that the part-loads are delivered to a warehouse where they are sorted and consolidated into full loads, and are then transported in full-loads to the customer. The extra cost of sorting and consolidation in the warehouse is more than recovered from the reduced cost of transport.

It may be difficult for a single company to consolidate loads in this way, but several companies working together could combine loads. More often, third parties organise the consolidation, and freight-forwarders do this for global logistics. Freight forwarders might book a number of containers on a ship travelling between Hong Kong and Rotterdam, and then consolidate loads from a number of companies around Hong Kong who all want to ship relatively small amounts. The forwarders make their money by paying full-container rates, and charging somewhat more than this but obviously less than small load rates.

New Words and Expressions

1. sophisticated [sə'fɪstɪketɪd] *adj.* 复杂的,精致的,完善的,久经世故的,富有经验的,深奥微妙的
2. variation ['vɛrɪ'eʃən] *n.* 变化,[生物]变异,变种
3. marshalling ['mɑːʃəlɪŋ] *adj.* 编组的,集结待发的
   n. 信号编集
4. vendor ['vɛndə] *n.* 卖主,小贩,供应商,[贸易]自动售货机
5. centre ['sɛntə] *vi.* 以……为中心
   vt. 集中,将……放在中央
   n. 中心
   adj. 中央的
6. consumable [kən'suməbl] *n.* 消费品,消耗品
   adj. 可消耗的,可消费的
7. raw materials warehouse 原料库
8. finished goods warehouse 产成品库

Notes

[1] Traditionally, it is kept in warehouses — and this gives a convenient label for any storage areas.

传统上,它(指货物)被存放在仓库中——这就给任何存储区域赋予了一个方便的标签。

[2] Reflecting the different physical arrangements, people use different names for the stores, with the most common being distribution centres and logistics centres.

人们使用不同的名称命名存储,反映不同的物理布置,最常见的是配送中心和物流中心。

[3] So a typical configuration has materials arriving from suppliers and put into a raw materials warehouse, moving through operations, and then put into a finished goods warehouse before being sent to customers.

因此一个典型的配置包括从供应商处运抵物料,放入原料库,经过操作移动,然后在发送给客户之前(将物料)放入成品库。

[4] By looking at their ability to reduce overall costs, add value (and generally increase utility) managers can see warehouses as an asset rather than a necessary overhead.

鉴于仓库具有降低总成本、增值的能力(通常增加效用),管理者们可以将仓库视为资产而不是必需的开销。

[5] The broader role of warehouses has developed from their traditional jobs. For instance, they have always been the places where organizations do most sorting of materials.

仓库的广义作用已经从其传统的工作中扩展出来。例如,仓库一直是各种组织机构进行物料分类最多的地方。

[6] Here part-loads are amounts that do not fill the transport used, so a part-load might be part of a container, some of a tanker of liquid, or less than a full van load.

此处零担是指不能装满所用载运工具的运输量,所以零担可能是集装箱的一部分、液体罐车的一部分或少于整个车厢装载量的一部分。

Passage B Material Handling

Everytime an item is moved it costs money, takes time, and gives an opportunity for damage or mistake. So efficient warehouses reduce the amount of movement to a minimum, and make the necessary movements as easy as possible. [1] A reasonable set of aims for material handling includes:

(1) moving materials around a warehouse as required;

(2) moving materials quickly, reducing the number and length of movements;

(3) increasing storage density, by reducing the amount of wasted space;

(4) reducing costs, by using efficient operations;

(5) making few mistakes, with efficient material management systems.

To a large extent, these aims depend on the choice of handling equipment, as this affects the speed of movement, type of materials that can be moved, costs, layout, number of people employed, and so on. This handling equipment can range from something as simple as a supermarket basket, through to industrial robots and automated vehicles.

Imagine a store of, say, medicines, where each item is small and light. Material handling is done by hand, with little equipment except for trolleys and baskets. This gives the first level of technology, which is almost entirely manual. Another warehouse might store engineering equipment that is moved by fork-lift trucks or other tools. This gives a second level of technology, which is mechanized. Now imagine a warehouse where all movements are controlled by a central computer and hardly anything is done by hand. This gives a third level of technology, which is automated. These three levels of technology give warehouses with completely different characteristics.

1. Manual Warehouses

This is probably the easiest arrangement to imagine, and is still one of the most common. Items are stored on shelves or in bins. People go round picking items from the shelves, and putting them into some sort of container for movement like a supermarket trolley. There may be some aids, perhaps hand trucks for moving pallets, or carousels to bring materials to pickers but, essentially, people control all aspects of movements. You can get an idea of these operations by looking around a supermarket, which is very similar to a manual warehouse.

Manual warehouses only work if the items are small and light enough to lift and then shelves must be low enough for people to reach and close together to reduce the distance they walk. The warehouse must be heated, well lit, and allow people to work safely and comfortably.

Manual systems have the benefit of low capital cost and all the other advantages of involving people in the operations, but they can only be used for certain types of materials as they have high unit handling costs.[2]

2. Mechanized Warehouses

Mechanized warehouses replace some of the muscle power of manual warehouses by machines. But the feature of mechanized systems is that these machines are still driven and operated by people. There is a huge range of mechanized equipment available, but typical examples include followings.

(1) Fork-lift trucks, by far, is the most widely used vehicle that you can see in almost any store, with estimates that they are used in up to 94% of companies. They come in many different versions and are used to move pallets and equivalent loads for short distances. They are very manoeuvrable, flexible, and can be adapted for many jobs.[3] On the other hand, they need space to work, and are fairly expensive to use.

(2) Reach trucks, which are usually electrically powered and move pallets and similar loads up to higher storage racks. A driver controls the truck, which raises loads and places them in the racks. These trucks are quite small, slow, and with limited facilities, but they work well in confined spaces.

(3) Order-picking machines are a variation on reach trucks, where the driver is lifted with the materials to pick, or deliver, at high locations.

(4) Cranes or turret trucks is a general term to describe a family of vehicles that can lift materials up to very high storage racks. They work in confined spaces, often limited to a single aisle, so they allow high density with narrow aisles.

(5) Towlines are continuous cables that pull trailers or similar vehicles around a fixed path, rather like ski lifts. They are useful for moving large numbers of packages to, say, a departure dock, but their operations are much less flexible than free moving equipment.

(6) Conveyors are belts that materials are placed on and taken around a fixed path. They can move large quantities of goods, and you can see examples of conveyor belts moving items that range from iron ore to letters.

(7) Tractors or trains are power units that pull a chains of trailers containing materials and they work like small articulated lorries or tugs and barges.

(8) Carousels have a series of bins going round a fixed track. At some point on the journey items are put into a bin, and the bins are emptied when they pass another chute or collection point. These are typically used for picking, where materials are added at the picking store and emptied at a packing area.

Different types of equipment needs different warehouse layout. For instance, conveyors and towlines need regular fixed routes, fork-lift trucks need wide aisles to manoeuvre, and cranes are most efficient with very high racks.[4]

3. Automated Warehouses

In a mechanized warehouse equipment is still controlled by people, but the essence of an automated warehouse is that the control is transferred to a computer. As usual, there are many forms of automation ranging from modest levels through to sophisticated complete systems. These do the usual standard activities of a warehouse, but have:

(1) storage areas that are accessed by automatic equipment — with narrow aisles and racks up to, say, 40m tall to get a high density of materials and minimize the distances moved;

(2) automated storage and retrieval equipment to find materials, and move them into and out of storage, these are typically high speed stacker cranes that can reach any point in the narrow aisles very quickly;

(3) equipment to move materials around the warehouse, and these are typically Automated Guided Vehicles (AGVs) which are controlled through guide wires in the floor, but they might include conveyors, tractors, and a range of other equipment;

(4) transfer equipment to move materials between the different types of equipment, and these automatic loaders and unloaders might include industrial robots;

(5) a warehouse management system to control operations, including transactions, stock locations, and all movements.

Automated systems clearly need some way of tracking materials, and for many years the standard method has used bar codes. Then readers around a warehouse can monitor all the movement. Alternatives are available, such as magnetic strips, and the latest development is RFID. This is not a passive label, but is an active transmitter that responds to a reader. An RFID lag is essentially a semi-conductor chip which stores information (about its current location, status, associated material, destination, customer, etc.) and when it receives a message from a scanner it responds by transmitting this information. This has the advantages of being readable at some distance without contact or being in line of sight, faster reading speeds, greater security, more information, and so on.[5] On the down side, there are still problems with cost and agreeing standards.

The benefits of automation include faster movement, lower unit costs, fewer errors, higher productivity, greater throughput, improved space utilisation, less handling, better control of movements, support of EDI, improved stock records and better customer service. An obvious point is that no people work in the storage areas, so there is no need for heat, light or other comforts the people need. On the other hand, some of the disadvantages of automation are the high capital costs, lime needed for maintenance and repairs, inflexibility to deal with change, obsolescence, need to integrate systems, extra training, and so on.

New Words and Expressions

1. automated ['ɔ:toʊmeɪtɪd]   adj. 自动化的
                                v. 自动化(过去分词)
2. articulated [aː'tɪkjulitɪd]   adj. 铰接(的),枢接(的),有关节的
3. carousels [kærə'selz]   n. pl 回转机构,旋转木马
4. manoeuvrable [mə'nuvərəbl:]   adj. 可调动的,可移动的
5. confined [kən'faɪnd]   adj. 有限的,受限制的
6. towline ['toʊlaɪn]   n. 拖链,拖绳
7. aisle [aɪl]   n. 过道,通道,侧廊
8. rack [ræk]   n. 行李架,支架,导轨,滑轨
                                 v. 把……放在架子上,推压,震动,倾斜,变形
9. AGV (Automated Guided Vehicle) 自动导引车
10. throughput ['θru:put]   n. 生产量,生产率,生产能力,吞吐量,容许量
11. inflexibility [ɪnfleksə'bɪlɪti] n. 不屈性,顽固,不变性

Notes

[1] So efficient warehouses reduce the amount of movement to a minimum, and make the necessary movements as easy as possible.
因此,高效的仓库将移动降低到最低限度,并使必要的移动尽可能容易。

[2] Manual systems have the benefit of low capital cost and all the other advantages of involving people in the operations, but they can only be used for certain types of materials as they have high unit handling costs.
人工系统具有低资本费用的优点以及操作时与人有关的其他优点,但由于其单位搬运

成本高,只能用于一定类别的物料。

[3] They are very manoeuvrable, flexible, and can be adapted for many jobs.

他们非常容易移动、灵活,并能适应很多种工作。

[4] For instance, conveyors and towlines need regular fixed routes, fork-lift trucks need wide aisles to manoeuvre, and cranes are most efficient with very high racks.

例如,输送机和拖缆需要固定的路径,叉车需要宽阔的道路进行操作,带有高架导轨的起重机是最有效率的。

[5] This has the advantages of being readable at some distance without contact or being in line of sight, faster reading speeds, greater security, more information, and so on.

其(RFID)优点有:在一定距离内无需接触或处于视线范围内就可读取、读取速度更快、安全性更高、信息更丰富等。

Part 4 Other Key Logistics Activities

Unit 14

Passage A Inventory Management(I)

1. Reasons for Holding Stock

All organizations hold stocks of some kind, whether it is a shop that stocks goods for customers to look at, a chef with stocks of ingredients in the pantry, a market research company with stocks of information in a database, or a bank with stocks of cash held in reserve.[1] An inventory is a list of things held in stock (but there is some confusion and people often use it to mean the actual stock).

Every organization holds stocks, even those offering intangible services but manufacturers hold particularly large amounts. In the UK, manufacturing industry contributes less than 20% of the GNP, but it holds 40% of the stocks. At the same time, the amount of stock held by manufacturers has fallen much faster than in other sectors of industry, suggesting that they have been at the forefront of stock reduction and also that they are in the best position to reduce stocks.

Not all organizations can eliminate, or even reduce, their stocks. For instance, retailers need stocks of items for their customers to look at, and they often find that bigger stocks give higher sales. Wholesalers have to react quickly to replace items that customers buy, which generally needs stocks near the end of supply chains. Farmers grow hay in the summer, and then store it to feed their animals in the winter; a distillery stores barrels of whisky for at least three years before selling it; a library buys books and keeps them in stock until someone borrows them; Fort Knox keeps the USA's strategic reserve of gold. These organizations do not want to eliminate stocks, but they want to control them properly and they do this by efficient stock control. This function is known by several names, particularly inventory control, or inventory management.

MRP and JIT as dependent demand systems for controlling materials. These automatically define ordering policies and set stock levels. In particular, JIT places an order through a kanban when operations are ready to start work; MRP schedules an order needed to meet production specified in the master schedule.

The alternative approach assumes independent demand, where the total demand for an item is made up of lots of separate demands that are not related to each other. For instance, the overall demand for bread in a supermarket is made up of lots of demands from separate customers who act independently. With independent demand systems there is no obvious ordering policy, and managers have to decide when to place orders and how much to order.[2] This is a part of their work in designing short-term schedules. A number of standard models can help with these ordering decisions, generally by finding the best balance between various costs. In particular, they look for answers to three basic questions.

(1) What items should we stock? No item, however cheap, should be stocked unless the benefits outweigh the costs. So organizations should never add unnecessary, new items to stock, and they should make regular searches to remove obsolete or dead items.

(2) When should we place an order? This depends on the inventory control system used, type of demand (high or low, steady or erratic, known exactly or estimated), value of the item, lead time between placing an order and receiving it into stock, supplier reliability, and a number of other factors.

(3) How much should we order? Large, infrequent orders give high average stock levels, but low costs for transport and administering orders; small, frequent orders give low average stocks, but high costs for transport and administering orders.

The first of these questions is a matter of good housekeeping, simply avoiding stock that is not needed. The rest of this unit looks for answers to the other two questions.

2. Stock as a Buffer

As so many people consider stocks to be a waste of resources, we should ask why all organizations still hold them. The answer is that they provide an essential buffer between supply and demand. Both the supply of materials and demand can be variable and uncertain, and stocks give a cushion between them.

Imagine the food delivered to a supermarket. This comes in large quantities—perhaps a truckload a day—but it is sold in much smaller quantities to individual customers throughout the day. There is clearly a mismatch between supply and demand, and stocks are needed to give a cushion between them. Stocks held on the shelves and in storerooms allow the supermarket to continue working efficiently, even when delivery vehicles are delayed, or there is unexpectedly high demand from customers.

We can be a bit more specific and list the following reasons for holding stocks:

(1) to act as a buffer between different parts of the supply chain;

(2) to allow for demands that are larger than expected, or at unexpected times;

(3) to allow for deliveries that are delayed or too small;

(4) to take advantage of price discounts on large orders;

(5) to allow the purchase of items when the price is low and expected to rise;

(6) to allow the purchase of items that are going out of production or are difficult to find;

(7) to allow for seasonal operations;

(8) to make full loads and reduce transport costs;

(9) to provide cover for emergencies;

(10) to generate profit when inflation is high.

3. Types of Stock

Just about everything is held as stock somewhere, whether it is raw materials in a factory, finished goods in a shop or tins of baked beans in your pantry. We can classify these stocks as:

(1) raw materials—the materials, parts and components that have been delivered to an organization, but are not yet being used;

(2) work in progress—materials that have started, but not yet finished their journey through the organization's operations;

(3) finished goods—goods that have finished the process and are waiting to be shipped out to customers.

Nationally, there are roughly equal amounts of raw materials, work in progress and finished goods stored. But this is a fairly arbitrary classification, as one company's finished goods are another company's raw materials. Some organizations (like retailers and wholesalers) notably have stocks of finished goods only, while others (like manufacturers) have all three types in different proportions. Some items do not fall easily into these categories, so we can define two other types:

(1) spare parts for machinery, equipment, etc. ;

(2) consumables such as oil, fuel, paper, etc. .

4. Costs of Carrying Stock

The usual approach with independent demand has managers analyzing the inventory system and looking for ordering policies that minimize the total cost a rule of thumb says that the total cost of holding stock is around 25% of its value a year. You might think that minimizing this cost is the same as minimizing the stock, but this is not necessarily true. If a shop holds no stock at all, it certainly has no inventory costs—but it also has no sales and effectively incurs another cost of losing customers.[3] Then a reasonable option is to balance the costs of holding stock and making sales, with the costs of having no stock and losing sales.[4] Before going into more details; we should look at the different costs of stock these are usually divided into four types.

(1) Unit cost: the price of an item charged by the supplier, or the cost to the organization of acquiring one unit of the item. It may be fairly easy to find this by looking at quotations or recent invoices from suppliers, but it is more difficult when several suppliers offer slightly different products, or offer different purchase conditions. If a company makes the item itself, it may be difficult to get a reliable production cost or set a transfer price.

(2) Reorder cost: the cost of placing a repeat order for an item. This might include allowances for preparing an order, correspondence, delivery, insurance, receiving, unloading, checking, testing, use of equipment and follow-up. Sometimes a range of other costs can be included, such as quality control, sorting, repackaging, movement of received goods, and so on. In practice, the best estimate for a reorder cost often comes from dividing the total annual cost of the purchasing department by the number of orders it sends out.

(3) Holding cost: the cost of holding one unit of an item in stock for a unit period of lime (for example, the cost to Air France of holding a spare engine in stock for a year). The obvious cost is tied-up money, which is either borrowed (in which case there are interest payments) or it is cash that could be put to other uses (in which case there are opportunity costs). Other holding costs are for storage space (warehouse rent, financing, taxes, equipment, building maintenance, etc.), risks (deterioration, damage, loss, obsolescence, etc.) and services (insurance, handling, utilities, special treatment such as refrigeration, administration, etc.).

(4) Shortage cost: occurs when an item is needed but it cannot be supplied from stock. In the simplest case a retailer loses direct profit from a sale. But the effects of shortages are usually much wider and include lost goodwill, loss of reputation, and loss of potential future sales. Shortages of raw materials for production can cause disruption, rescheduling of production, re-timing of maintenance periods, and laying off employees. Shortage costs might also include payments for positive action to remedy the short-age, such as expediting orders, sending out emergency orders, paying for special deliveries, storing partly finished goods, or using more expensive suppliers.

It can be difficult to get reliable figures for any inventory costs, but shortage costs cause particular problems. These can include so many intangible factors—such as lost goodwill—that it is difficult to agree a reasonable value. Most organizations take the view that shortages are expensive, so it is generally better to avoid them. In other words, they are willing to pay the relatively lower costs of carrying stock to avoid the relatively higher costs of shortages. Unfortunately, this defensive approach tends to increase the amount of stock, particularly when there is uncertainty.

New Words and Expressions

1. ingredient [ɪŋˈriːdɪrnts]   *n.* 组成成分,原料,要素
2. intangible [ɪnˈtændʒəbəl]   *adj.* 触摸不到的,难以理解的,无法确定的
3. distillery [dɪˈstɪləri]   *n.* 酿酒厂,蒸馏间
4. schedule [ˈskedʒuːl]   *n.* 时刻表,进度表,清单
                                       vt. 安排,计划,编制目录,将……列入计划表
                                       n. 时间表,计划表,一览表
5. obsolete [ˌɑːbsəˈliːt]   *adj.* 过时的,老式的,废弃的
6. buffer [ˈbʌfə(r)]   *n.* 缓冲器,起缓冲作用的人(或物),缓冲剂
7. mismatch [mɪsˈmætʃ]   *v.* 使配错,失配,使配合不当
8. inflation [ɪnˈfleʃən]   *n.* 膨胀,通货膨胀
9. incur [ɪnˈkɜː(r)]   *v.* 遭受,招致,引起
10. arbitrary [ˈɑːrbətreri]   *adj.* 随意的,任性的
11. quotation [kwoʊˈteɪʃn]   *n.* 引用,引证,[商业]行情
12. estimate [ˈestɪmət]   *n.* 估计,报价
                                      v. 评估,估计,预算
13. financing [fɪˈnænsɪŋ]   *n.* 筹措资金,理财,筹集资金,融资

Notes

［1］All organizations hold stocks of some kind, whether it is a shop that stocks goods for customers to look at, a chef with stocks of ingredients in the pantry, a market research company with stocks of information in a database, or a bank with stocks of cash held in reserve.
无论是一个存储客户看得见货物的商店,一个拥有食材存储的厨师,一家数据库中有信息存储的市场研究公司,或是一家持有储备现金的银行,所有的组织机构都持有某种库存。

［2］With independent demand systems there is no obvious ordering policy, and managers have to decide when to place orders and how much to order.
独立需求系统没有明显的订货策略,管理者必须决定订货时间和订货数量。

［3］If a shop holds no stock at all, it certainly has no inventory costs but it also has no sales and effectively incurs another cost of losing customers.
如果一家商店根本没有库存,它当然没有存货成本,但也没有销售,事实上招致丢失客户而产生了其他成本。

［4］Then a reasonable option is to balance the costs of holding stock and making sales, with the costs of having no stock and losing sales.
那么一个合理的选择就是用没有存货和失去销售的成本来平衡持有库存和销售的成本。

Passage B Inventory Management (Ⅱ)

1. Changing Value Over Time

At first sight, the value of something held in stock seems to remain constant over time, so this is its value. But it is easy to see that the value really changes. If you have a stock of newspapers, they have no value when the next edition arrives; food gets out of date and conversely a tank of oil might rise in price; and inflation might increase the cost of materials. A particular problem here is obsolescence, which refers to stock that has been kept in storage so long that it has little or no value.[1] You can imagine this with spare parts for equipment that has been replaced, or food that is past its sell-by date. There is a general trend for products to have shorter life cycles and a corresponding increase in the risks of obsolescence.[2] Managers dearly want to avoid obsolescence, and the way to do this is not to keep materials for long periods, but to keep them moving as fast as possible. The rate of movement is usually measured in terms of turnover.

If the value of an item changes over time, this raises questions about the value of stock held. A company must know this, as stock forms part of the assets that are recorded in its accounts. Is the stock worth the amount you actually paid for it, the amount you would have to pay to replace it, the amount you can sell it for, or some other value? In practice, there are several accounting conventions, with the most common based on the amount actually paid. Variations on this are illustrated as follow.

(1) Actual cost—when it is possible to identify each unit remaining in stock and the amount paid for it. This works with small numbers of expensive items, such as cars and antiques, but most stocks have larger numbers of identical units.

(2) FIFO (first-in first-out)—assumes that stock is sold in the order it was bought, so the remaining stock consists of the most recent purchases.

(3) LIFO (last-in first-out)—assumes that the latest stock is used first, so the remainder is valued at earlier acquisition costs.

(4) Replacement cost—this is the full cost of replacing units at the current price.

(5) Average cost—this finds the average cost over some period.

2. Economic Order Quantity

The economic order quantity (EOQ) is the optimal size for an order in a simple inventory system. This analysis for this was done early in the last century and it remains the best way of controlling many stocks with independent demand. It is flexible and easy to use, and gives good guidelines for a wide range of circumstances.

3. Timing of Orders

When an organization buys materials, there is a lead time between placing the order and having the materials arrive in stock. This is the time taken to prepare an order, send it to the supplier, allow the supplier to make or assemble the materials and prepare them for shipment, ship the goods back to the customer, allow the customer to receive and check the materials and put them into stock. Depending on circumstances, this lead time can vary between a few minutes and months or even years.

In practice, inventory control systems keep a continuous record of the stock hand, updating this with every transaction and sending a message when it is time to place an order. Ordinarily, this message is sent to a purchasing department with E-procurement the message is sent directly to the supplier.

4. Weaknesses of the EOQ

The EOQ has been around for a long time and it is still the basis of most inventory systems for independent demand.

Among its advantages are that it: (1) is easy to understand and use; (2) gives good guidelines for order size; (3) finds other values such as costs and cycle lengths; (4) is easy to implement and automate; (5) encourages stability; (6) is easy to extend, allowing for different circumstances.

On the other hand, there are a number of weaknesses, as it: (1) takes a simplified view of inventory systems; (2) assumes demand is known and constant; (3) assumes all costs are known and fixed;(4)assumes a constant lead time and no uncertainty in supplies;(5)gives awkward order sizes;(6)assumes each item is independent of others;(7)does not encourage improvement, in the way that JIT does.

We can overcome some of these problems by developing more complicated models and in the next section lake one step in this direction.

5. Uncertain Demand and Safety Stock

The economic order quantity model assumes that demand is constant and known exactly. In practice it can vary widely and unpredictably. For instance, a company selling a new DVD does not know in advance how many copies will sell, or how sales will vary over time. When the variation is small, the EOQ model still gives useful results but as the variation increases its results get worse. You can see why this happens from the reorder level. An order is placed when stock falls to the reorder level, which is calculated as the average lead time demand. But when the actual demand in the lead time is above average, stock will run out before the next delivery arrives. By definition, demand is above average half the time, so this means that there are shortages in half the stock cycles. Conversely, demand is below average half the time, so there will be unused stock at the end of the other half of stock cycles.

The shortages give most concern, as few managers would be pleased by a system that only met the demands of half their customers. A way around this is to hold extra stocks—above the expected needs—to add a margin of safety. Then organizations increase their holding costs by a small amount, to avoid the higher shortage costs.

Higher safety stocks give a greater cushion against unexpectedly high demand and reduce shortages, but they also increase holding costs. So managers have to balance the costs of holding safety stock with the cost of shortages. Unfortunately, shortage costs are so difficult to find that they are usually little more than guesses. An alternative approach relies on managers' judgment to set a service level. which measures the likelihood that a demand can be met from stock. An organization typically gives a service level of 95%, which means that it meets 95% of orders from stock and accepts that 5% of orders cannot be met. The service level needs a positive decision by managers, based on their experience, competition, and knowledge of customer expectations.[3]

When demand varies widely, the standard deviation of lead time demand is high and very high safety stocks are needed to give a service level anywhere dose to 100%. Managers usually choose service levels that reflect the importance of each item, so very important items might have levels around 99%, while less important ones are 95% or even lower.

6. Periodic Review Systems

The EOQ analysis defines a fixed quantity that is always ordered when stock falls to a certain level. A heating plant may order 25,000 litres of oil whenever the amount in the tank falls to 2500 litres. These systems need continuous monitoring of stocks to notice when they fall to the reorder levels, so they are best suited to low, irregular demand for relatively expensive items. An alternative periodic review system orders varying amounts at regular intervals. For instance, at the end of each day a shop might order replacements few everything that was sold during the day. The operating cost of this system is generally lower and it is better suited to high, regular demand of low-value items.

Demand varies. We can show this by extending the last analysis, and looking at a periodic review system where demand is normally distributed. Then we are looking for answers to two questions.

Firstly, how long should the interval between orders be? This can be any convenient time, and organizations typically place orders at the end of every week, or every morning, or at the end of a month. If there is no obvious cycle they might aim for a certain number of orders a year, or some average order size. One approach is to calculate an economic order quantity, and then find the period that gives orders of about this size. This decision is largely a matter for management judgment.

Secondly, what is the target stock level? The system works by looking at the stock on hand when an order is due, and ordering an amount that brings this up to a target stock level.

$$\text{order quantity} = \text{target stock level} - \text{stock on hand}$$

At the end of a month a company might have 10 units remaining of an item with a target stock level of 40, so it orders 30 more units.

We can calculate the target stock level by extending our previous analyses. Suppose the lead time is constant at a point. When an order is placed, the stock on hand plus this order must last until the next order arrives.

Supermarkets traditionally use periodic review, and every night the tills pass messages to suppliers to replenish products that were sold during the day.[4] But the system becomes more responsive and reduces stock levels. If it sends messages more frequently, say, two or three times a day. Suppliers consolidate these orders and send deliveries as often as necessary. But why stop at two or three messages a day, when the tills can send messages every time they make a sale. This is the approach of continuous replenishment, which has reduced stocks in Tesco by 10%, while increasing availability by 1.5% and significantly increasing productivity.

7. ABC Analysis

Even the simplest and most automated inventory control system needs some effort to make it run smoothly. For some items, especially cheap ones, this effort is not worthwhile, so very few organizations include routine stationery or consumables in their automated systems. At the other end of the scale are very expensive items that need special care above the routine calculations. For instance, aircraft engines are very expensive, and airlines have to control their stocks of spare engines very carefully.

An ABC analysis puts items into categories that show the amount of effort worth spending on inventory control. This is a standard Pareto analysis or "rule of 80/20", which suggests that 20% of inventory items need 80% of the attention, while the remaining 80% of items need only 20% of the attention. ABC analyses define:

(1) A items as expensive and needing special care;
(2) B items as ordinary ones needing standard care;
(3) C items as cheap and needing little care.

Typically an organization might use an automated system to deal with all B items. The system might make some suggestions for A items, but decisions are made by managers after reviewing all the circumstances. C items might be excluded from the automatic system and controlled by ad hoc methods.

The categories are defined in terms of the value of annual demand, so an ABC analysis starts by calculating the annual use by value of each item. This means that it multiplies the number of units used in a year by the unit cost. Inevitably, a few expensive items account for a lot of use, while many cheap ones account for little. So listing the items in order of decreasing annual use by value, leaves A items at the top of the list, B items in the middle, and C items at the bottom.

Although they are useful for focusing attention on important items, ABC analyses can be misleading, as the annual use by value of an item is often a poor measure of its importance.[5] For instance, essential safety equipment must be available, even if it is never used; an assembly line can only keep going if all materials are available, even the cheapest; a medicine may be both cheap and rarely used, but patients hope that it is still available when they need it.

8. Vendor Managed Inventory

If an organization is trying to reduce the amount of effort it puts into inventory control, one option is to outsource some activities. For instance, as a start, a company might outsource some of the information systems that control stocks. so that a third party stores and manages all stock and makes sure that materials are available whenever needed. Between these two extremes are various alternatives for sharing responsibility, often with a third party managing the stocks without actually holding them. We have already mentioned another common arrangement of vendor managed inventory. You can imagine this in a department store, which holds stocks of, say, shoes. Then a supplier controls the stocks, and delivers new shoes when they are needed. The benefits of such arrangements are that the supplier can coordinate stocks over a wider area, use optimal inventory policies, organize transport more efficiently, increase integration in the supply chain, collect more information about demand patterns, and give a consistent customer service. The drawbacks include more reliance on a single supplier, differing aims and objectives, unclear responsibility for some aspects of stock, the need for more sophisticated information systems, and less flexibility.

New Words and Expressions

1. FIFO (first-in first-out)　　　　　　　　先进先出

2. LIFO (last-in first-out)　　　　　　　后进先出
3. EOQ (economic order quantity)　　　经济起订量；经济订货批量
4. guideline ['gaɪdˌlaɪn]　　　　　　　　n. 指导方针，指导原则
5. deviation [diːviˈeɪʃ(ə)n]　　　　　　n. 偏差，偏离，离经叛道的行为，误差，背离
6. interval ['ɪntevl]　　　　　　　　　　n. 间隔时间，间隔
7. stationery ['steɪʃəneri]　　　　　　　n. 文具，办公用品，信封，文房四宝
8. inevitably [ɪnˈevɪtəbli]　　　　　　　adv. 不可避免地，自然而然地；必然地，无疑的；难免；终于只好
9. assembly line　　　　　　　　　　　装配作业线，流水作业装配线
10. drawback ['drɔːbæk]　　　　　　　n. 缺点，障碍

Notes

[1] A particular problem here is obsolescence, which refers to stock that has been kept in storage so long that it has little or no value.
一个特别的问题是过时被淘汰，指的是已经保存太长时间而有很少或几乎没有价值了的库存。

[2] There is a general trend for products to have shorter life cycles and a corresponding increase in the risks of obsolescence.
存在产品具有更短生命周期以及产品过时风险相应的增加的总体趋势。

[3] The service level needs a positive decision by managers, based on their experience, competition, and knowledge of customer expectations.
基于管理者的阅历、竞争力和对客户期望的了解，服务水平需要管理者作出一个积极的决策。

[4] Supermarkets traditionally use periodic review, and every night the tills pass messages to suppliers to replenish products that were sold during the day.
超市一般都采用定期盘库，并且每晚传递消息给供应商以补充白天所卖的货品。

[5] Although they are useful for focusing attention on important items, ABC analyses can be misleading, as the annual use by value of an item is often a poor measure of its importance.
虽然 ABC 分类法对把注意力集中到重要货物上很有用，但 ABC 分类法会有误导，因为由一种货物价值的年使用量来评价其重要性通常是不恰当的。

Part 4 Other Key Logistics Activities

Unit 15

Passage A Scheduling

1. Introduction

Scheduling determines what will be made or shipped next. Many consider scheduling the absolute domain of operations, but it affects and is affected by marketing, human resource management, finance and accounting, and integrated logistics. This Passage concentrates on two functional interactions with scheduling: marketing and integrated logistics. Sales forecasts help schedule production and coordinate material flow into, through, and out of a facility.[1] Integrated logistics deals with scheduling primarily in inventory control for material requirements planning (MRP I), manufacturing resources planning (MRP II), JIT manufacturing, and distribution requirements planning (DRP).

2. Scheduling Concepts and Sales

Sales and marketing information triggers scheduling. Marketing provides the forecasts to determine component requirements. These forecasts are refined up to the moment of the sale. When orders are received, they replace the forecasts in determining the master schedule. The more closely final orders to suppliers match sales, the more accurately inventory will match production demand.

Customer service performance is limited by the length of time customers will wait for their orders and the time from order placement to the delivery of the goods.[2] If lead time is less than the time customers will wait, demand will pull orders through the supply chain smoothly. The closer the link between sales, marketing, and scheduling, the better the chance that production scheduling is accurate.

3. Scheduling Concepts and Integrated Logistics

Integrated logistics interfaces with operations, in particular with materials management, to ensure that the right product is available for manufacturing.[3] Without the efficient and effective flow of inbound product, manufacturing cannot produce goods when the customer wants them.

To achieve this flow, integrated logistics must cooperate with operations in several key areas. First, integrated logistics supports operations equipment and computer investments. These investments can lead to more operational flexibility and shorter lead time. Second, integrated logistics must cooperate in operations scheduling to reduce the planning cycle time. Integrated logistics can also assist in better production scheduling and system requirements. Third, operations and integrated logistics should eliminate the need for long production runs by reducing run times, setup times, and lead times. This offers lower inventory levels and reduced stockouts. Fourth, both functions must establish strategies to decrease supplier lead times for parts and supplies. Finally, integrated logistics needs to work with operations to produce goods with high turnover ratios.

4. Scheduling

Scheduling is making sure that operations produce the right products at the right time and in the right amount to meet customer demand.[4] Good scheduling requires:

(1) a dear, well-defined plan and schedule that recognize the interdependence of jobs that share equipment and facilities;

(2) communication of plans to those who carry out the plan;

(3) updates on production progress;

(4) revisions of plans and schedules.

It also involves on-time supply to the plant, adequate staffing to meet production requirements, and smooth product flow through operations. The two basic goals of scheduling are:

(1) meeting customer delivery windows or inventory delivery dates;

(2) meeting the first objective with the minimum required resources.

To achieve these goals jobs must first be planned. First, each finished product should be described in terms of the components necessary to make it. This includes choosing suppliers, determining the sequence of steps for manufacturing the product, and estimating the time required in each operation. Second, items must be scheduled (placed) in order so operations knows which job to make first, second, third, and so on. Third, the items must be released or dispatched in accordance with the schedule, available material and available capacity. Finally, status information must be kept to track the work against the scheduling requirements.

Scheduling varies depending on the type of manufacturing setting. The three basic manufacturing processes are repetitive manufacturing, batch processing, and job shop.[5]

5. MRP I

MRP I is a manufacturing planning tool. It is a computer-based production and inventory control system that minimizes inventory while ensuring that adequate materials are available for production. MRP I performs three functions.

(1) Order planning and control: when to release orders and for what quantity.

(2) Priority planning and control: how the expected date of availability compares to the need date for each item.

(3) Planning capacity requirements and development of broad business plans.

Although the principles of MRP I can be applied to distribution, job shops, and process industries, it fits best in continuous assembly of standard products like automobiles and electrical equipment.

MRP I pushes products through manufacturing and distribution processes on a schedule to meet forecasted demand. As processes improve, the integrated logistics pipeline becomes shorter, so orders replace forecasts earlier and earlier. When the lime between the start of production and customer delivery is acceptably short, then each job is an order.

The MRP I system consists of five interdependent components: the master production schedule, the bill of materials file, the inventory status file, the MRP I package, and output reports.[6]

6. MRP II

While MRP I addresses the inbound flow of inventory, MRP II adds finance, marketing, and integrated logistics. Like MRP I, MRP II is a push inventory model. However, it adds to the basic model. MRP II considers not only the inbound flow of material but also plant capacity. Additionally, it handles production scheduling, labor needs, and inventory budgets. MRP II benefits could include fewer shortages and stockouts, which should increase customer service, improve delivery, allow better response to demand changes reduce inventory levels and costs, and allow more planning flexibility.

7. JIT Manufacturing

JIT manufacturing has many different definitions. The formal definition of JIT is: produce and deliver finished goods just in time to be sold, subassemblies just in time to be assembled into finished goods, fabricated parts just in time to go into subassemblies, and purchased materials just in time to be transformed into fabricated parts.

JIT is a disciplined approach to improve manufacturing quality, flexibility, and productivity through the elimination of waste and the total involvement of people. JIT is not simply reducing inventory; rather its overall objective is increased quality. If properly developed, a number of potential benefits can follow. To realize these benefits, certain conditions must prevail. The goals must include the respect for people and the elimination of waste.

8. DRP

DRP applies MRP II principles to the flow of finished goods to field warehouses and customers. Although MRP II improved on MRP I by taking into account both materials management and production scheduling, it failed to account for this outbound movement DRP adjusts ordering patterns if inventory needs vary, responds more readily to system wide inventory needs, and better deals with product availability and receipt timing. DRP II helps plan the entire movement and storage of inventory by marrying MRPII and DRP.

New Words and Expressions

1. stockout [ˈstɒkaʊt]   n. 缺货,存货售完,无存货
2. elimination [ɪˌlɪmɪˈneɪʃn]   n. 排除,除去,根除,淘汰
3. fabricated [ˈfæbrɪˈkeɪt]   adj. 焊接的,组合的装配式的(fabricate 的过去分词)
                                  v. 制造,组装,伪造,捏造,装配
4. prevail [prɪˈveɪl]   vi. 盛行,流行,战胜,获胜,占优势,说服,劝说
5. MRP Ⅱ (manufacturing resources planning)   制造资源计划
6. DRP (distribution requirements planning)   配送需求计划
7. receipt timing   收货时间

Notes

[1] Sales forecasts help schedule production and coordinate material flow into, through, and out of a facility.
销售预测有助于安排生产和协调物料流入、流过和流出一个工厂。

[2] Customer service performance is limited by the length of time customers will wait for their orders and the time from order placement to the delivery of the goods.
客户服务性能受限于客户等待其订单签到的时间长短以及订单搁置到货物交付的时间长短。

[3] Integrated logistics interfaces with operations, in particular with materials management, to ensure that the right product is available for manufacturing.
一体化物流与各种操作,特别是与物料管理,相互衔接以保证正确的产品可供制造加工。

[4] Scheduling is making sure that operations produce the right products at the right time and in the right amount to meet customer demand.
调度就是确保按照客户的需求在合适的时间以合适的数量操作生产正确的产品。

[5] Scheduling varies depending on the type of manufacturing setting. The three basic manufacturing processes are repetitive manufacturing, batch processing, and job shop.
调度随制造类型不同而不同。三种基本制造过程是重复制造、批次处理和车间作业。

[6] The MRP Ⅰ system consists of five interdependent components: the master production schedule, the bill of materials file, the inventory status file, the MRP Ⅰ package, and output reports.
MRP Ⅰ 系统由五个相互独立的零部件组成:主生产计划、物料文件清单、库存状态文件、MRP Ⅰ 包以及产量报告。

Passage B Procurement

1. Purchasing and Procurement

People often assume that "procurement" is the same as "purchasing" but strictly speaking there is a difference.[1] Purchasing describes the actual buying, while procurement has a broader meaning that can include different types of acquisition (purchasing, rental, contracting, and so on) as well as the associated work of selecting suppliers, negotiazing, agreeing terms, expediting, monitoring supplier performance, arranging delivery, organising transport, checking arrivals, clearing payment, and so on. Procurement arranges the change of ownership of materials, organises the delivery, and does all the related administration. Another function—usually transport—actually delivers them, so procurement is largely concerned with processing information. At every point in the supply chain, procurement passes messages backwards to describe what customers want, and it passes messages forwards to say what suppliers have available.[2]

2. Importance of Procurement

Every organisation needs a reliable supply of materials, and as procurement is responsible for organising this supply it is an essential function within every organisation.[3] More specifically, it forms an essential link between vendors and purchasers, and provides the mechanism that triggers the movement of materials.

Not only is procurement essential, but it is also responsible for a lot of expenditure. Procurement is responsible for much of a company's spending, so a relatively small improvement can give substantial benefits.[4] Suppose that a company buys raw materials for €60, spends €40 on operations and then sells the product for €110. It clearly makes a profit of 110 − (60 + 40) = €10 a unit. Now suppose that procurement negotiates a 5% discount on materials. Materials now cost 60 × 0.95 = €57, and with the same selling price the €3 saving goes straight to profit. The profit on each unit now jumps to €13, so a 5% decrease in material costs raises profit by 30%. Using this calculation Philips Electronics found that a 2% reduction in their purchasing expenditure increased their return on assets by almost 16%.

3. Organisation of Procurement

The way that procurement is organised clearly depends on the type and size of the organisation. In a small organisation, a single buyer might be responsible for all purchases, policy and administration. A medium-sized organisation might have a department with buyers, expeditors, storekeepers, and clerks. A large organisation might have hundreds of people coordinating huge amounts of purchases.

Usually procurement is organised as a single department to get the benefits of centralised purchasing. These benefits can be considerable, but centralised purchasing has its critics. An alternative view says that organisations which work over a wide geographical should also consider local purchasing. Local offices are likely to have better knowledge of local conditions and culture, better relations with suppliers, more flexible operations, lower transport costs, and so on. The benefits from local contacts might more than offset the costs of less centralisation. In practice, most organisations use a combination of centralised purchases (typically for larger items) and local (typically for smaller items).

4. Activities in Procurement

The aim of procurement is to ensure that an organisation has the materials that its operations need. This generally means guaranteed deliveries of high quality products from reliable suppliers. So procurement managers consider questions about what to buy, how much to buy, when to buy, from whom buy, at what price, with what quality, with what conditions, and so on. Typically, this involves the following activities: (1) identifying users' needs for materials; (2) describing the materials; (3) deciding whether to acquire the materials; (4) deciding the type of purchase; (5) reviewing market conditions; (6) forming a long list of suppliers; (7) forming a short list of suppliers; (8) evaluating the short list; (9) choosing the supplier; (10) ordering the materials; (11) recording the arrival; (12) expediting; (13) reviewing the purchase.

This list shows typical activities for procurement, but the details of any single transaction vary with conditions. It would not be worth going through this type of procedure to buy a few envelopes, but if you want to buy a computer you will probably do more of the steps. When a company wants to buy a new oil tanker it adds many other analyses, particularly about design, financing and delivery.

5. Make or Buy Decision

The simplest form of the make-or-buy decision asks whether it is cheaper to make a certain item or to buy it. The argument in favour of outsourcing is that efficient operations and economics of scale often mean that specialised suppliers can deliver products efficiently at the lowest possible prices. The providers give the benefits of specialisation, access to greater expertise, lower stock levels, reduced risk, flexibility, and so on. On the other hand, internal operations can be more reliable, give greater control over supply, tailor products, have short lead times, use spare resources, protect designs, keep value-adding operations, and increase the size of the company. In practice, the three main considerations in such decisions are:

(1) financial factors—particularly the total acquisition costs;

(2) operational factors—relating to capacity, responsiveness, flexibility, reliability;

(3) strategic factors—relating to the long-term implications of the decision.

As there is a considerable move towards outsourcing, the arguments in its favour are clearly more convincing.

Considering the increasing number of materials that are bought in, a much simplified view says with the three core tasks of procurement defining what you want, identifying a supplier and negotiate the terms.[5] The aim is to find the combination of products and suppliers that best satisfies your needs.

6. Choosing a Supplier

Arguably, the most important part of procurement is finding the right supplier.

Most organisations have a list of approved suppliers who have given good service in the past, or who are otherwise known to be reliable. If there is no acceptable supplier on file, procurement managers have to search for one. For low-value items they probably look in catalogues, trade journals, or through business contacts. More expensive items need a thorough search, and this can be very time consuming. We have hinted at the procedure for identifying a qualified supplier in the list of procurement activities, and can list a reasonable set of steps explicitly:

(1) review market conditions to get a clear view of the conditions of supply;

(2) build a long list of qualified suppliers who can deliver the materials;

(3) compare organisations on this long list and eliminate those who are, for any reason, less desirable;

(4) continue eliminating organisations until you have a short list (usually four or five) of the most promising suppliers;

(5) prepare an enquiry, or request for quotation, and send it to the short list;

(6) receive bids from the short list;

(7) do a preliminary evaluation of bids and eliminate those with major problems;

(8) do a technical evaluation to see if the products meet all specifications;

(9) do a commercial evaluation to compare the costs and other conditions;

(10) arrange a pre-award meeting to discuss bids with the remaining suppliers;

(11) discuss and negotiate specific conditions that have to be met;

(12) choose a preferred supplier that is most likely to win the order;

(13) arrange a pre-commitment meeting to sort out any last-minute details;

(14) finalise details and award an order to the preferred supplier.

7. Monitoring Performance

Most organisations monitor their suppliers to make sure that they continue to give satisfactory service. This is called supplier rating or vendor rating, this might be done informally by a subjective review or it might use measures for virtually every aspect of performance.[6] Most organisations use a compromise that gives a reasonable view of performance, but with an acceptable amount of effort. They typically use a checklist of important factors to see if the supplier meets an acceptable standard in each of these. The checklist might ask whether deliveries have been made on lime, the quality is high enough, the price is still competitive, there have been complaints, and so on.

When a supplier does not meet any criterion, the customer may discuss performance with the vendor, ask for specific improvements, and then look for ways of achieving these improvements. It takes time to find a good supplier, so a customer should only start looking for a new one as a last resort.

8. Number of Suppliers

An important question for procurement concerns the best number of suppliers to use. In the extreme, a firm might move to single suppliers where it buys each material, or related materials, from only a single supplier. The argument for single sourcing is that it allows trading partners to develop mutually beneficial relationships over the long term, and typically brings benefits.

There is a strong trend towards the use of fewer suppliers, so there is little doubt that these benefits are convincing. However, the alternative view is that a firm becomes too vulnerable when it relies on a single supplier, and it can become vulnerable to events over which it has no control. To avoid this, some organisations have a policy of buying the same materials from a number of competing suppliers.

Multi-sourcing gives one way of avoiding potential problems, but an alternative uses forward buying. This makes an arrangement now, for a number of deliveries phased over different points in the future. This guarantees supplies over some period in the future and minimises the effects of possible disruptions. Because the purchases are at fixed costs, it also reduces the risks from price rises. Of course, things can still go wrong. A company that signs a long-term contract can still go out of business, or a warehouse can bum down, but the chances of a problem are much smaller.

9. Steps in Procurement

Once they have chosen a supplier, managers have to set about the actual procedure of procurement. Despite the inevitable differences in detail, we can give a general approach to procurement. In practice, the procedure for buying often includes the selection of the supplier. So the procurement starts with a user identifying a need for materials, moves through supplier selection and then arranges the purchase. The whole procedure finishes when materials are delivered and paid for. This is the typical procedure steps.

New Words and Expressions

1. negotiating [nɪˈgəʊʃɪeɪtɪŋ]　　　　n. 谈判
2. outsourcing [ˈaʊtˈsɔːsɪŋ]　　　　n. 外包,外购,外部采办
3. subjective [səbˈdʒɛktɪv]　　　　adj. 主观上的,个人的,自觉的
　　　　　　　　　　　　　　　　　n. 主观事物
4. mechanism [ˈmɛkənɪzəm]　　　　n. 机制,原理,途径,进程,机械装置,技巧
5. geographical [dʒɪəˈgræfɪkl]　　　adj. 地理的,地理学的
6. pre-commitment [kəˈmɪtmənt]　　n. 预先承诺(/许诺/委任/委托/致力/献身),承担义务

Notes

[1] People often assume that "procurement" is the same as "purchasing" but strictly speaking there is a difference.

人们通常认为"采购"和"购买"是一样的,但严格来说两者之间存在差异。

[2] At every point in the supply chain, procurement passes messages backwards to describe what customers want, and it passes messages forwards to say what suppliers have available.

在供应链中的每一个环节,采购都是逆向传递信息以描述客户的需求,并且正向传递信息告知供应商可供的货物。

[3] Every organisation needs a reliable supply of materials, and as procurement is responsible for organising this supply it is an essential function within every organisation.

每个组织机构都需要可靠的物料供应,由于采购负责组织此供应,它就成为每个组织机构内部的基本职能。

[4] Procurement is responsible for much of a company's spending, so a relatively small improvement can give substantial benefits.

采购占据了一个公司的大部分开支,因此一个相对较小的改进也能带来充实的效益。

[5] Considering the increasing number of materials that are bought in, a much simplified view says with the three core tasks of procurement defining what you want, identifying a supplier and negotiate the terms.

考虑到购入的物料日益增多,一个非常简单的观点来说明采购的三个核心任务,即你想要什么、确定供应商和谈判条款。

[6] This is called supplier rating or vendor rating, this might be done informally by a subjective review or it might use measures for virtually every aspect of performance.

这被称为供应商评级或卖方评级,可以非正式地进行主观评价,也可以采用绩效对每个方面来实际评价。

Unit 16

Passage A Outsourcing Considerations

1. Introduction

Organizations outsource to address specific business issues and opportunities. Executives need to be conscious of their organization's specific motivations for outsourcing. What business issues are you looking to solve and how will outsourcing enable you to solve them? Every subsequent outsourcing decision is rooted in a clear understanding of what an organization is trying to accomplish because the motivations drive the selection of candidates, expectations, and outcomes. Typically, the issues and opportunities an organization faces will fall in one or more of three general categories: tactical, strategic, and transformational. [1] These categories represent ways in which outsourcing is typically used.

2. Tactical Reasons for Short-term Outsourcing

(1) Freeing capital for investment.
(2) Cash infusion.
(3) Unavailability of resources internally.
(4) Function difficult to manage or out of control. .

3. Strategic Reasons for Long-Term Outsourcing

(1) Provide access to world-class capabilities
(2) Provide acceleration to reengineering efforts.
(3) Shared risks.
(4) Free resource for other purposes.
(5) Every organization has limited resources available to it.

4. Transformational Reasons for Outsourcing

(1) Bring new and faster solutions to customers.
(2) Help respond to shortening product life cycles.
(3) Redefine relationships with suppliers and business partners.
(4) Help in surpassing the competitors.

(5) Help to enter new markets with reduced risks.

(6) Concept of outsourcing.

When an enterprise identifies a need for a specific product or service, it must decide whether to make the product and perform the service internally or to purchase the requirement from an external source.

5. Advantages of Specialization

(1) Typically provide cost advantages through economies of scale.

(2) Provide strategic benefits.

(3) Due to the above capabilities, the transport company can take decision to reroute or reconsign material to an alternate destination while enroute to its original destination.[2]

6. Issues in Outsourcing Decision

While making outsourcing decisions two important factors that should be considered are: (1) economic factors, and (2) strategic factors.

Economic factors mainly refer to transaction costs. Its analysis suggests that logistics activities can be performed internally if the transaction costs are lower than expenses associated with outsourcing.[3] Moreover, the fear of loss of internal control encourages firms to perform activities internally, because outsourcing may create a situation where external firms may become opportunistic at the expense of their customer, such as a service provider with holding poor performance information to ensure its operational success.

For the company to undertake the task in-house, internal costs should be lower since it affects outsourcing decisions. This will be possible when:

(1) only a few potential suppliers are available for outsourcing;

(2) transaction specific assets such as dedicated trucks, buildings or work force are required.

For alternative opportunity cost of capital, there are the cost factors involved in outsourcing but not easily visible.

For instance, to evaluate whether the company should own the fleet of trucks or outsource, the company needs to determine the opportunity cost of capital.[4] It should assess that to own private trucking fleet requires substantial equipment investment. It needs to consider alternative uses of capital that would be invested in a private fleet of vehicle.[5] The same amount of money could be used to increase manufacturing capacity, improve logistics facilities, or expand other areas of business. The enterprise must determine which type of investment offers the best long-term advantage.

For cost associated with obsolescence, the internal performance of logistics activities requires a firm to invest in technologies that may become obsolete before the enterprise can amortize the cost fully. In this case, technology gets replaced before it has paid for itself in productivity and efficiency. It needs to be understood that outsourcing logistics activities would imply that third party service provider becomes responsible for technology investments thereby reducing the risk of obsolescence by spreading replacement cost across a large number of customer base. Because of high-volume usage the service providers would be able to amortize the cost of technology investments before they become obsolete. Further, if the equipment becomes outdated, service providers will be forced to update their technology to maintain attractiveness to their customer base.

For cost related to labour, moving from internal to external performance of logistics, the labour requirements and management responsibilities of the enterprise will be reduced or shifted to the service supplier.

While deciding to perform logistics activity either in-house or through a third party service provider, the key considerations are: hiring, training, internal labour availability, and implementation lime.

7. Strategic Factors

Strategic factors involve evaluating which supplier is the most capable of performing the service at best practice level.

An enterprise requires to evaluate the potential outsource services in terms of their contribution to a firm's core and non-core activities. Typically, a firm will not dilute its core competencies by having external firms perform highly sensitive activities. Once the enterprise has isolated those activities that are its core activities, the balance of required activities or the non-core requirements become candidates for outsourcing.

8. Desirability of Outsourcing

Based partially on the concept of specialization we need to understand that the specialization would mean better utilization of facilities, equipment, or labour consequently doing more with less.

If required service can be improved or an enterprise can reduce its overall investment or operating requirements, then outsourcing is an attractive alternative. Specialization can result in economies of scale thereby achieving reduced cost and improved services simultaneously. Thus outsourcing is justified if visible costs decrease and services improve.

New Words and Expressions

1. infusion [ɪnˈfjuʒn]   *n.* 灌输,浸泡,注入物,激励
2. reroute [riˈraʊt]   *vt.* 变更旅程,按新的特定路线运送
3. dilute [daɪˈlut]   *adj.* 稀释的,淡的
                       vt. 稀释,冲淡,削弱
                       vi. 变稀薄,变淡
4. amortize [ˈæmətaɪz]   *vt.* 摊销(等于 amortise),分期偿还

5. dedicated ['dɛdə'ketɪd]　　　*adj.* 专用的,专注的,献身的
　　　　　　　　　　　　　　　　v. 以……奉献,把……用于
6. dedicated trucks　　　　　　专用卡车
7. motivation ['motə'veʃən]　　 *n.* 动机,积极性,推动
8. candidate ['kændədet]　　　 *n.* 候选人,申请者,应征人员

Notes

[1] Typically, the issues and opportunities an organization faces will fall in one or more of three general categories: tactical, strategic, and transformational.
通常,一个组织机构所面临的问题和机遇会落入常见的三种类别之一或多个:战术、战略和转型。

[2] Due to the above capabilities, the transport company can take decision to reroute or reconsign material to an alternate destination while enroute to its original destination.
由于以上的能力,运输公司可以在向原始目的地运货的途中决定变更运输路线或把物料重新托运到另一个目的地。

[3] Its analysis suggests that logistics activities can be performed internally if the transaction costs are lower than expenses associated with outsourcing.
其分析表明,如果业务成本低于外包的相关费用,则物流活动可以由内部执行。

[4] For instance, to evaluate whether the company should own the fleet of trucks or outsource, the company needs to determine the opportunity cost of capital.
例如,为了评估是应该拥有车队还是将其外包,公司需要确定资本的机会成本。

[5] It needs to consider alternative uses of capital that would be invested in a private fleet of vehicle.
需要考虑投资于私人车队的资本的另一种用途。

Passage B　Facility Location

1. Location Decisions

In practice, location decisions are needed whenever there are major changes. For instance, manufacturing costs were lower in China before 2010, so many companies were moving their manufacturing plants; in the same way, call centres were locating in Mumbai, India; financial services in London; high technology companies in Silicon Valley; oil wells in Siberia, and so on. As manufacturing cost are increasing in China recently, many companies are moving away their manufacturing plants, say, to Vietnam.[1] The reasons for such moves include:

(1) the end of a lease or tenure on existing premises;

(2) expansion of the organisation into new geographical areas;

(3) changes in the locations or requirements of customers or suppliers;

(4) changes to operations, such as JIT production or an electricity company;

(5) moving from coal generators to gas;

(6) reorganisations, perhaps reducing the number of tiers in a supply chain;

(7) improved facilities, perhaps introducing new technology;

(8) changes to transport, such as a switch from rail to road;

(9) changes to the transport network, such as the opening of the Channel Tunnel or the road bridge between Sweden and Denmark.

2. Importance of Location Decisions

As you can imagine, choosing the best location is an old problem, which people have been working on for many years. Early villages were built in good growing areas, settlements grew near to river crossings, and castles were built on promontories. Then when industry arrived, weavers set up near water power, steel mills were built near iron ore deposits and coal mines, ports appeared near deep water inlets, and so on. In the 19th century Von Thunen did some formal analyses for the value of crops at different locations in terms of the costs of land and transporting the crops to market. In the 20th century analysts such as Weber built on this work to consider a wide range of location problems.

The underlying message behind location decisions is that choosing the right site does not guarantee success, but choosing the wrong site certainly guarantees failure.[2]

3. Alternatives to Locating New Facilities

In practice, when an organisation wants to change its facilities either expand, move or contract it has three alternatives:

(1) expand or change operations at an existing site;

(2) open additional facilities at another site, while maintaining operations at the existing site (perhaps modified in some way);

(3) close down existing operations and move all operations to a new site.

4. Trends in Location

When organisations look at their operations and business environment, it is not surprising that they often see similar conditions and come to similar choices about locations. This is the reason that certain regions, countries, towns or trading estates become popular, as many organisations recognise independently that they are the best place to locate.[3]

Apart from the growing popularity of specific regions and areas, there are other types of trend in location, such as a growing number of out-of-town shopping malls, supermarkets and retail estates. This, together with the growth of E-business, means that traditional high streets often find it difficult to compete, and are in a relative decline.[4] At the same time, the move towards shorter supply chains means that layers of intermediaries are disappearing and logistics is concentrated into fewer facilities that serve wider areas.

5. A Hierarchy of Decisions

Location decisions are always difficult. Managers have to consider many different factors and there are serious consequences for making mistakes. Some of the factors in location decisions can be measured or at least estimated such as operating costs, wage rates, taxes, currency exchange rates, economic growth, number of competitors, distances from customers and suppliers, development grants, population and reliability of supplies.[5] Other factors are non-quantifiable, such as business strategics, quality of infrastructure, political stability, social attitudes, industrial relations, legal system, culture, lifestyle, climate, and so on.

6. Choosing a Geographical Region

The broadest decisions about geographical regions and countries come from the business strategy. For instance, an organisation with a strategy of global operations or expansion must continually look for new locations, while other strategies might specify operations in a particular market, or dose to suppliers.

Another problem is added when organisations want low operating costs, as these often come at sites that are some way from both customers and suppliers. Then firms have to make sure that lower operating costs are not swamped by higher logistics costs.

7. Models for Location

After making a decision about the geographical region, an organisation has to look in more detail at areas and then individual sites. There are many analyses to help with this decision, usually based on some kind investigation of costs.

One approach that is not recommended is personal preference. Managers often seem to be subjective and choose sites they like perhaps in the town where they live or grew up in, or where they spend their holidays. These decisions may be successful, but they are unreliable and often lead to very poor choices because you like spending your holidays in a particular town, and it does not mean that this is the best location for a business.

An infinite set approach finds the best location in principle, and then managers can look for an available site nearby; a feasible set approach compares sites that are currently available and chooses the best.[6]

These approaches are often used together, with an infinite set approach homing in on the best area to locate, in principle, and then a feasible set approach comparing available sites nearby.

New Words and Expressions

1. deposit [dɪˈpɑzɪt]   *n.* 存款,押金,订金,保证金,沉淀物,堆积物,存放物
                                                vt. 使沉积,存放,堆积
2. estate [ɪˈstet]   *n.* 房地产,财产,身份
3. hierarchy [ˈhaɪərɑrki]   *n.* 层级,等级制度
4. investigation [ɪnˈvɛstɪˈgeʃən]   *n.* 调查,调查研究

5. infinite [ˈɪnfɪnət]　　　　　　*adj.* 无限的,无穷的,无数的,极大的

　　　　　　　　　　　　　　　n. 无限,[数] 无穷大,无限的东西(如空间,时间)

Notes

[1] In practice, location decisions are needed whenever there are major changes. For instance, manufacturing costs were now lower in China before 2010, so many companies were moving their manufacturing plants; in the same way, call centres were locating in Mumbai, India; financial services in London; high technology companies in Silicon Valley; oil wells in Siberia, and so on. As manufacturing cost are increasing in China recently, many companies are moving away their manufacturing plants, say, to Vietnam.

实际上,每当有重大变化时就需要选址决策。例如,2010年之前中国制造成本低,所以许多公司正在把其制造厂搬迁到此;同理,客服中心正在落户印度孟买;金融服务正在落户伦敦;高科技公司正在落户硅谷;石油钻井正在落户西伯利亚等。近年来,由于中国制造成本增加,许多公司正在把他们的制造厂搬离于此,比如搬至越南。

[2] The underlying message behind location decisions is that choosing the right site does not guarantee success, but choosing the wrong site certainly guarantees failure.

选址决策背后的信息是,选择正确的地点并不能保证成功,但选择错误的地点肯定会导致失败。

[3] This is the reason that certain regions, countries, towns or trading estates become popular, as many organisations recognise independently that they are the best place to locate.

这就是某些地区、国家、城镇或贸易地产变得流行的原因,因为许多组织机构都独立地认识到它们是最好的选址地点。

[4] This, together with the growth of E-business, means that traditional high streets often find it difficult to compete, and are in a relative decline.

它与电子商务一起增长,并意味着传统的繁华街区往往难以竞争,并处于相对下降趋势。

[5] Some of the factors in location decisions can be measured or at least estimated such as operating costs, wage rates, taxes, currency exchange rates, economic growth, number of competitors, distances from customers and suppliers, development grants, population and reliability of supplies.

选址决策考虑的一些因素能被评价或者至少能被估计,如:经营成本、工资率、税收、货币汇率、经济增长量、竞争对手数量、客户与供应商间的距离、开发补助金、人口以及供应商可靠性。

[6] An infinite set approach finds the best location in principle, and then managers can look for an available site nearby; a feasible set approach compares sites that are currently available and chooses the best.

无限集法基本上找到最佳位置,然后管理人员可以在它附近寻找一个可用地点;可行集法与目前可用的地点比较并选出最佳地点。

Part 5 Logistics Machine and Equipment

Unit 17

Unit 18

Unit 19

Unit 20

Part 5 Logistics Machine and Equipment

Unit 17

Passage A Material Handling Equipment (I)

Effective materials handling requires the effective use of different types of equipment, including the dock, conveyors and cranes, guided vehicles, and order-picking and storage equipment.

1. Dock Equipment

Materials handling begins at the loading dock when a truck containing the goods arrives and needs to be unloaded. The faster the distribution center unloads the goods, the greater its throughput capability. Due to the constant activity, both the receiving and shipping dock activities need to be efficient. To load or unload the goods safely and quickly, the distribution center should utilize dock equipment. There are many kinds of dock equipment, such as forklifts, dock bumpers, dock levelers, dock seals, trailer restraint systems, pallets and ect..

(1) Forklifts.

One type of dock equipment common to many materials-handling systems is the forklift truck, see Figure 17-1, a very versatile piece of equipment that a company can provide at a very reasonable cost. Able to perform several useful materials-handling tasks, the forklift is individually powered and is available with various lift arrangements. Warehouses usually use forklifts in conjunction with pallets.

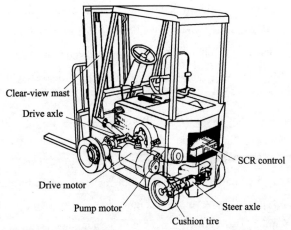

Figure 17-1 Forklift truck

The forklift truck operates very efficiently, and companies can use it in a variety of ways. Its major disadvantage is that it requires an operator, who may often be idle when the forklift is not in use. But, all things considered, it is probably the most popular type of materials-handling equipment in existence. Even the smallest firm with the simplest materials-handling system can often afford a forklift truck. Its biggest advantage is its versatility in moving goods from one distribution center section to another or in transferring goods into and out of transportation equipment.

(2) **Dock Bumpers.**

Dock bumpers are molded rubber pieces that protect the building from the impact of a docking trailer backing into it and from a trailer shifting in weight during loading or unloading.

(3) **Dock Levelers.**

Dock levelers level out the angle between the dock and the trailer by providing a ramp that enables the forklift to drive into the trailer safely.[1] The greater the ramp angle, the greater the chance of an accident.

(4) **Dock Seals.**

A dock seal is a cushioned frame around the dock door opening that connects the trailer to the dock. Its purpose is to create a seal blocking any outside weather, smoke, and fumes from entering the warehouse.

(5) **Trailer Restraint Systems.**

Vehicle restraints prevent the trailer from drifting away from the dock during loading or unloading. Since this drifting causes many dock accidents, the Occupational Safety and Health Administration (OSHA) must approve a warehouse's restraining system. While a company can use wheel chocks or wedge molded rubber under tires of a truck, these methods are ineffective on ice, snow, or gravel. The best system is an automated one that uses a lighting or sound system to communicate the trailer's safety status between the dock worker and the truck driver.

(6) **Pallets.**

Pallets are both basic and essential to materials-handling operations. A pallet's main function is to provide a base to hold individual items together. Once the items are stacked on the pallet, materials-handling equipment, most often a forklift, can move the pallet to the proper storage location. Companies also use pallets when shipping products from the distribution center to the customer.

2. Conveyors

Conveyors, popular form of materials-handling equipments, play an important role in advancing productivity and improving bottom-line operating results, particularly in the mechanized distribution center or warehouse. These systems decrease handling costs, increase productivity of workers and equipment, and provide an interface with management information systems.

There are two basic types of conveyors, see Figure 17-2. The first, a roller conveyor, basically uses the gravity principle. The conveyor is inclined, and goods move down the conveyor by force of their own weight, typically at a slow pace depending on the conveyor's incline.[2] The other type is the wheel conveyor, or belt or towline conveyor, which requires power equipment.

Part 5　Logistics Machine and Equipment

Such conveyors move goods either on a level or up inclines to a warehouse section. Companies use a roller conveyor wherever possible to minimize their operating costs.

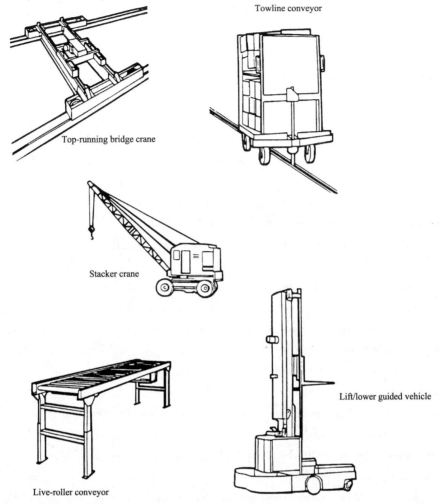

Figure 17-2　Materials-handling equipment

　　Many companies consider conveyors advantageous because they can be highly automatic and, therefore, can eliminate handling costs. They also may save space since they can use narrow aisles and operate on multiple levels in the same area.[3] Conveyor systems often have low operating costs.

　　Conveyors equipped with scanners and other automatic devices enable companies to move goods very efficiently and quickly from one distribution center area to another. Scanners can keep inventory records by recording packages moving on conveyors and also track storage locations. Finally, scanners enable managers to use computers to rapidly locate goods.

　　A modern conveyor system is very expensive and requires a large capital investment. It is also fixed in location; that is, it lacks versatility. Designing a conveyor system requires much time and effort, particularly with reference to a company's future needs. If conditions change, changing the conveyor system may be necessary, often at a very high cost. Organizations that invest in complex conveyor system are usually large manufacturing and retailing firms. Using conveyors to automate a large distribution center, for example, generally requires a significant investment of funds in a very complex and sophisticated conveyor system. However, companies can install some very simple conveyors at a very reasonable cost.

In analyzing the possibility of using conveyor systems, an organization must decide whether its materials-handling approach should be capital intensive or labor intensive. Many large companies with sophisticated logistics requirements find capital-intensive systems such as elaborate conveyors to be extremely worthwhile because of reduced labor costs and possible improvements in distribution time. However, such approaches are not necessarily right for all companies. More labor-intensive approaches may be much more appropriate. Comparing labor-intensive and capital-intensive materials-handling methods is analogous to comparing private and 3PL distribution. In other words, conveyor systems have a very important fixed-cost segment, and a company must have throughput volume sufficient to defray or spread the fixed costs.

One disadvantage of conveyors is the possibility of equipment malfunction, which could cause supply chain delays. However, conveyor users can minimize operational problems. To avoid exceeding the equipment's capacity and causing breakdowns, the company using conveyors must consider the dimensions and weight of each unit the conveyors will carry. The company must consider the load's center of gravity when loads travel on inclined or declined conveyors, are handled in start-stop operations, or are transferred while in motion. To avoid problems, a company must operate a conveyor at the rate for which the company intended it. This rate may vary, depending on unit sizes, and these sizes will be mixed.

Conveyors can handle loads of almost any size, shape, weight, or fragility. However, users must determine, before they purchase equipment, the items a specific conveyor will handle and its expected functions-sortation. Following the guidelines this section suggests will contribute to an effective conveyor system.

Trends show that conveyor usefulness will continue to increase as automation technologies develop. Already, conveyors can be valuable tools in data generation and product-monitoring systems, and their use in computerized inventory control is quite common.[4]

New Words and Expressions

1. versatility [ˌvɜːsəˈtɪləti]　　　　　　n. 多用途,多功能,多才多艺
2. ramp [ræmp]　　　　　　　　　　n. 斜坡,斜道,匝道
3. malfunction [ˌmælˈfʌŋkʃn]　　　　n. 失灵,故障,功能障碍
4. dock bumper　　　　　　　　　　月台缓冲器,船坞缓冲器
5. elaborate [英][iˈlæbəreit][美][ɪˈlæbəret]　vi. 详尽说明,变得复杂
　　　　　　　　　　　　　　　　　vt. 详细制定,详尽阐述,[生理学]加工,尽心竭力地做
　　　　　　　　　　　　　　　　　adj. 复杂的;精心制作的;(结构)复杂的;精巧的

Notes

[1] Dock levelers level out the angle between the dock and the trailer by providing a ramp that enables the forklift to drive into the trailer safely.
通过提供一个使叉车安全地开到拖车里的斜坡,月台轧平机消除了月台与拖车之间的角度。

[2] The conveyor is inclined, and goods move down the conveyor by force of their own weight, typically at a slow pace depending on the conveyor's incline.
输送机是倾斜的,货物凭借自重沿输送机向下移动,通常(货物)以一个取决于输送机倾斜度的缓慢速度移动。

[3] They also may save space since they can use narrow aisles and operate on multiple levels in the same area.
它们(输送机)还可以节省空间,因为它们可以使用狭窄的过道并且能在同一区域多个高度工作。

[4] Already, conveyors can be valuable tools in data generation and product-monitoring systems, and their use in computerized inventory control is quite common.
在数据时代和生产监控系统中,输送机已经能够成为有价值的工具,而且输送机应用于计算机库存管理也十分普遍。

Passage B Material Handling Equipment (Ⅱ)

1. Cranes

Companies can utilize a variety of cranes in warehouses, see Figure 17-2 in last Passage. The two basic types are fridge cranes and stacker or wagon cranes. Bridge cranes are more common in physical supply warehouses or where companies have to move, store, and load heavy industrial goods such as steel coils or generators.

Stacker cranes are popular because they can function in narrow aisles, effectively utilizing cubic capacity. This equipment is also very adaptable to automation. Fully automated stacker cranes on the market today can put stock into and take it out of storage areas without an operator. The computer equipment such systems utilize can select the best storage placement and recall this placement later. Stacker cranes are commonly used in conjunction with elaborate shelving systems.

Though not usually as expensive as conveyor systems, cranes are also capital-intensive equipment. Handling very heavy items may require bridge cranes; a company should justify stacker cranes on a cost basis. The advantage of bridge cranes is the ability to lift heavy items quickly and efficiently. The advantages of stacker cranes are the effective use of space and the possibility for automation.

Companies can utilize a variety of cranes in warehouses, see Figure 17-2 in last Passage. The two basic types are fridge cranes and stacker or wagon cranes. Bridge cranes are more common in physical supply warehouses or where companies have to move, store, and load heavy industrial goods (such as steel coils or generators). [1]

Stacker cranes are popular because they can function in narrow aisles, effectively utilizing cubic capacity. This equipment is also very adaptable to automation. Fully automated stacker cranes on the market today can put stock into and take it out of storage areas without an operator. The computer equipment such systems utilize can select the best storage placement and recall this placement later. Stacker cranes are commonly used in conjunction with elaborate shelving systems.

Though not usually as expensive as conveyor systems, cranes are also capital-intensive equipment. Handling very heavy items may require bridge cranes; a company should justify stacker cranes on a cost basis. The advantage of bridge cranes is the ability to lift heavy items quickly and efficiently. The advantages of stacker cranes are the effective use of space and the possibility for automation.

2. AGV Systems

AGVs are machines that connect receiving, storing, manufacturing, and shipping. Firms can track these vehicles, either roaming freely or on a fixed path, with computers that make traffic control decisions. [2] Essentially, AGVs travel around the warehouse or manufacturing plant carrying various items to a particular programmed destination. Since these AGVs do not require a driver, labor costs are reduced.

The double-pallet jack, another vehicle that does not require a driver, can transport two pallet loads between distribution center areas. As with AGVs, a computer can guide the double-pallet jack to its destination along a floor-wired guide. [3]

Also available is a variety of other, more specialized equipment, including draglines that pull carts in a continuous circle in a warehouse, elevators, hoists, and monorails.

3. Order-Picking and Storage Equipment

One of the main functions in a distribution center is order picking. Although order picking by nature is labor intensive, an effectively designed order-picking and storage system can enhance the speed, accuracy, and cost-effectiveness of the order-picking process. Most storage systems primarily try to use distribution center space effectively. Because the cost of labor, equipment, and space for order picking equals about 65% of total distribution operating costs, any improvement that reduces these costs is greatly important. This section covers two main equipment types: picker-to-part and part-to-picker. Picker-to-part systems include bin shelving, modular storage drawers, flow racks, mobile storage systems, and order-picking vehicles. Part-to-picker systems include carousels and miniload ASRS (see Unit 2) Figure 17-3 illustrates these systems.

Part 5 Logistics Machine and Equipment

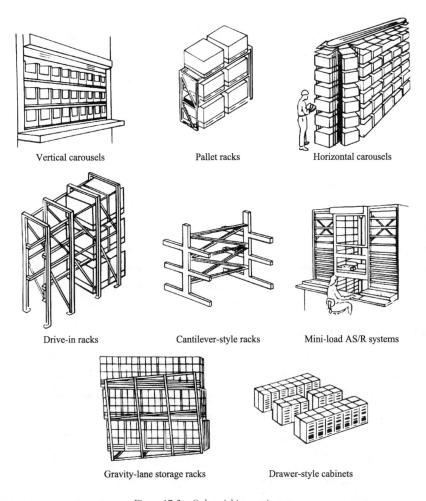

Figure 17-3 Order-picking equipment

1) Picker-to-Part Systems

In picker-to-part systems, the order picker must travel to the pick location within the aisle.

(1) Bin Shelving.

Bin shelving is the oldest and most basic storage system available for storing small parts. The main advantages of bin shelving are the low initial cost and the ability to divide units into various compartments. However, the system underutilizes cubic space by not using a bin's full size and by requiring shelf height to be within a person's reach.

(2) Modular Storage Drawers.

Modular storage drawers are cabinets that are divided into drawers and further subdivided into compartments. Their main advantage is their ability to hold a large number of SKUs. Their main drawback is height: the drawers cannot be more than approximately 5ft high because the order picker must look into them when picking an order.

(3) Flow Racks.

Flow racks store items in cartons having a uniform size and shape. The cartons, which warehouse personnel replenish from the rack's back end, flow on rollers, by gravity, to the rack's front or aisle end for order picking. A main advantage to this system is that the back-to-front item movement ensures FIFO inventory turnover. Flow racks can also hold full pallets of items.

(4) Mobile Storage Systems.

Mobile storage systems need only one order-picking aisle because a motorized system can slide the racks, shelves, or modular drawers to the left or right. The order picker can slide the racks apart to expose the aisle in which he or she needs to pick an order. Slower picking speed due to the shift time offsets the advantage of high storage density.

(5) Order-Picking Vehicles.

Order-picking trucks and person-aboard storage and retrieval (S/R) vehicles increase order-picking rates and maximize cubic space utilization. The order picker rides or drives the vehicle horizontally or vertically to the pick location. Some of these vehicles move automatically, allowing the order picker to perform another task while traveling.

2) Part-to-Picker Systems

In part-to-picker systems, the pick location travels through an automated machine to the picker. These systems have a higher initial cost than picker-to-part systems, but utilizing automated storage and retrieval equipment speeds up order-picking operations, improves inventory control, and increases profits. Part-to-picker systems minimize travel time. By comparison, in static shelving systems, workers spend up to 70% of their time traveling.

(1) Carousels.

Carousels are shelves or bins linked together through a mechanical device that stores and rotates items for order picking. The two main types of carousels are horizontal and vertical.

Horizontal carousels are a linked series of bins that rotate around a vertical axis. A computer locates a needed part and rotates the carousel until the part location stops in front of the order picker's fixed position. Automated systems attempt to minimize wait times and maximize order-picking times. For this reason, an order picker usually works two carousels. In this way, the picker can pick from one carousel while waiting for the other carousel to rotate to a needed item. Industries that use horizontal carousels include aviation, electronic, paper, and pharmaceutical.

Vertical carousels differ from horizontal ones in two ways: ① the bins are enclosed for cleanliness and security, and ② the carousel rotates around a horizontal axis. The vertical carousel operates on a continuous lift principle, rotating the necessary items to the order picker's work station. This vertical storage approach cuts floor space use by 60% and increases picking productivity by up to 300% over racks and shelving of equal capacity. Some industries that use vertical carousels include electronics, automotive, aerospace, and computer.

(2) Miniload ASRS.

The most technically advanced order-picking system is the miniload ASRS, which efficiently uses storage space and achieves the highest accuracy rate in order picking. The ASRS machine travels both horizontally and vertically to storage locations in an aisle, carrying item storage containers to and from an order-picking station at the end of the aisle. At the order-picking station, the order picker programs the correct item-picking sequence. The ASRS machine retrieves the next container in the sequence, while the order picker obtains items from the present container. The miniload ASRS utilizes vertical space and requires few aisles, but this system is very expensive.

New Words and Expressions

1. stacker['stækə]   n. 堆码机,堆码工,叠式存储器
2. jack[dʒæk]   n. 千斤顶,升起
3. hoist[hɔist]   n. 提升间,
4. S/R (storage and retrieval)   存储和拣货
5. picker-to-part system   人到货前系统
6. part-to-picker system   货到人前系统

Notes

[1] Bridge cranes are more common in physical supply warehouses or where companies have to move, store, and load heavy industrial goods (such as steel coils or generators).
桥式起重机在实体供应仓库或须移动、存储以及装载笨重工业货物(如钢铁卷材或发电机)的公司中是最常见的。

[2] Firms can track these vehicles, either roaming freely or on a fixed path, with computers that make traffic control decisions.
公司可以用做出交通控制决策的计算机跟踪这些车辆,不论车辆是自由选径或是在一个固定的路径上。

[3] As with AGVs, a computer can guide the double-pallet jack to its destination along a floor-wired guide.
和自动导引车一样,一台计算机可以把双托盘千斤顶沿着地面导线导向其目的地。

Unit 18

Passage A Hoisting Machines

Mechanisms for raising and lowering material with intermittent motion while holding the material freely suspended. Hoisting machines are capable of picking up loads at one location and depositing them at another anywhere within a limited area. In contrast, elevating machines move their loads only in a fixed vertical path, and monorails operate on a fixed horizontal path rather than over a limited area.

The principal components of hoisting machines are sheaves and pulleys, for the hoisting mechanism; winches and hoists, for the power units; and derricks and cranes, for the structural elements.[1]

1. Block and Tackle

Sheaves and pulleys or blocks are a means of applying power through a rope, wire, cable, or chain. Sheaves are wheels with a grooved periphery, in appropriate mountings, that change the direction or the point of application of a force transmitted by means of a rope or cable. Pulleys are made up of one or more sheaves mounted in a frame, usually with an attaching swivel hook, eye, or similar device at one or both ends. Pulley systems are a combination of blocks (Figure 18-1).

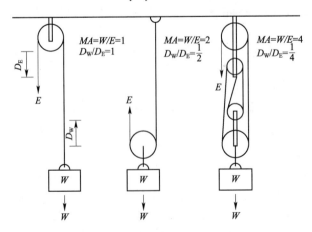

Figure 18-1 Mechanical advantage of pulley systems

Sometimes used alone, sheaves and pulleys find their most usual application as the hoisting tackle of derricks and cranes.

2. Winches and Hoists

Normally, winches are designed for stationary service, while hoists are mounted so that they can be moved about, for example, on wheel trolleys in connection with overhead crane operations.

A winch is basically a drum or cylinder around which cordage is coiled for hoisting or hauling. The drum may be operated either manually or by power, using a worm gear and worm wheel, or a spur gear arrangement. A ratchet and pawl prevents the load from slipping; large winches are equipped with brakes, usually of the external band type. Industrial applications of winches include use as the power element for derricks and as the elevating mechanism with stackers (Figure 18-2).

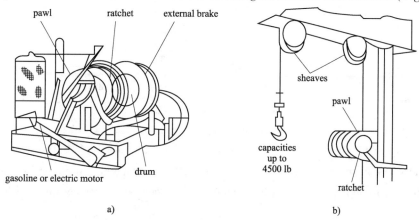

Figure 18-2 Powered and hand winches
a) Heavy-duty single-drum winch; b) Wire-rope hand winch (4500lb = 2042kg)

Floor and wall-mounted electric hoists are used for many hoisting and hauling jobs from fixed locations in industrial plants and warehouses.[2]

Heavy-duty types are standard equipment for powering ship's gear in cargo handling. They are also mounted on over-the-road carriers to facilitate the moving of heavy bulky loads, and serve as the power units of power cranes and shovels. A railroad car puller employs the same principle; however, the drum is mounted vertically and is used for spotting railroad cars in freight yards.

Hoists are designed to lift from a position directly above their loads and thus require mobile mountings. Hoists are classified by their power source, such as hand, electric, or pneumatic.

Hand hoists-are chain operated. There are four types: spur geared, worm geared, differential, and pull-lift or lever (Figure 18-3). The last, with its lever for operation and its ratchet for holding, is the simplest and most economical. However, since the operating lever is located on the anchor end of the hoist, it is not as convenient for vertical lifting as it is for horizontal pulling.

The spur-gear type costs the most but is the most economical to operate, with an efficiency as high as 85%. Where hoists are to be used frequently, it is the type most recommended. Worm-gear hoists transform about one-third to one-half the input energy to useful work. Offsetting this low efficiency is the locking characteristic of the worm drive: the load cannot turn the mechanism; consequently the load is at all times restrained from running away. In contrast, with a ratchet the load is locked only at positions where the pawl engages a step of the ratchet. Differential hoists use only about one-third the energy input; they too prevent loads from running away during lowering. Spur-gear hoists are more efficient, but require a brake to restrain loads during lowering or holding.

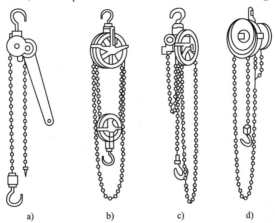

Figure 18-3　Chain hand hoists

a) Lever (pull-lift); b) Differential; c) Worm geared; d) Spur geared

Electric hoists lift their loads by either cable or chain (Figure 18-4). The cable type has a drum around which a wire cable is coiled and uncoiled for hoisting and lowering. Chain models have either a roller chain and sprocket or a link chain and pocketed wheel for hoisting and lowering.

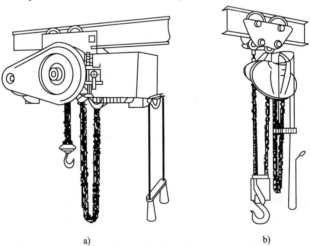

Figure 18-4　Hoists

a) Chain; b) Roller chain

There are innumerable below-the-hook attachments, such as slings, hooks, grabs, and highly specialized devices to facilitate practically any handling requirement. Many of these devices are designed to pick up and release their loads automatically. All chain hoists are designed with the lower hooks as the weakest parts; not being interchangeable with the anchor hook, therefore, if the hoist is overloaded, the lower hook spreads or opens up. If the inside contour of the hook is not a true arc of a circle, this is an indication that the hook has been overloaded.

Part 5 Logistics Machine and Equipment

Pneumatic or air hoists are constructed with cylinders and pistons for reciprocating motion and air motors for rotary motion. Compressed air is the actuating medium in both. Various arrangements admit air to and discharge it from cylinders mounted to operate vertically or horizontally. Pneumatically operated hoists provide smooth action and sensitive response to control; these characteristics account for their wide use in handling fragile materials, such as molds in foundries. In addition, freedom from sparking makes them useful in locations where the presence of explosive mixtures make electrical equipment hazardous.[3]

3. Derricks and Cranes

A derrick is distinguished by a mast in the form of a slanting boom pivoted at its lower end and carrying load-supporting tackle at its outer end.[4] In contrast, jib cranes always have horizontal booms.

Derrick masts are supported by guy lines or stiff legs; some are arranged to rotate 360°. Winches, hand or powered, usually in conjunction with pulleys, do the lifting. Derricks are standard equipment on construction jobs; they are also used on freighters for loading and unloading cargo, and on barges for dredging operations.

Jib cranes, when carried on self-supporting masts, are called pillar cranes; those mounted on walls are called wall-bracket cranes. Cranes with jib like booms are frequently used in shops, mounted on columns or walls, but have limited coverage. They may have their own running gear or be mounted on trucks. Mobile types for heavier service are called yard cranes or crane trucks. They may or may not be able to rotate their booms. More powerful machines of this type belong to the power crane and shovel group (Figure 18-5).

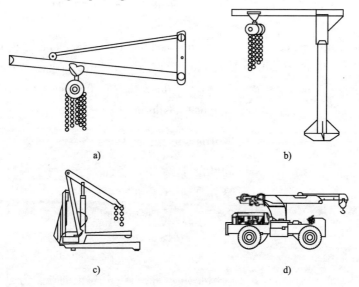

Figure 18-5 Four types of jib cranes
a) Wall-bracket crane; b) Pillar crane; c) Movable hydraulic crane; d) Crane truck

4. Overhead-Traveling and Gantry Cranes

Hoisting machines with a bridge like structure spanning the area over which they operate are overhead-traveling or gantry cranes. In the overhead-traveling type, the bridge is carried by, and moves along, overhead trackage which is usually fixed to the building structure itself. The gantry crane is normally supported by fixed structures or arranged for running along tracks on ground level. Gantry cranes are standard equipment in shipside operations. Basic arrangements of overhead-traveling cranes are top running and under-hung. In the former, the bridge's end trucks ride on top of the runway rails; in the latter, the end trucks carry the bridge suspended below the rails. Types for relatively light duty can be made of elements used in the construction of overhead track.

Both overhead-traveling and gantry cranes are called bridge cranes. These cranes span a rather large area and differ among themselves primarily only in the construction of the bridge portion of the crane, and in the method of suspension of the bridge. Where smaller areas are to be spanned, standard beams are used for the bridge structure; however, built-up girders or truss-like bridge structure are used for larger spans. A full gantry crane has both its supporting elements erected on the ground, usually riding on tracks. A half-gantry crane has a supporting structure at one end of the bridge that reaches to the ground, and the other end is carried directly on overhead tracks. Selection of either type depends primarily on building design and the areas in which the crane is to be used.

Any one or several of the hoists described earlier may be attached to the bridge, usually suspended from a trolley attached to an I-beam track. The combination of a hoist on a track and the bridge crane itself moving on tracks provides for usable movement of equipment within a rectangular area governed only by the length of the bridge and the total horizontal movement of the bridge or gantry crane.[5]

Another type of lifting mechanism, used on a modified type bridge crane, is a fork-lift attachment suspended from the overhead truck or bridge; it is referred to as a stacker crane. This unit is especially used for such locations as stock rooms, die racks, or finished-goods storage because it has the advantage of being able to handle unit loads in narrow aisles.

New Words and Expressions

1. intermittent motion　　　　　间歇运动
2. elevating machine　　　　　举升机械,提升机械
3. pulley['puli]　　　　　　　　n. 滑车,滑轮,辘轳,皮带轮,滚筒
4. winch[wintʃ]　　　　　　　　n. 绞盘,卷扬机,曲柄
5. shipside['ʃipsaid]　　　　　　n. 码头
6. derrick['derik]　　　　　　　n. [机]起重机,[矿]井口上的铁架塔,悬臂式起重机
7. groove[gru:v]　　　　　　　n. (唱片等的)凹槽,惯例,最佳状态
　　　　　　　　　　　　　　　vt. 开槽于

Part 5　Logistics Machine and Equipment

8. periphery [pə'rifəri]　　　　　　　n. 外围,四周,边缘,周边
9. trackage ['trækidʒ]　　　　　　　n. 轨道,轨长,铁路轨道线路,线路使用权
10. mounting ['mauntiŋ]　　　　　　n. 装备,衬托纸,登上,乘骑
　　　　　　　　　　　　　　　　　adj. 上升的,增长的
　　　　　　　　　　　　　　　　　v. 登上,骑上(mount 的现在分词);增加,上升;上演;准备
11. hook [huk]　　　　　　　　　　n. 钩,吊钩
　　　　　　　　　　　　　　　　　v. 钩住,沉迷,上瘾
12. swivel hook　　　　　　　　　　转钩
13. ratchet ['rætʃit]　　　　　　　　n. [机](防倒转的)棘齿
14. pneumatic [nju(:)'mætik]　　　　adj. 装满空气的,气动的,风力的
　　　　　　　　　　　　　　　　　n. 气胎
15. pawl [pɔ:l]　　　　　　　　　　n. [机]棘爪,制转杆
　　　　　　　　　　　　　　　　　vt. 用制转杆使停转
16. spur gear　　　　　　　　　　　直齿轮
17. worm gear　　　　　　　　　　蜗轮
18. recommend [rekə'mend]　　　　vt. 推荐,介绍,劝告,使受欢迎,托付
19. anchor ['æŋkə]　　　　　　　　v. 抛锚,锚定
　　　　　　　　　　　　　　　　　n. 锚
20. spur-gear hoist　　　　　　　　直齿轮提升机
21. sprocket ['sprɔkit]　　　　　　　n. 链轮齿
22. attachment [ə'tætʃmənt]　　　　n. 附件,附加装置,配属
23. sling [sliŋ]　　　　　　　　　　n. 投掷器,弹弓,悬带,吊索[绳,环,链,具],吊重装置
　　　　　　　　　　　　　　　　　v. 投掷,用悬带吊挂
24. interchangeable ['intə'tʃeindʒəbl]　adj. 可互换的
25. contour ['kɔntuə]　　　　　　　n. 轮廓,周线,等高线
26. reciprocating [ri'siprəkeitiŋ]　　adj. 往复的,交替的,互换的摆动的
27. in the form of　　　　　　　　　用……的形式
28. shovel ['ʃʌvl]　　　　　　　　　n. 铲,铁铲,挖斗机,铁锹
　　　　　　　　　　　　　　　　　v. 铲,挖,舀,翻动
29. loading and unloading　　　　　装载和卸载
30. hydraulic 英[haɪ'drɔ:lɪk]　　　　adj. 水力的,水压的;用水发动的;[建]水硬的;水力学的
　　　美[haɪ'drɔlɪk]
31. girder ['gə:də]　　　　　　　　　n. 梁,钢桁的支架
32. trolley ['trɔ:li]　　　　　　　　　n. 小车,手推车,触轮,(有轨)电车
33. be attached to　　　　　　　　　把……放(系/连)在……上
34. I-beam　　　　　　　　　　　　工字梁

Notes

[1] The principal components of hoisting machines are sheaves and pulleys, for the hoisting mechanism; winches and hoists, for the power units; and derricks and cranes, for the structural elements.

升降机的主要部件有作为起重机构的绳束和滑轮、作为动力单元的绞盘和提升装置、作为结构件的塔架和起重机构。

[2] Floor and wall-mounted electric hoists are used for many hoisting and hauling jobs from fixed locations in industrial plants and warehouses.

落地式和壁挂式电动升降机用于许多从工厂和仓库中的固定地点吊装和搬运作业。

[3] In addition, freedom from sparking makes them useful in locations where the presence of explosive mixtures make electrical equipment hazardous.

另外,不受火花的影响(绝缘)使得它们(指上句中所说的气动式升降机)在有易爆混合物而使得电子装置有危险的那些场合下可以使用。

[4] A derrick is distinguished by a mast in the form of a slanting boom pivoted at its lower end and carrying load-supporting tackle at its outer end.

悬臂式起重机是以桅杆而著名的,以一个斜的起重臂的形式出现,臂下端绕着枢轴旋转且臂外端承载着荷载承重滑轮。

[5] The combination of a hoist on a track and the bridge crane itself moving on tracks provides for usable movement of equipment within a rectangular area governed only by the length of the bridge and the total horizontal movement of the bridge or gantry crane.

在一条轨道上的升降机和自身在轨道上移动的桥式起重机组合,保证装置在一个矩形区域内移动,矩形区域仅仅受起重桥的长度、起重桥或门式起重机的总的水平方向(横向)移动的限制。

Passage B Elevating Machines

Materials-handling machines are the ones that lift and lower a load along a fixed vertical path of travel with intermittent motion. In contrast to hoisting machines, elevating machines support their loads instead of carrying them suspended, and the path they travel is both fixed and vertical. They differ from vertical conveyors in operating with intermittent rather than continuous motion. Industrial lifts, stackers, and freight elevators are the principal classes of elevating machines.

1. Industrial Lifts

A wide range of mechanically, hydraulically, and electrically powered machines are classified simply as lifts. Figure 18-6 shows some examples of industrial lifts.

Part 5 Logistics Machine and Equipment

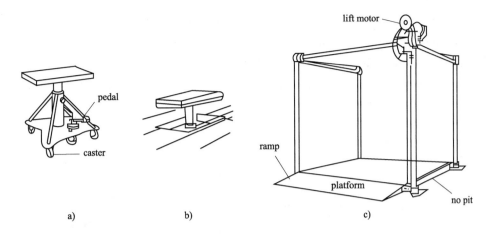

Figure 18-6 Industrial lifts

a) Hydraulic elevating work table; b) Hydraulic lift floor leveler; c) Motor-driven floor leveller

They are adapted to such diverse operations as die handling and feeding sheets, bar stock, or lumber. In some locations with differences in floor level between adjacent buildings, lifts take the form of broad platforms to serve as floor levelers to obviate the need for ramps. They are also used to raise and lower loads between the ground and the beds of carriers when no loading platform exists. Lifting tail gates attached to the rear of trucks are similarly used for loading or unloading merchandise on sidewalks or roads and at points where the lack of a raised dock would make loading or unloading difficult.[1] These units are usually driven by battery-operated motors or a power taken off from the drive transmission of the vehicle. Adjustable loading ramps are necessary because heights of truck and trailer beds vary. Advances in mechanized loading and unloading of vehicles have made necessary sturdier, more efficient dock boards or bridge plates, mechanically or hydraulically operated.

2. Stackers

Tiering machines and portable elevators used for stacking merchandise are basically portable vertical frames that support and guide the carriage, to which is attached a platform, pair of forks, or other suitable lifting device (Figure 18-7).[2] The operation of these units varies in the sense that the carriage can be raised and lowered by hand, by an electrically driven winch, or by a hydraulic cylinder, which actuates the system of chains or cables, operative by hand lever, pedal, or push button. Early electric motors used on stackers were plugged into adjacent power lines to receive current. This limited the flexibility of the stackers. Since the trend is to make the machines independent of this sources, there are now models powered by either storage batteries or by small gasoline or gas engines. Horizontal movement is effected by casters on the bottom of the vertical frame, and can be accomplished manually, or mechanically, by using the same power source as the lifting mechanism. These casters are usually provided with floor locks bolted in position during the elevating or lowering operation. The three types of stackers are shown as Figure 18-7.

The basic type of stackers can be varied in several particulars. Masts, which are part of the frame, can be hinged or telescopic, and the platforms can be plain, equipped with rollers, or constructed specially to handle a specific product. Some stackers have devices for tilting barrels and drums or for lifting and dumping free-flowing bulk materials. Used in conjunction with cranes, they are widely applied to the handling of materials on storage racks and die racks. Stackers have a significant place in the development of materials-handling equipment. They are the prototypes of completely powered noncounter balanced platform and forklift trucks.

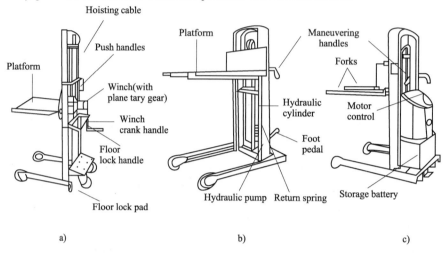

Figure 18-7　Three types of electric and hydraulic stackers
a) Hand type; b) Hydraulic foot type; c) Electric lift type

3. Industrial Elevators

Examples of industrial elevators range from those set up temporarily on construction jobs for moving materials and personnel between floors to permanent installations for mechanized handling in factories and warehouses.[3] Dumbwaiters are a type of industrial elevator, having capacities up to approximately 500 lb (227 kg), with a maximum floor space of 9 ft^2 (0.8 m^2); they carry parts, small tools, samples, and similar small objects between buildings, but are not permitted to carry people.

Oil hydraulic plunger electric elevators are designed for low-rise, light- or heavy-duty freight handling. Although they can be installed without special building alterations, they are restricted to buildings with only a few floors because of the limitations of the plunger length and design.

The most common and economical elevator employs electric motors, cables, pulleys, and counterweights (Figure 18-8). Powered machines impose a severe operating condition on elevators. Elevator platforms and structures are subjected to impact loading, off-balance loading, and extra static loading. To meet these forces, in addition to load forces, freight elevator design and construction provide greatly increased ruggedness over that of passenger units.

Special-purpose freight-handling elevators are equipped with platform or arms for carrying specific articles such as rolls of paper, barrels, or drums. Some of these elevators load and discharge automatically and are arranged so that they can operate at any selected floor by means of remote control.[4]

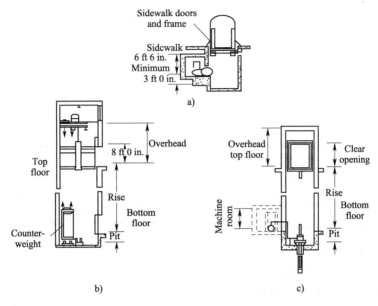

Figure 18-8 Three types of industrial elevator

a) Sidewalk elevator type; b) Heavy-duty freight elevator type; c) Hydraulic electric elevator type

New Words and Expressions

1. leveller[ˈlevələ]　　　　　　　　　n. 使平等(或平均)者,校平机
2. adjacent[əˈdʒeisənt]　　　　　　　adj. 邻近的,接近的
3. obviate[ˈɔbvieit]　　　　　　　　　vt. 消除,排除(危险、障碍等),预防,避免
4. sidewalk[ˈsaidwɔ:k]　　　　　　　n. 人行道
5. caster[ˈka:stə]　　　　　　　　　　n. 投手,(家具的)脚轮,调味瓶
6. prototype[ˈprəutətaip]　　　　　　n. 原型
7. noncounterbalance[ˈnɔnˈkauntəˈbæləns]　vt. 使不平均,使不平衡
　　　　　　　　　　　　　　　　　　n. 不平衡量,不平衡力,非势均力敌
8. range from　　　　　　　　　　　　分布在……范围,从……延伸到
9. dumbwaiter[美]　　　　　　　　　(楼上楼下之间)送饭菜的小升降机
10. oil hydraulic plunger electric elevator　油压柱塞式电力升降机/油压柱塞式电梯
11. counterweight[ˈkauntəweit]　　　n. 平衡物,秤锤,平衡力
12. freight elevator　　　　　　　　　货运电梯
13. remote control　　　　　　　　　遥控,遥控装置,遥控操作
14. hydraulic[haiˈdrɔ:lik]　　　　　　adj. 水力的,水压的
15. temporarily[ˈtempərerili]　　　　adj. 暂时地
16. ruggedness[rʌgidnis]　　　　　　n. 险峻,粗野/强度,耐久性,坚固性,坚固度
17. freight-handling　　　　　　　　　货物搬运

Notes

[1] Lifting tail gates attached to the rear of trucks are similarly used for loading or unloading merchandise on sidewalks or roads and at points where the lack of a raised dock would make loading or unloading difficult.

连接在货车尾部的后升降门也同样适用于下列场合装卸货物:在人行道或路边,以及在那些缺少升降台使货物装卸困难的地方。

[2] Tiering machines and portable elevators used for stacking merchandise are basically portable vertical frames that support and guide the carriage, to which is attached a platform, pair of forks, or other suitable lifting device.

用来堆垛货物的堆踩机和轻便升降机本质上是一些轻便垂直的框架,该框架支撑并导引着托架,其上连接有一个平台、一对叉子或其他合适的升降装置。to which 是把 is attached to 中的 to 提前了。

[3] Examples of industrial elevators range from those set up temporarily on construction jobs for moving materials and personnel between floors to permanent installations for mechanized handling in factories and warehouses.

工业电梯的例证从建筑工地上临时建造的用于楼层间运输物料和人员的电梯,延伸到在工厂和仓库里长期使用的、进行机械化装卸的电梯。

[4] Some of these elevators load and discharge automatically and are arranged so that they can operate at any selected floor by means of remote control.

一些电梯能自动地装卸货物,并被安排成依靠遥控使其在任意选定的楼层工作。

Unit 19

Passage A Up and Away with Overhead Cranes

Whether a load weighs 25 pounds or 100t, overhead cranes gets them off the floor and to their destination.

Make best use of the cube. It has been said so many times, and has never had greater value than now. Yet, so many managers think only of higher racks and new mezzanines to minimize footprints and maximize vertical space usage. But their options do not stop there.

Quite literally, overhead cranes add a new dimension to the movement of materials in a facility. While conveyors and lift trucks are focused on moving inventory, work-in-process, and finished goods at or near floor level, cranes do most of their work well above the floor and often at ceiling height. This, in turn, frees up the floor for other activities, making overhead cranes a space saver in addition to being an efficient way to move loads.

Long known for their ability to transport loads of many tons from one end of a facility to another, cranes are equally adept at moving much lighter loads within the relatively small area of an individual workstation.[1]

In fact, the latter has taken on increasing importance as the ergonomics of handling loads has received greater scrutiny. 25 pounds is now considered to be at the high end of the manual lifting range, not 50 pounds. Similarly, it is estimated that nine out of ten loads handled in industry weigh 300 pounds or less, considerably less than what was once the case.[2]

The end result is that enclosed-track workstation cranes are now much more widely used than they once were. At the same time, jib and gantry cranes are often used at workstations as well as other applications. Bridge cranes, the fourth type, are the heavy lifters, handling not only the largest loads but those that need to travel the greatest distance in the least amount of time.

All four types of cranes can be used in warehousing/distribution operations as well as manufacturing. Except for steel service centers and similar operations, however, cranes are most often associated with manufacturing operations.

Regardless of the specific application, each crane type offers its own range of movement, both directionally and in distance, while handling loads of various dimensions and weights. In addition, the frequency of moves differs by crane type.

While most cranes are either electric or air powered, some are operated manually. As with other types of materials handling equipment, manual operation is generally confined to applications handling the lightest loads and the least frequency of use.

In all of this lifting, lowering, and moving of loads, cranes cannot do it all. They are typically used with hoists tailored to the job at hand.

Bridge cranes make the biggest impression of the four types because they move loads of many tons from one end of a large facility to another. The standard configuration is two steel girder runways attached to the building at ceiling height. In some cases, the crane is positioned further down the wall of the building. Either one or two additional girders span the two runways, creating the bridge. The bridge girders are attached on each side to an end truck that travels along the runway.

Applications run from heavy manufacturing, fabrication shops, and steel service centers to large paper roll handling. The various designs are suitable to specific requirements.

Top-running double-girder bridge cranes generally carry the heaviest loads, as much as 100t. True to its name, this design has two parallel girders mounted on top of the runway beams. The hoist is mounted on a trolley that runs atop the girders, maximizing the lifting height of loads. As with all other bridge cranes, the combination of hoist, runway, and bridge movement provides six directions of travel for any load.

Top-running single-girder bridge cranes are much the same but have only one bridge between runways. This design requires the hoist's trolley to run along the lower flange of the girder, reducing lifting height somewhat as well as carrying capacity.

There are also two underhung bridge crane designs. Rather than having the girder on top of the runway, these have the bridge girder trolley running along the lower flange of the runway. Capacities of both single- and double-girder underhung cranes are less than the top-running ones. Lifting height is reduced also.

Traditionally, overhead bridge cranes, especially top running ones, have been under the control of an operator that rides in a cab attached to the bridge. Unfortunately, the frequency of moves often leaves the operator idle a significant portion of the shift. With that in mind, many users are looking at other control options—pendant or radio remote control.

Both put the operator on the floor, and allow maximum use of that person's time. Pendant controls are hard wired to the crane, requiring the operator to walk with the crane as it moves. The drawback here is the inherent inflexibility of movement and potential for accidents as a result.[3] Radio remote control eliminates that inflexibility and potential danger, allowing the operator to remain in one position as the crane moves. Both pendant and radio remote control can be used with other types of cranes too.

A cousin of the bridge crane is known as the gantry. This floor-mounted type uses either a single or double leg to support the bridge that the hoist trolley runs along. While the double leg design supports both sides of the bridge, a wall rail provides the support on the other side of the single leg. In both cases, the leg travels along a floor rail.

The enclosed-track workstation crane is another takeoff on the overhead bridge. Much like the double-leg gantry, these can be built anywhere in the plant or warehouse. It consists of four vertical columns that are anchored to the floor to create the four corners of the crane's work envelope.

Two parallel runways connect the columns on each side. An underhung bridge in the form of an enclosed track with a hoist on a trolley moves from one end of the runway to the other, providing the range of motion for the workstation. Loads under 50 pounds or greater than 1000 pounds can be easily lifted and moved with great precision within the work envelope.

The final category of cranes is the jib, which is not a derivation of the bridge crane. As with the other types, jibs come in several different designs.

The simplest is the wall-mounted jib crane. It consists of a horizontal girder that attaches to the wall with a pivot. A steel cable extends from the end of the horizontal beam at a 45° angle to an anchor point on the wall above the crane, providing support. The pivot allows the beam to swing 180°. The range of motion of the hoist and its trolley as well as the load is limited to the length of the beam.

A floor-mounted jib replaces the wall with a vertical column that can be placed anywhere in the facility. Depending on the pivot mount, the jib can swing 180° or 270°. A floor-mounted, free-rotating column design provides 360° range of movement, as does a ceiling-mounted rotating column jib. Another floor-mounted version places the vertical column on a floor-mounted runway, allowing the jib to travel some distance. Similarly, a wall-traveling design allows the horizontal beam and its load to move along a runway mounted above the beam.

As can be seen, not only do cranes add a new dimension to materials handling, but they are a match for a load of any size.[4]

New Words and Expressions

1. underhung['ʌndə'hʌŋ]   adj. 支承在(下方的)轨上的
2. adept['ædept, ə'dept]   n. 老手,擅长者
   adj. 熟练的,拿手的
3. ergonomics['ə:gəu'nɔmiks]   n. 人类工程学,生物工程学,工效学
4. scrutiny['skru:tini]   n. 详细审查,详尽的研究,推敲,细看
5. girder['gə:də]   n. 梁,钢桁的支架
6. truck[trʌk]   n. 载货汽车,手推车,(铁路)无盖货车,滚轮,转向轮
7. parallel['pærəlel]   n. 平行线,平行面
   adj. 平行的
8. trolley['trɔli]   n. 电车,(电车)滚轮,台车,小车
   vt. 用手推车运
9. flange[flændʒ]   n. 边缘,轮缘,[机]凸缘,法兰
10. derivation[deri'veiʃən]   n. 引出,来历,出处
11. pivot['pivət]   n. 枢轴,支点
12. be a match for   和……匹敌,敌得过

Notes

[1] Long known for their ability to transport loads of many tons from one end of a facility to anoth-

er, cranes are equally adept at moving much lighter loads within the relatively small area of an individual workstation.

长期以来已知起重机具有将大荷载从一个设施的某端运输到另一端的能力,同样地,起重机擅长在一个面积相对较小的单独工作间内运送非常轻的荷载。

[2] Similarly, it is estimated that nine out of ten loads handled in industry weigh 300 pounds or less, considerably less than what was once the case.

同样地,据估计工业上所要装卸的荷载约十分之九重为300磅或更小,比以前此种情形下的荷载要小得多。此句为主语从句,it 为形式主语;此句中 weigh 为动词。

[3] The drawback here is the inherent inflexibility of movement and potential for accidents as a result.

此处弊端是固有的刚性运动及由此造成的偶然事故。

[4] As can be seen, not only do cranes add a new dimension to materials handling, but they are a match for a load of any size.

正如所见到的,起重机不仅给物料装卸增加了一个新的维度,而且它们还和任意尺寸的荷载相匹敌。此句是 not only 引起的倒装句。

Passage B Containerization

1. General Introduction

Containerization is a system of intermodal cargo transport using standard containers that can be loaded on container ships, freight train wagons, and trucks. It is an important element of the logistics revolution that changed freight handling in the 20th century. Malcolm McLean invented the shipping container in the 1930s in New Jersey. And containerized traffic, which was formally introduced in 1955 principally in rail haulage, has, during the past two decades, extended to land-sea through transportation, or intermodal transportation, as it is generally called in western counties, and is becoming increasingly important in the field.

This system of transportation implies moving of commodities in unit loads as opposed to the conventional individual packing or break bulk cargo, by unit loads are meant the placing of cargo on pallets or consolidating of cargo into containers when being carried by ship or by land conveyance of various types-lorries, wagons and others. This is generally known as palletization and containerization.[1] Transportation by this mode paves the way for more extensive use of mechanical equipment in loading and unloading as well as in transshipment, achieving a saving in time and labor.

Containerization consists of stowing large amounts of cargo into strongly constructed, standard-sized and reusable vans at the manufacturer's plant inland, or at the container freight station (CFS), and shipping the cargo in unit loads to its destination. From the moment the container is locked and sealed, the cargo is undisturbed until it reaches the consignee. It is loaded aboard lorries, railcars and ships by mechanical devices that speed shipping and reduce labor costs. During the time the cargo is in its container, the box acts also as a warehouse.

There are two standard sizes, one 20ft long and the other twice as long at 40 ft. Container capacity is measured in TEU. A TEU is a measure of containerized cargo equal to one standard 20ft × 8.5ft × 8.5ft container (approximately 40.92 m^3). Most containers today are of the 40ft variety and thus are 2 TEU. 2 TEU are referred to as one Forty-foot Equivalent Unit (FEU). These two terms of measurement are used interchangeably.

Containerization revolutionized cargo shipping. Today, approximately 90% of cargo moves by containers stacked on transport ships. Over 200 million containers per year are now moved between those ports.

2. Advantages of Containerization

The use of container, though an improvement over the conventional mode, does not dispense with the individual packing required for the cargo, and the cost of packing remains unreduced. This mode of carriage does not minimize the exposure to various risks in the course of transit, which include theft and pilferage. However, the saving in the operation cost of substantial when the carriage involves sea voyage only.

Use of this efficient process can be made even in situations where full container-load is not possible. In such cases, individual shipments coming to berths as breakbulk cargo, i.e., traditionally packed cargo, can be loaded into containers before being hoisted aboard the ship. At destination port the containers can be opened and the cargo stored for customs clearance and subsequent delivery to the consignee. Ships can be loaded and unloaded by cranes in a fraction of time needed for handling the general breakbulk cargo.

This mode of transportation provides the shipper with seagoing strong vans which not only protect shipments from damage and theft but also can be used repeatedly, thus reducing the expense of export packaging.[2]

Tankers and ore carriers are now highly mechanized in both loading and unloading and thus involve fewer hands. But conventional cargo ships place reliance on manual labor in the handling of cargo, including stacking, loading, stowing and unloading. This process oftentimes costs a ship of, say, 10,000t approximately one-third of her time in a trading year, leaving her only about 200 days at sea. This slow turnover in trading implies higher cost and less freight income.

However, a different picture will present itself in the case of container ships. A rough comparison will bear this out. On a conventional cargo ship, the rate of loading by a gang of from 16 to 18 hands is approximately 35t an hour, while a total of twenty containers weighing 20t each can be lifted by one crane in an hour. In one shift lasting 21 hours, only 735t can be loaded by sling, while in the same shift one crane can life 410 containers weighing 8400t. Besides, due to mechanized loading, the number of hands can be greatly reduced.

There is another case in point. When containerized traffic was first initiated in China, a trail trip was made by a Chinese ship from Shanghai to Japan, which carried a total of 30 containers. The loading was done by nine wharf workers only and completed in one hour, while the loading of the same consignment, if shipped as breakbulk cargo, would have taken around 16 hours by a team of 19 workers.

The above clearly shows that containerized traffic is far more efficient than the traditional mode of transportation. It achieves not only a saving in the time for operations but also a saving in labor, thus greatly reducing the operational cost and enabling the ship to be put to better and more profitable use.[3]

The other advantages derivable from containerized traffic comprise minimization of losses and simpler packaging.

Containers being weather proof metal vans are capable of withstanding most of the risks while in transit and the cargo packed therein is always much safer than when conveyed in separate packing. Damage to cargo in the course of handling can also be well avoided, and the risk of theft and pilferage can be reduced to a large extent. This will reduce the chance of claims on the carrier even though certain of the claims are not answerable due to the immunities conferred on him under the contract of carriage.

Since cargo is consolidated into containers which usually serve as sort of outer packing, the traditional packaging normally required for breakbulk cargo can be dispensed with. Simpler packaging connotes a saving in the packing cost which is definitely of benefit to the cargo owner.

The high efficiency of containerized traffic will contribute considerably to the substantial saving in the carrier's overheads, thus rendering it possible for him to fix the freight rate at a more attractive level.[4]

On the other hand, the capital investment that will be required for the operation of containerized traffic will be quite substantial.

First, the carriage of containers necessitates specific accommodations in the ship. Whilst conventional cargo ships are not absolutely unfit for the carriage of containers, the broken space that will ensue in the stowage due to the dimension of the hold, will prove uneconomical to the carrier. Container ships are therefore designed with a view to making the best possible use of the container.

Second, the manufacture or purchase of containers involves a considerable sum of money, especially when the number required is taken into account. A container ship carrying 750 containers which sails once a week on a fixed route requires triple that number of containers. A 20ft size container costs approximately USD 2000 and 2250 containers will cost USD 4,500,000. The more container ships are employed, the bigger the number of containers that will have to be made ready, though not in like proportion, and the cost for this item alone will be fairly considerable.

Third, to meet the specific requirements for container ships, a special type of terminal different from traditional berths is required. Such terminal normally calls for a space 3~6 times the traditional terminal for handling a similar volume of inward and outward cargo. Whilst fewer sheds and go downs are needed at such terminal because most containers, being constructed of metals, can withstand any climate, the foundation of the terminal is to be so built as to be capable of sustaining the weight of straddle carriers having a lifting capacity of 30t each and gantry cranes along the berths to lift containers onto or out of ships.[5] Further, there are always a great number of containers at the container yard and the container freight station, if it is situated within the framework of the terminal. In addition, there are containers spread out at the marshalling yard and along the apron, the frontage of the berth, ready for loading. The higher standard required in the construction of this type of terminal will cost considerably more than the traditional berth for conventional cargo ship.

The foregoing would, at first sight, appear to be a deterrent in the way of growth of containerization, particularly in countries in the third world whose financial resources might not permit of such a gigantic project, but the whole world is now well cognizant of the advantages of this renovated mode of transportation, and a steady development can be expected.[6]

3. Operations

This normally relates to cargo packed or consolidated into the container in full load by the shipper himself at the plant or at his place of business where customs inspection is made before the container is locked and sealed.[7] In technical terms such container is called "full container load (FCL)". And on the other side, the cargo packed or consolidated into the container is less than the full container load by the shipper. In such situation, a term is called "less than the full container load (LCL)".

Where the cargo to be forwarded is less than a full load, it is to be sent by the shipper to the carrier's container freight station for consolidation into the container by the carrier with other cargo destined for the same port of discharge. In such case, the customs inspection is made at the station before the container is locked and sealed. And the carrier's liability commences once the cargo is in his custody.

When the ship arrives at the destination terminal, it is also at the container freight station that the less than a full load. Containers in full load are normally delivered at the container yard at the terminal if through traffic has not been arranged.

When there is loss of or damage to containerized cargo for which the carrier is liable, the carrier's liability can, in most cases, be limited according to the provision in the covering bill of lading in the same manner as when loss or damage occurs to cargo in conventional packing.[8] But the application of the carrier's limit is, according to the existing international codes covering this matter, open to two alternatives.

New Words and Expressions

1. as opposed to   与……相反,与……相对(比)
2. CFS(container freight station)   集装箱货运站
3. operational cost   经营成本,营业成本

4. place reliance on   依靠
5. connote [kɔ'nəut]   v. 意味着
6. CY (container yard)   集装箱货柜堆场
7. marshalling yard   铁路货运编组站
8. apron ['eiprən]   n. 挡板,护栏
9. gigantic [dʒai'gæntik]   adj. 巨大的
10. dispense with   免除,省却,无需
11. berth [bəːθ]   n.(车、船、飞机等的)铺位,停泊处,泊位
12. seagoing 英['siːgəʊɪŋ] 美['sɪ'goɪŋ]   adj. 适于远航的
13. consolidated [kən'sɔlideitid]   adj. 加固的,整理过的,统一的
14. godown ['gəudaun]   n. 仓库
15. at first sight   乍看起来,初看起来
16. appear to be   看来像是
17. bill of lading   提单
18. FCL (full container load)   整箱货
19. LCL (less than the full container load)   拼箱货

Notes

[1] This system of transportation implies moving of commodities in unit loads as opposed to the conventional individual packing or break bulk cargo, by unit loads are meant the placing of cargo on pallets or consolidating of cargo into containers when being carried by ship or by land conveyance of various types-lorries, wagons and others. This is generally known as palletization and containerization.

与传统的单件包装或散装运输不同,这种运输系统是指以成组运输来运送货物。以成组运输意思是在海洋运输或各种载货汽车、铁路货车及其他方式陆路运输时,把货物放置在托盘上或压实后置于集装箱内。这种方式通常称为托盘化和集装箱化。

[2] This mode of transportation provides the shipper with seagoing strong vans which not only protect shipments from damage and theft but also can be used repeatedly, thus reducing the expense of export packaging.

这种运输方式为托运人提供了一种适于海洋运输的坚固的货物包装形式,它不但能防止货损和货盗,而且还可以重复使用,从而降低了出口包装的费用。

[3] It achieves not only a saving in the time for operations but also a saving in labor, thus greatly reducing the operational cost and enabling the ship to be put to better and more profitable use.

这不仅可以节省装卸搬运的作业时间,还能节约劳动力,从而大大降低经营成本,能使船舶以更好、更大利润地装卸。

[4] The high efficiency of containerized traffic will contribute considerably to the substantial saving in the carrier's overheads, thus rendering it possible for him to fix the freight rate at a

more attractive level.

集装箱化运输的高效率有助于承运人节省相当可观的一笔日常管理费用,从而使承运人把运费率确定在一个更有吸引力的水平成为可能。

[5] Whilst fewer sheds and go downs are needed at such terminal because most containers, being constructed of metals, can withstand any climate, the foundation of the terminal is to be so built as to be capable of sustaining the weight of straddle carriers having a lifting capacity of 30t each and gantry cranes along the berths to lift containers onto or out of ships.

同时大多数由金属构成的集装箱能经受得住任何气候条件,集装箱装卸区只需要极少的货棚和仓库,而集装箱装卸区的地基应该建造得能够承受得住每侧起升量为30t的集装箱吊车的重量,并且能够承受得住沿着泊位的桥吊进行集装箱装船或卸船。

[6] The foregoing would, at first sight, appear to be a deterrent in the way of growth of containerization, particularly in countries in the third world whose financial resources might not permit of such a gigantic project, but the whole world is now well cognizant of the advantages of this renovated mode of transportation, and a steady development can be expected.

乍看起来,前面所述看来像是集装箱化发展的一个制约因素,特别是在财政资源可能不允许投资巨大项目的第三世界国家里,但全世界现在都很好地认识到这一创新的运输模式的优点,并期望其稳固发展。

[7] This normally relates to cargo packed or consolidated into the container in full load by the shipper himself at the plant or at his place of business where customs inspection is made before the container is locked and sealed.

这通常涉及由托运人自己在工厂或在其业务所在地进行货物包装或把货物合并成整箱货,并在锁上集装箱或封装集装箱之前,在工厂或在其业务所在地进行海关检验。

[8] When there is loss of or damage to containerized cargo for which the carrier is liable, the carrier's liability can, in most cases, be limited according to the provision in the covering bill of lading in the same manner as when loss or damage occurs to cargo in conventional packing.

如果承运人所负责的集装箱货物有货损或货差,在大多数情况下,与传统包装的货物发生货损或货差时同样,按照所涉及的提单上的条款,承运人的责任会受到限制。

Unit 20

Passage A Automated Guided Vehicle (AGV)

An AGV is a computer-controlled, driverless vehicle used for transporting materials from point to point in a manufacturing setting.[1] They represent a major category of automated materials handling devices. An AGV can be used for any and all materials handling tasks from bringing in raw materials to moving finished products to the shipping dock.[2]

In any discussion of AGVs, three key terms are heard frequently: (1) guide path; (2) routing; (3) traffic management.

The term guide path refers to the actual path the AGV follows in making its rounds through a manufacturing plant. The guide path can be one of two types. The first and oldest type is the embedded wire guide path. With this type, which has been in existence for over 20 years, the AGV follows a path dictated by a wire that is contained within a path that runs under the shop floor.[3] This is why the earliest AGVs were sometimes referred to as wire-guided vehicles. The more modern AGVs are guided by optical devices.

The term routing is also used frequently in association with AGVs. Routing has to do with the AGVs ability to make decisions that allow it to select the appropriate route as it moves across the shop floor. The final term, traffic management, means exactly the same thing on the shop floor that it means on the highway. Traffic management devices such as stop signs, yield signs, caution lights, and stop lights are used to control traffic in such a way as to prevent collisions and to optimize traffic flow and traffic patterns.[4] This is also what traffic management means when used in the context of AGVs.

1. Rationale for Using AGVs

Some manufacturing plants still use traditional materials handling systems. Some use ASRs, some use AGVs, and many use all of these together. Why manufacturing firms use AGVs? Five of the most frequently stated reasons are as follows:

(1) because they can be computer controlled, AGVs represent a flexible approach to materials handling;

(2) AGVs decrease labor costs by decreasing the amount of human involvement in materials handling;

(3) AGVs are compatible with production and storage equipment;

(4) AGVs can operate in hazardous environments;

(5) AGVs can handle and transport hazardous materials safely.

Of the various reasons frequently given for using AGVs, perhaps the two that are the most important to the future of manufacturing are flexibility and compatibility.[5] Because they are so versatile, they can be adapted to be compatible with most production and storage equipment that might exist in a typical manufacturing setting.[6] Their flexibility and compatibility allow AGVs to fit in with trends in the world of manufacturing, including automation and integration of manufacturing processes.[7]

2. Types of AGVs

Automated guided vehicles are called on for use in a variety of different manufacturing settings. Consequently, there is no one type that will meet the needs of every setting. Figure 20-1 and Figure 20-2 show typical AGVs. In the current state of development, there are six different types of AGVs: (1) towing vehicles; (2) unit load vehicles; (3) pallet trucks; (4) fork trucks; (5) light load vehicles; (6) assembly line vehicles. These AGVs are the Work Horese.

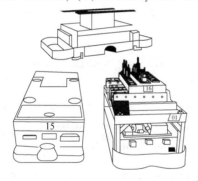
Figure 20-1 AGV and dock configuration

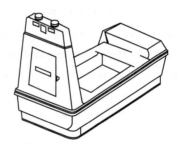
Figure 20-2 Sample of AGVs

(1) Towing Vehicles.

Towing vehicles are the most widely used type of AGVs. Their most common use is in transporting large amounts of bulky and heavy materials from the warehouse to various locations in the manufacturing plant. A popular approach is to arrange a series of vehicles into a train configuration. In such a configuration, each vehicle can be loaded with material for a specified location and the train can be programmed to move throughout the manufacturing facility, stopping at each location.[8]

(2) Unit Load Vehicles.

Unit load vehicles represent the opposite extreme from towing vehicles. Whereas towing vehicles are used in settings requiring the movement of large amounts of material to a variety of different locations, unit load vehicles are used in settings with short guide paths, high volume, and a need for independent movement and versatility.[9] Warehouses and distribution centers are the most likely settings for unit load vehicles. An advantage of unit load vehicles is that they can operate in an environment where there is not much room and movement is restricted.

(3) Pallet Trucks.

Pallets trucks is different from other AGVs in that they can be operated manually. Pallet trucks are used most frequently for materials handling and distribution systems. They are driven along a guide path from location to location and are unloaded as they go. Because they can be operated manually, Pallet trucks represent a very flexible approach to materials handling.

(4) Fork Trucks.

The fork truck type AGV is to the automated manufacturing plant what the fork lift is to a traditional materials handling setting. Fork trucks are designed for use in highly automated manufacturing plants. They are used when it is necessary to pick material up at the shop floor level and move it to a location at a higher level or to pick up material at a higher level and move it down to the shop floor level. Unlike the traditional fork lift, however, fork truck type AGVs travel along a guide path.

(5) Light Load Vehicles.

Light load vehicle technology is simply the miniaturization of unit load vehicle technology. Light load vehicles, as the name suggests, are used in manufacturing settings where the material to be moved is neither heavy nor bulky.

(6) Assembly Line Vehicles.

As the name implies, assembly line vehicle type AGVs are used in conjunction with an assembly line process. Their most common use is in the assembly of automobiles. Assembly line vehicles can be used to transport major subassemblies (e.g., automobile engines, transmissions, doors, and other associated subassemblies) to the proper location on an assembly line. Using such vehicles can enhance the flexibility of an automobile assembly line.

New Words and Expressions

1. embedded [em'bedid]		n. 装入的,压入的,嵌入的
2. optical ['ɔptikəl]		adj. 光学的
3. yield sign		让路标志
4. in such a way as to		以这样的方式,通过以下方式
5. versatile ['və:sətail]		adj. 通用的,万能的,多才多艺的
6. be compatible with		与……不矛盾,与……兼容
7. fork truck		叉车,叉式运货车
8. unit load vehicle		组合运货车
9. towing vehicle		拖曳车,牵引车
10. pallet truck		码垛车,托盘式小车
11. light load vehicle		轻载运货车,轻便式小车
12. assembly line		装配作业线,流水作业装配线
13. a variety of		各种各样的,种种
14. unit load		成组运输

Notes

[1] An AGV is a computer-controlled, driverless vehicle used for transporting materials from point to point in a manufacturing setting.

AGV 是由计算机控制的、在生产场所中点到点运输物料的无人驾驶车。

[2] An AGV can be used for any and all materials handling tasks from bringing in raw materials to moving finished products to the shipping dock.

AGV 可用于从搬运原材料到将产成品运到装卸码头的所有物料的搬运作业。

[3] With this type, which has been in existence for over 20 years, the AGV follows a path dictated by a wire that is contained within a path that runs under the shop floor.

这种类型的自动导引车已存在了 20 多年,它沿着一条受钢丝绳控制的轨道运行,此钢丝绳被牵制于车间地板底下的一条轨道内。

[4] Traffic management devices such as stop signs, yield signs, caution lights, and stop lights are used to control traffic in such a way as to prevent collisions and to optimize traffic flow and traffic patterns.

这些交通管理设施,例如停车指示牌、让路标志、警示灯和停车灯,被用来以下述方式进行交通控制,即防止车辆碰撞、优化交通流和交通模式。

[5] Of the various reasons frequently given for using AGVs, perhaps the two that are the most important to the future of manufacturing are flexibility and compatibility.

在时常给出的使用自动导引车的各种理由中,对于未来生产最为重要的两个理由也许是其灵活性和兼容性。

[6] Because they are so versatile, they can be adapted to be compatible with most production and storage equipment that might exist in a typical manufacturing setting.

因为自动导引车如此通用,所以它们能够与典型制造业场所中可能有的大部分产品和存储设备相兼容。

[7] Their flexibility and compatibility allow AGVs to fit in with trends in the world of manufacturing, including automation and integration of manufacturing processes.

自动导引车的灵活性和兼容性使得它们适应世界制造业的发展趋势,该趋势包括制造过程的自动化和集成化。

[8] In such a configuration, each vehicle can be loaded with material for a specified location and the train can be programmed to move throughout the manufacturing facility, stopping at each location.

在这种配置中,每辆(自动导引)车能在一种特定场所进行物料装载,而且能对列车进行编程以使其移动遍及所有的制造设施设备,并在每个工位处停车。

[9] Whereas towing vehicles are used in settings requiring the movement of large amounts of material to a variety of different locations, unit load vehicles are used in settings with short guide paths, high volume, and a need for independent movement and versatility.

成组运输的货车适用于短途、大体积且需要独立运送和灵活性的场所,而牵引车适用于需要将大量物料运往多种不同地点的场所。

Passage B Palletizers: Man Versus Machine

Many companies are realizing big savings and fewer injuries by switching to automated palletizers.

These are just a few of the benefits automated palletizing systems have over manual stacking of pallets: higher throughputs, fewer injuries, more consistent stacking, improved accuracy.

When labor savings and injury reductions are factored in, it is easy to see economic justification for automation for those companies that build a large number of pallets daily.[1] Most can see paybacks on systems in a short amount of time.

Another advantage is reliability. Machines are going to be more reliable day in and day out than a person doing manual palletizing is going to be.

As with any materials handling project, the key is to match the right equipment to the job. Palletizers should be considered as a part of the overall materials handling system, as they must be able to easily integrate with other systems and maintain the same rate of throughput as equipment feeding them.[2] They must also integrate well with conveyors and lift trucks that will pick up the loads that they build.

There are two primary types of palletizing systems: in-line and robotic. With a dedicated in-line system you get speed. With robotics, you get flexibility.

In-line systems move a layer of product, an stock keeping unit (SKU) at a time. Row strippers and vacuum heads are the most widely used systems. These systems build pallet loads the fastest, but are also the most expensive. They are typically chosen for high-flow needs.

Robotics systems build the load several cartons at a time. While slower, they are very versatile. Typical robotic systems include selective compliant articulated robot arm (SCARA), articulated arm, and gantry. Here is a brief look at each type of system.

1. In-line Palletizers

Row stripper palletizers are the most commonly installed in-line systems and possess very high stacking speeds. They typically consist of a central staging area that accumulates one row at a time of an individual product SKU. It is here that pushers rotate, slide, or grab each carton until it is aligned with other cartons into a tight load layer. The group of cartons are then pushed or "stripped" onto the base of the pallet or onto other layers already on the pallet. Some units build from the bottom up while others form loads from the top down.

There are basically two types of row stripper designs: high-level and low-level.

High-level row strippers are faster, usually topping out at 160 cartons/minute, and build from the top down. After being accumulated, a transport mechanism vertically lifts the cartons, moves them over the pallet, and then lowers the newly built layer so it can be slid into place. These units occupy less floor space than low-level row strippers since they accumulate and build the load overhead at 7 ~ 12 ft above floor level.

Low-level units spread out their accumulation and load building over a greater footprint at or near floor level. These palletizers build bottom up and tend to run slightly slower with peak rates of 140 cartons/minute. The unit builds an initial layer, which is held in place while another layer is built below it. The process is repeated until all layers have been built.

Vacuum head systems use a similar system of pushers and mechanical devices to accumulate and build layers. Instead of pushing the load onto a pallet, however, this system uses a vacuum head to pick up the cartons together as a row and place them upon the stack. These units typically use suction, though clamshell grippers may also be used for grabbing and placement duties.

Vacuum head palletizers are good for loading pails, drums, bags, and other odd shaped items that may not slide easily in row strippers. Vacuum heads are slower, typically handling between 10 ~ 25 cases/minute, but cost about one-third of the price of a row stripper.

2. Robotic Palletizers

SCARA palletizers consist of a single, fixed-mast robot with an arm able to rotate at the knuckles. This provides a wide range of movement along an X/Y radius. It is also designed for a high amount of flexibility, and can build as many as six pallets at a time. Unlike in-line systems which typically handle only one incoming line composed of one SKU, robotic systems can palletize multiple lines feeds and mixed SKUs. Built in bar code readers define incoming SKUs and determine how loads should be built on each of the surrounding pallets.

Speeds tend to be about 10 ~ 30 cases/minute, but they can handle a box 5 in × 5 in × 5 in in one moment and then lift and deposit a load that is 36 in × 24 in × 12 in in the next move. The end effectors that lift the load vary among various vacuum and gripper types.

Articulated arm systems are similar to SCARA palletizers except that the arm is jointed, offering a wider range of motion and flexibility. Of course, this means that they are more expensive.

When you desire flexibility, you have to reach for more dollars. If you have a complicated intermix load situation, then articulated arm is the robot of choice. As with SCARA systems, there are a variety of end effectors available, including grabbers, vacuum, clamp, and units that offer dual combinations of the above. Articulated arm robots have greater reach and are good for palletizing complex mixed SKU loads. Stacking speeds are generally about 10 ~ 30 cartons/minute.

Gantry palletizers are comprised of a robot attached to a moving carriage that rides suspended from an overhead I-beam.[3] Typically, a central conveyor line feeds into the system. The robot picks up a carton with an end effector. Then the gantry slides along cells of in-process pallets and stops at the chosen cell to add the carton upon the load. Following deposit, it returns to the pick-up station to retrieve another carton.

Robots feature from two to four rotating axis and are ideal for heavier loads, supporting cartons up to 900 lb. Speed is somewhat sacrificed for flexibility, as systems typically achieve rates of 10 ~ 30 cartons/minute.

Gantry systems can easily build mix SKU loads and offer support to flexible manufacturing and specialty packaging needs. Up to 40 pallets can be served at one time per robot, making them ideal for building loads to customer specifications.

3. Five Steps for Palletizer Selection

Regardless of the reasons for moving to an automated palletizing system, companies need to define how palletizing fits into their overall processes.

"They should view it as a part of the packaging or materials handling system," says Michael Hernan of Horizon Automation.

Hernan has defined five steps to consider before installing a palletizer.

(1) **Define the Load.**

What makes up the load and how should it stack? How high will it be? Will items be labeled or wrapped? These questions should be considered for each SKU and customer.

(2) **What Rates are Desired.**

What throughputs are desired for the palletizer? Also determine if the conveyors and systems before and after the palletizer can keep up with that rate, or will other modifications be required.

(3) **What will It Cost.**

Compare actual expenditure of the system against both hard and soft costs. Hard costs are those easily measured, such as labor savings. Soft costs are a bit harder to define but can add up to large amounts, such as injury reductions, floor space savings, increased throughput, more consistent loads sent to customers, etc..[4]

(4) **What Is the Budget.**

Once hard and soft costs are factored in, it should be easier to see anticipated cost savings. This should become the basis for establishing a budget with a reasonable return on investment.

(5) **Select System.**

Approach palletizer suppliers with the above information to determine the most cost-effective solution for gaining the desired throughputs.[5] The system must fit the available space and be within the determined budget.

New Words and Expressions

1. palletizer['pælitaizə]　　　　　　　　　n. 堆积机,堆码机
2. rate of throughput　　　　　　　　　　物料通过速率
3. in-line　　　　　　　　　　　　　　　在线,串联
4. stripper['stripə]　　　　　　　　　　　n. 剥离器,卸料器,拆卸机,刨煤机
5. palletize['pælitaiz]　　　　　　　　　vt. 把……放在货盘上,码垛堆集,用货盘装运
6. compliant[kəm'plaiənt]　　　　　　　adj. 顺从的,适应的
7. vacuum['vækjuəm]　　　　　　　　　n. 真空,空间,真空吸尘器

	adj. 真空的,产生真空的,利用真空的
8. suction['sʌkʃən]	*n.* 吸入,吸力,吸引
9. knuckle['nʌkl]	*n.* 指节,关节
10. clamp[klæmp]	*n.* 夹子,夹具,夹钳
	vt. 夹住,夹紧
11. specialty['speʃəlti]	*n.* 专业
12. clamshell['klæmʃəl]	*n.* 蛤壳式挖泥机
13. SCARA(selective compliant articulated robot arm)	有选择适应的铰接机器手
14. floor space(设备的)	占地面积
15. cost effective	有成本效益的,合算的,划算的

Notes

[1] When labor savings and injury reductions are factored in, it is easy to see economic justification for automation for those companies that build a large number of pallets daily.

若考虑到节省劳动力、减少工伤两方面因素,对于那些每天造成大量货盘的公司而言,自动化堆垛机的经济合理性是显而易见的。

[2] Palletizers should be considered as a part of the overall materials handling system, as they must be able to easily integrate with other systems and maintain the same rate of throughput as equipment feeding them.

应该把堆码机作为整个物料搬运系统的一部分来考虑,因为它们必须能够容易地与其他系统集成在一起,并且在其他设备向其进料时与之保持相同的物料通过速率。

[3] Gantry palletizers are comprised of a robot attached to a moving carriage that rides suspended from an overhead I-beam.

龙门堆垛机由一个移动小车上的机器人构成,此移动小车悬跨在头顶上的工字梁上。

[4] Soft costs are a bit harder to define but can add up to large amounts, such as injury reductions, floor space savings, increased throughput, more consistent loads sent to customers, etc..

软成本是比较难以确定的,但能合计到巨大的总额中,如工伤的减少、(设备)占地面积的节省、生产能力的提高、更为一致的发往客户的装载等。

[5] Approach palletizer suppliers with the above information to determine the most cost-effective solution for gaining the desired throughputs.

向堆码机供应商提出上述信息以确定取得预期生产能力的最合算的解决方法。

Part 6   Recent Trends

Unit 21
Unit 22
Unit 23
Unit 24

Unit 21

Passage A Just-in-time (JIT)

JIT, referred as just-in-time, is actually a broad philosophy of management that seeks to eliminate waste and improve quality in all business processes. JIT is put into practice by means of a set of tools and techniques that provide the cutting edge in the "war on waste". The application of JIT to logistics is focused on here. This partial view of JIT has been called little JIT: there is far more to this wide-ranging approach to management than we present here. Nevertheless, little JIT has enormous implication for logistics, and has spawned several logistics versions of JIT concepts.

The partial view of JIT is an approach to material control based on the view that a process should operate only when a customer signals a need for more parts from that process.[1] When a process is operated in the JIT way, goods are produced and delivered just in time to be sold. This principle cascades upstream through the supply network, with subassemblies produced and delivered just in time to be assembled, parts fabricated and delivered just in time to be built into subassemblies, and materials bought and delivered just in time to be made into fabricated parts. Throughout the supply network, the trigger to start work is governed by demand from the customer— the next process. A supply network can be conceived of as a chain of customers, with each link coordinated with its neighbors by JIT signals. The whole network is triggered by demand from the end-customer. Only the end-customer is free to place demand whenever he or she wants; after that the system takes over.

The above description of the flow of goods in a supply chain is characteristic of a *pull* system.[2] Parts are pulled through the chain in response to demand from the end-customer.[3] This contrasts with a *push* system, in which products are made whenever resources (people, material and machines) become available in response to a central plan or schedule. The two systems of controlling materials can be distinguished as follows.

(1) *Pull scheduling*: a system of controlling materials whereby the user signals to the maker or provider that more material is needed. Material is sent only in response to such a signal.

(2) *Push scheduling*: a system of controlling materials whereby makers and providers make or send material in response to a pre-set schedule, regardless of whether the next process needs them at the time.

The push approach is a common way for processes to be managed, and often seems a sensible option. If some of the people in a factory or an office are idle, it seems a good idea to give them work to do. The assumption is that those products can be sold at some point in the future. A similar assumption is that building up a stock of finished goods will quickly help to satisfy the customer.[4] This argument seems particularly attractive where manufacturing lead times are long, if quality is a problem, or if machines often break down. It is better and safer to make product, just in case there is a problem in the future. Unfortunately, this argument has severe limitations. Push scheduling and its associated inventories do not always help companies to be more responsive. All too often, the very products the organization wants to sell are unavailable, while there is too much stock of products that are not selling.[5] And building up stock certainly does not help to make more productive use of spare capacity. Instead it can easily lead to excess costs, and hide opportunities to improve processes.

New Words and Expressions

1. philosophy [fi'lɒsəfi] *n.* 哲学,哲理
2. implication ['ɪmplɪ'keʃən] *n.* 含义,暗示,牵连,卷入,可能的结果,影响
3. spawn [spɔːn] *v.* 大量生产
4. cascade [kæ'skeid] *v.* 流注,大量落下
   n. 串联,倾泻;瀑布
5. trigger ['trigə] *v.* 引发,引起,触发
6. conceive [kən'siːv] *v.* 构思,以为,持有
7. whereby [英][hwɛə'bai][美][hwɛr'bai, wɚ‐] *adv.* 凭借,通过,借以,与……一致
8. sensible ['sensib(ə)l] *adj.* 明智的,通情达理的,意识到的
   n. 可感觉到的东西,敏感的人
9. assumption [ə'sʌm(p)ʃ(ə)n] *n.* 假定,设想,担任,采取
10. break down 分解,发生故障,失败,毁掉,制服

Notes

[1] The partial view of JIT is an approach to material control based on the view that a process should operate only when a customer signals a need for more parts from that process.
准时制生产(JIT)的部分观点是一种基于下述观点的物料控制方法,此观点认为仅仅当顾客在某生产流程发出多个零部件的需求时该流程才会运作。

[2] The above description of the flow of goods in a supply chain is characteristic of a *pull* system.
供应链中货物流的上述描述特点是一个拉动系统。

[3] Parts are pulled through the chain in response to demand from the end-customer.
通过供应链拉动零部件以响应终端客户的需求。

[4] A similar assumption is that building up a stock of finished goods will quickly help to satisfy the customer.
一个相似的假设是建立一个产成品库存将会利于迅速满足客户。

[5] All too often, the very products the organization wants to sell are unavailable, while there is

too much stock of products that are not selling.

很多时候,恰恰是组织机构想要卖的产品难以获得,而卖不掉的产品却有大量库存。本句中,very 表示:恰好是,恰恰是。

Passage B Lean Thinking and Six Sigma

1. Lean Thinking

Lean thinking developed by Krafcik and Mac Duffie in 1989 as a term used to contrast the JIT production methods used by Japanese automotive manufacturers with the mass production methods used by most Western manufacturers.[1] Suffering shortages and lack of resources, Japanese car manufacturers responded by developing production processes that operated with minimum waste. Gradually the principle of minimizing waste spread from the shop floor to all manufacturing areas, and from manufacturing to new product development and supply chain management. The term *lean thinking* refers to the elimination of waste in all aspects of a business.

Lean thinking is a route to seeking perfection by eliminating waste and thereby enriching value from the customer perspective. The end-customer should not pay for the cost, time and quality penalties of wasteful processes in the supply network.[2] The following four principles are involved in achieving the fifth, seeking perfection.

(1) **Specify Value.**

Value is specified from the customer perspective. From the end-customer's perspective, value is added along the supply network as raw materials from primary manufacture are progressively converted into finished product bought by the end-customer, such as the aluminium ore being converted into one of the constituents of a can of cola. From a marketing and sales perspective the can of cola should be "always within reach of your thirst". That is an attempt to define value from the end-customer's perspective. Another is Porter's concept of the *value chain* proposed by Porter in 1985, which sees two types of activity that are of value to the customer. The first is the primary value activities of transforming raw materials into finished products, then distributing, marketing and servicing them. The second is support activities, such as designing the products and the manufacturing and distribution processes needed to underpin primary activities.

(2) **Identify the Value Stream.**

Following on from the concept of value, the next principle is to identify the whole sequence of process along the supply network.

(3) **Make Value Flow.**

Minimizing delays, inventories, defects and downtime supports the flow of value in the supply networks.[3] Simplicity and visibility are the foundations to achieving these key factors.[4]

(4) **Pull Scheduling.**

Make only in response to a signal from the customer that more is needed. This implies that demand information is made available across the supply chain. Where possible, supply from manufacturing, not from stock. Where possible, use customer orders not forecasts.

While some of these concepts may be distant from current practice, lean thinking shares the philosophy of "big JIT": seek perfection. This is the fifth principle, and is achieved by gradually getting better at everything, squeezing waste out at every step.

2. Six Sigma

In the recent years, the six-sigma program for quality and process improvements has been adopted by many of the larger firms in the United States and around the world.[5] From statistics, the term "sigma" refers to standard deviation of values for the output a process and is an indicator of variability. While traditional quality management programs defined three sigma as the objective, in a six-sigma approach, the goal is to achieve a process standard deviation that is six times smaller than the range of outputs allowed by the product's design specification. A primary objective of six-sigma programs is to design and improve products and processes so that variability is reduced. For example, imagine a grinding process that automatically grinds metal parts to a specified width. As the grinding wheel wears, the average width of the processed parts increases. It is this type of movement that creates quality problems. When a process is stable and centered within specification limits a three-sigma quality level means that the firm produces defect-free product 99.74% of the time. A six-sigma process that is centered produces defect-free product 99.99966% of the time. Thus, a six-sigma process produces only 3.4 defects per million parts, while a three-sigma process produces 66,807 defects per million parts.

The six-sigma approach is actually a structured process for first identifying sources of variability and then reducing them.[6] Early developers of the six-sigma approach at Motorola originally chose six standard deviations as an appropriate goal given the nature of their manufacturing processes. In truth, very few business operations ever attain a six-sigma level of quality. More important than the absolute goal are the quality improvement processes that comprise a six-sigma program.

New Words and Expressions

1. aluminium [ˌæljəˈmɪniəm]　　　　　*n.* 铝
2. constituent [kənˈstɪtjuənt]　　　　*n.* 选民,成分,构成部分,委托人
　　　　　　　　　　　　　　　　　　adj. 构成的,组成的,选举的,有选举权的
3. underpin [ˌʌndəˈpɪn]　　　　　　*v.* 用砖石结构等从下面支撑(墙等),加强……的基础
4. grinding [ˈɡraɪndɪŋ]　　　　　　　*adj.* 磨的,摩擦的,碾的
　　　　　　　　　　　　　　　　　　v. 磨碎,旋转开动,压迫
5. delay [dɪleɪ]　　　　　　　　　　*vi.* 延期,耽搁
　　　　　　　　　　　　　　　　　　vt. 延期,耽搁
　　　　　　　　　　　　　　　　　　n. 延期,耽搁,被耽搁或推迟的时间

6. downtime ['dauntaim] n. (工厂等由于检修,待料等的)停工期
　　　　　　　　　　　　　[电子]故障停机时间
7. deviation [diːvi'eiʃ(ə)n] n. 偏差,误差,背离
8. lean thinking 精益生产

Notes

[1] Lean thinking developed by Krafcik and MacDuffie in 1989 as a term used to contrast the JIT production methods used by Japanese automotive manufacturers with the mass production methods used by most Western manufacturers.
1989 年 Krafcik 和 MacDuffie 提出了精益生产这一术语,该术语用来对比日本汽车制造商使用的准时制生产方法和大多数西方制造商使用的大批量生产方法。

[2] The end-customer should not pay for the cost, time and quality penalties of wasteful processes in the supply network.
终端客户不应该支付供应链网络中浪费的流程产生的成本惩罚、时间惩罚及质量惩罚。

[3] Minimizing delays, inventories, defects and downtime supports the flow of value in the supply networks.
最小化延误、库存、不合格品以及故障停机时间支撑着供应网络中的价值流。

[4] Simplicity and visibility are the foundations to achieving these key factors.
简单化和可视化是实现这些关键因素的基础。

[5] In the recent years, the six-sigma program for quality and process improvements has been adopted by many of the larger firms in the United States and around the world.
近年来,美国及世界各地的许多大型公司都已经采用了六西格玛程序用以提高质量和改进流程。

[6] The six-sigma approach is actually a structured process for first identifying sources of variability and then reducing them.
六西格玛方法实际上是首先识别变化性的来源然后再减少这些来源的一种结构化过程。

Unit 22

Passage A Vendor Managed Inventory (VMI) and Joint Managed Inventory (JMI)

1. Vendor Managed Inventory (VMI)

Vendor managed inventory (VMI), is an approach to inventory and order fulfillment whereby the supplier, not the customer, is responsible for managing and replenishing inventory.[1] This appears at first sight to counter the principle of pull scheduling, because the preceding process (the manufacturer) is deciding when and how many to send to the next process (the retailer). In practice, the basis on which decisions will be made is agreed with the retailer beforehand, and is based on the retailer's sales information. Under VMI, the supplier assumes responsibility for monitoring sales and inventory, and uses this information to trigger replenishment orders. In effect, suppliers take over the task of stock replenishment.

Automated VMI originated in the late 1980s with department stores in the United States as a solution to manage the difficulties in predicting demand for seasonal clothing. This manual VMI had existed for many years—particularly in the food industry. Under manual VMI, the manufacturer's salesman took a record of inventory levels and reordered product for delivery to the customer's store, where the manufacturer's representative would restock the shelves. As product variety has increased and life cycles have shortened, manual VMI has been replaced by automated VMI.[2]

The supplier tracks product sales and inventory levels at their customers, sending goods only when stocks run low. The decision to supply is taken by the supplier, not the customer as is traditionally the case. The supplier takes this decision based on the ability of the current level of inventory to satisfy prevailing market demand, while factoring in the lead time to resupply.

The smooth running of VMI depends on a sound business system.[3] It also requires effective teamwork between the retailer and the manufacturer. In order for both parties to gain full benefit from the system, appropriate performance measures need to be used. The top priority measure is that of product availability at the retailer. It is in both parties' interests to maximize product availability, avoiding lost sales in the short term and building customer-buying habits in the long term. By emphasizing the supplier's responsibility for maximizing product availability, VMI aims to achieve this with minimum inventories. In order to combine both of these apparently conflicting goals, it is necessary to have access to real-time demand at the customer.

The most widely used technology for broadcasting demand data from the customer is EDI. This provides the means for exchanging data from customer to suppliers in a standard format. Internet-based applications using EDI protocols are increasingly popular, providing the same facility at lower cost. Customer demand and inventory data are often processed through software packages to automate the application of decision rules and identify stock lines that need replenishment.[4]

2. Joint-Managed Inventory (JMI)

Joint-managed inventory (JMI) is a kind of risk-sharing inventory management method on the basis of dealer integration, and it is used to solve the problem of demand amplification resulted by independent inventory operation mode of each enterprise in the supply chain system as well as to improve the degree of synchronization of the supply chain. It is different from VMI, in the JMI the suppliers and the buyers in the supply chain make the inventory control plan together, so inventory management links both suppliers and buyers, and promote the operation synchronization of the supply chain.[5] At the same time, information-sharing through the coordination of the management center reduces inventory uncertainty, and improve the operation stability of the supply chain. The implementation of joint inventory management has a lot of advantages, and the inventory of the dealer can be reduced, so that the inventory of the whole supply chain can be reduced and the manufacturer can make its focus to improve production ability and improve the quality of the products.

New Words and Expressions

1. VMI(vendor managed inventory)   供应商管理库存
2. protocols['prəutəkɒl]   n. 礼仪,(外交条约的)草案,(数据传递的)协议,科学实验报告(或计划)
  v. 把……写入议定书,在议定书中拟定(或颁布),拟定议定书,拟定草案
3. JMI(joint-managed inventory)   联合管理库存
4. amplification[ˌæmplifɪˈkeiʃən]   n. [电子]放大(率),扩大,详述

Notes

[1] Vendor-managed inventory (VMI), is an approach to inventory and order fulfillment whereby the supplier, not the customer, is responsible for managing and replenishing inventory.
供应商管理库存(VMI)是库存和订单履行的一种方法,该方法通过供应商而不是通过客户来负责管理和补充库存。

[2] As product variety has increased and life cycles have shortened, manual VMI has been replaced by automated VMI.
由于产品多样化的增加和生命周期的缩短,人工供应商管理库存已经被自动化供应商管理库存所取代。

[3] The smooth running of VMI depends on a sound business system.
供应商管理库存的平稳运行依赖于完好的商务系统。

[4] Customer demand and inventory data are often processed through software packages to automate the application of decision rules and identify stock lines that need replenishment.
客户需求和库存数据通常通过软件包进行处理,以自动应用决策规则并且识别需要补货的货垛行列。

[5] Contrary to VMI, in the JMI the suppliers and the buyers in the supply chain make the inventory control plan together, so inventory management links both suppliers and buyers, and promote the operation synchronization of the supply chain.
与供应商管理库存不同,在联合管理库存中供应链上的供应商和买方共同制定库存控制方案,这样库管理就把供应商和买方两者联系在一起,并且促进供应链运作同步化。

Passage B Efficient Consumer Response (ECR) and Collaborative Planning, Forecasting and Replenishment (CPFR)

1. Efficient Consumer Response (ECR)

Established as a grocery industry initiative, efficient consumer response (ECR) is designed to integrated and rationalize product assortment, promotion, new product development and replenishment across the supply chain.[1] It aims to fulfill the changing demands and requirements of the end-customer through effective collaboration across all supply chain members, in order to enhance the effectiveness of merchandising efforts, inventory flow and supply chain administration.

The origin of ECR can be traced back to work carried out by Kurt Salmon Associates for the apparel sector and, later, the grocery sector. Since then, ECR has increased industrial awareness of the growing problem of non-value-added supply chain costs.

Within the consumer products industry, ECR emerged partly because of the increased competition from new retail formats entering the traditional grocery industry in the early 1990s, as well as through the joint initiatives developed between Wal-Mart and Procter & Gamble. In Europe, ECR programs commenced in 1993 with the commissioning of a series of projects, for example the Coopers & Lybrand survey of the grocery supply chain.

The focus of ECR is to integrate supply chain management with demand management. This requires supplier-retailer collaboration—but in spite of the apparent emphasis on the end consumer, a lot of the early ECR studies focused on the supply side. Subsequent increased focus on demand and category management, however, has led to the adoption of a more holistic view of the supply chain when discussing ECR initiatives.[2] In addition, ECR has also stimulated collaborative efforts that have increased companies' emphasis on key areas such as EDI, cross-docking and continuous replenishment.

Other examples of studies of ECR initiatives include the Coca-Cola survey evaluating supply chain collaboration within 127 European companies; PE International's 1997 survey, and IGD's 1997 report. Generally, ECR initiatives aim to promote greater collaboration between manufacturers and retailers. Effective logistics strategies as well as administrative and information technology are essential for its successful implementation. These required techniques are available within most organizations, but the main problem facing most organizations is ensuring that people use these existing tools differently in order to secure or achieve their maximum potential.

2. Collaborative Planning, Forecasting and Replenishment (CPFR)

Collaborative planning, forecasting and replenishment (CPFR) is aimed at improving collaboration between buyer and supplier so that customer service is improved while inventory management is made more efficient.[3] The trade-off between customer service and inventory is thereby altered.[4]

The CPFR movement was originated in 1995. It was the initiative of five companies: Wal-Mart, Warner-Lambert, Benchmarking Partners, and two software companies (SAP and Manugistics). The goal was to develop a business model to collaboratively forecast and replenish inventory. An initial pilot was tested between Wal-Mart and Warner Lambert using the Listerine mouthwash product and focusing on stocks kept in the retail outlets. The concept and process was tested initially by exchanging pieces of paper.[5] This generated clear visibility of the process required and the requirements for the information technology (IT) specification. The two companies later demonstrated in a computer laboratory that the Internet could be used as a channel for this information exchange.

In 1998 the Voluntary Inter-Industry Commerce Standards Committee (VICS) became involved in the movement, which enabled it to make major strides forward. VICS was formed in 1986 to develop bar-code and EDI standards for the retail industry. The involvement of VICS meant that other organizations could participate in the validation and testing of the CPFR concept. With VICS support, organizations including Procter & Gamble and Kimberly Clark undertook pilots to test the idea of sharing information to improve inventory handling.

New Words and Expressions

1. rationalize [ˈræʃnəlaiz]　　　　　　v. 使合理化,据理解释,使消根,文饰
2. merchandise [ˈmɜːtʃəndais]　　　　n. 商品,货物
　　　　　　　　　　　　　　　　　　v. 销售,买卖,经商
3. apparel [əˈpærəl]　　　　　　　　v. 给……穿衣服(尤指华丽或特殊的服装)
　　　　　　　　　　　　　　　　　　n. (商店出售的)衣服,外观,外表,覆盖物
4. emerge [iˈmɜːdʒ]　　　　　　　　vi. 浮现,摆脱,暴露
5. holistic [həʊˈlistik]　　　　　　　adj. 全盘的,整体的,功能整体性的
6. strides [straid]　　　　　　　　　adj. 步幅,大步,阔步,进展,一跨(的宽度)
　　　　　　　　　　　　　　　　　　v. 跨过,大踏步走,跨

7. outlet [ˈaʊtlet]   n. 出口,批发商店,排水口,通风口,发泄(情感)的方法
8. bar-code [ˈbɑːkəud]   n. 条形码
   vt. 给……印(或标)上条形码
9. participate [pɑːˈtisipeit]   vi. 参与,参加,分享
   vt. 分享,分担
10. validation [ˌvæliˈdeiʃən]   n. 确认,批准,生效
11. ECR (efficient consumer response)   有效客户响应
12. trade-off   权衡

Notes

[1] Established as a grocery industry initiative, efficient consumer response (ECR) is designed to integrated and rationalize product assortment, promotion, new product development and replenishment across the supply chain.
由食品行业创始建立的有效客户响应(ECR),旨在使横穿供应链的产品分类、促销、新产品开发以及补货一体化和合理化。

[2] Subsequent increased focus on demand and category management, however, has led to the adoption of a more holistic view of the supply chain when discussing ECR initiatives.
然而,后来对需求和分类管理不断增多的关注已导致在讨论有效客户响应主动性时采用更加全面的供应链视角。

[3] Collaborative planning, forecasting and replenishment (CPFR) is aimed at improving collaboration between buyer and supplier so that customer service is improved while inventory management is made more efficient.
协同规划预测补货(CPFR)旨在改善买方和供应商之间的协作,从而在使得库存管理更为有效的同时,改善客户服务。

[4] The trade-off between customer service and inventory is thereby altered.
因此,客户服务和库存之间的权衡被改变了。

[5] The concept and process was tested initially by exchanging pieces of paper.
此概念和过程最初通过纸质记录单互换进行测试。

Unit 23

Passage A The Agile Supply Chain

The view of the agile supply chain is shown in Figure 23-1.

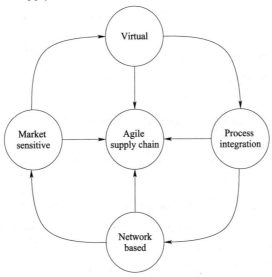

Figure 23-1 An integrated model for enabling the agile supply chain

First, the agile supply chain is *customer responsive*. The supply chain is capable of reading and responding to end-customer demand by coustomer responsive.[1] Most organizations are forecast-driven rather than demand-driven.[2] In other words because they have inadequate real-time data and cannot react fast enough anyway, they are forced to make forecasts based upon past sales or shipments and convert these forecasts into inventory.[3] The breakthroughs of the last decade in the form of such advances as ECR and the use of information technology to capture data on demand direct from the point-of-sale or point-of-use are transforming an organization's ability to hear the voice of the market. This throws down the challenge of how to develop the capabilities needed to respond.

Second, the supply chain should be viewed as a network of partners who have a common goal to collaborate together in order to respond to end-customer needs. The term "network" to refer to the cross-linking of partners that forms the basic model used in this text. Individual partners are viewed in terms of their contribution to the value being generated for the end-customer. Competitive strength comes from focusing the capabilities of a network of partners onto responding to customer need.

The third component of agility is viewing the network as a system of *business processes*. Nesting the capabilities of these process creates power and synergy for network.[4] "Stand alone" processes that do not support material flow create penalties in terms of time, cost and quality for the whole network.

Fourth, use of information technology to share data between buyers and suppliers creates, in effect, a virtual supply chain. Virtual supply chains are information-based rather than inventory-based. Conventional logistics systems seek to identify optimal quantities of inventory and their spatial location.[5] Complex formulae and algorithms exist to support this inventory-based business model.[6] Paradoxically, what we are now learning is that once we have visibility of demand through shared information, the premise upon which these formulae is based no longer holds. EDI and the Internet have enabled partners in the supply chain to act upon the same data—real demand—rather than being dependent upon the distorted and noisy picture that emerges when orders are transmitted from one step to another in an extended chain.[7]

As proposed in Figure23-1, enabling the agile supply chain requires many significant changes. As an example of such changes, consider the position of Li & Fung, an largest export trader in Hong Kong. The organization coordinates manufacturers in the Far East to supply major customers like the *Limited*, mostly in the United States. Chairman Victor Fung said that one of the key features of his approach was to organize for the customer, not on country units that ended up competing against each other.

So customer-focused divisions are the building blocks of Harrison's organization, and Harrison keeps them small and entrepreneurial. They do anywhere from $20 million to $50 million of business. Each is run by a lead entrepreneur.

And capabilities of the supply networks are "all about flexibility, response time, small production runs, smack minimum order quantities, and the ability to shift direction as the trends move".[8]

New Words and Expressions

1. formulae ['fɔːmjəliː] *n.* 配方,公式(formula 的名词复数),分子式,方案
2. paradoxically [ˌpærə'dɒksikli] *adv.* 自相矛盾,荒谬,反论,似非而可能是
3. premise ['premis] *n.* 前提,[复数]房屋,[复数][合同、契约用语]上述各点
   v. 预述(条件等),提出……为前提,假设,做出前提
4. emerge [i'mɜːdʒ] *vi.* 浮现,摆脱,暴露
5. smack [smæk] *v.* 拍,打,捆
   n. 掌掴(声),海洛因,(打的)一拳,打巴掌
   adv. 直接地,准确地,猛烈地,急剧地
6. the agile supply chain 敏捷供应链

Notes

[1] The supply chain is capable of reading and responding to end-customer demand by customer responsive.
通过顾客响应供应链能够看到终端客户的需求并对其做出响应。

[2] Most organizations are forecast-driven rather than demand-driven.
大部分组织机构是由预测驱动的而不是由需求驱动的。

[3] In other words because they have inadequate real-time data and cannot react fast enough anyway, they are forced to make forecasts based upon past sales or shipments and convert these forecasts into inventory.
换句话说,因为他们没有足够的实时数据,而且不能足够快地反应,所以他们被迫基于以往的销售额或发货量做出预测,并将这些预测转换成库存。

[4] Nesting the capabilities of these process creates power and synergy for network.
这些过程的嵌套能力为网络创造了动力和协同。

[5] Conventional logistics systems seek to identify optimal quantities of inventory and their spatial location.
传统的物流系统寻求确定库存的最佳数量及其空间位置。

[6] Complex formulae and algorithms exist to support this inventory-based business model.
复杂的公式和算法的存在用来支持这种基于库存的业务模式。

[7] EDI and the Internet have enabled partners in the supply chain to act upon the same data—real demand—rather than being dependent upon the distorted and noisy picture that emerges when orders are transmitted from one step to another in an extended chain.
电子数据交换和互联网使供应链中的合作伙伴能够根据相同的数据——实际需求——采取行动,而不是依赖于扩展链中订单从一步传送到另一步时形成的扭曲而嘈杂的图片。

[8] And capabilities of the supply networks are "all about flexibility, response time, small production runs, smack minimum order quantities, and the ability to shift direction as the trends move".
供应网络的能力是"所有关于灵活性、响应时间、小产量运营、准确的起订量以及随着趋势的变化而转换方向的能力。"

Passage B Benchmarking

It is critical for a company to know the strengths and weaknesses of its business and those of its order to continue to maintain and gain market, share and profits. Companies are generally aware of this during their early years but over time get more international focused and lose sight of the environment around them. This type of insulated environment benefits the competitors since they have a better understanding of the needs of the customers. Benchmarking refers to the act of comparing a company with word-class performers and competitors involved in similar functions and operations. It is important to do benchmarking every few years since world-class performance and competitors change conceptual framework for benchmarking is presented in Figure 23-2. The concept as illustrated in Figure 23-2 demonstrates that benchmarking identifies the gap in performance between a company and the best performer and seeks to identify ways and means to close or narrow the gap as much as possible.[1]

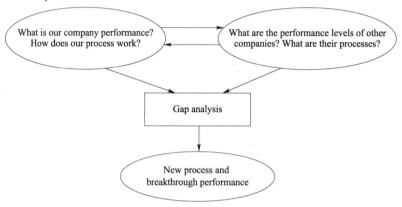

Figure 23-2 The concept of benchmarking

Benchmarking helps an organization to identify and learn the best practices in the world for a process or a function. Benchmarking can be very useful to evaluate a company's strategies, operating plans and processes. This will help to identify flaws in strategies as well as identify process that may require reengineering, resulting in better practices leading to superior performance.[2] Many big corporations and several progressive small companies use benchmarking to assess their standing against competitors in order continuously to improve their operations and processes.

Benchmarking can be classified into several different types, depending upon the type of process to be benchmarked, the scope of the process and the benchmark used. For instance, a company may want to benchmark the order filling process, and the scopes may be limited to the filling of in-company orders. The benchmark used may be based on world-class performance or industry-best performance. The type of process to be benchmarked may include one or more of the logistics functions or processes. Accordingly, one can have order picking benchmarking, benchmarking of truck dispatching or benchmarking of local pick-up and delivery scheduling. The scope of the process or function may include the location, type and number of in-company departments or customers. Examples include benchmarking of order picking at all the warehouses or only at the warehouses in, say, Singapore, dispatching of trucks that carry certain type of commodities to or from certain regions or the order fulfillment process for the top five customers.[3]

Benchmarking methods based on benchmark type is shown in Figure 23-3. This figure is also known as the analysis pyramid of benchmarking. This pyramid essentially lists the various types of benchmarks that can be used to compare and evaluate practices or processes. The lowest level is internal benchmarking and the highest is world-class benchmarking.[4] Comparing the performance of a function or process with the best practice of the function or process by another internal department is internal benchmarking.[5] A comparison of the same against the process of a world-class company is world-class benchmarking.[6]

Figure 23-3　Type of benchmarking: analysis pyramid

New Words and Expressions

1. insulate ['insjuleit]　　　　　　　　v. 使绝缘,隔离
2. order filling　　　　　　　　　　　订单填充
3. delivery scheduling　　　　　　　　日程安排

Notes

[1] The concept as illustrated in Figure 23-2 demonstrates that benchmarking identifies the gap in performance between a company and the best performer and seeks to identify ways and means to close or narrow the gap as much as possible.

图 23-2 所示的概念表明标杆管理能识别一个公司与最佳执行者之间的绩效差距,并且能找寻识别途径和方法,以尽可能地弥补或缩小这一差距。

[2] This will help to identify flaws in strategies as well as identify process that may require reengineering, resulting in better practices leading to superior performance.

这将有助于识别战略中的缺点以及可能要求流程再造的过程,形成更好的产生卓越绩效的实践。

[3] Examples include benchmarking of order picking at all the warehouses or only at the warehouses in, say, Singapore, dispatching of trucks that carry certain type of commodities to or from certain regions or the order fulfillment process for the top five customers.

例子包括在所有仓库或只在某些仓库中(比如说在新加坡),对按单拣货的货车调度进行的标杆管理,这些货车装载一定类别的货物运往或运自一定区域,或者对前五名客户的订单执行过程进行的标杆管理。

[4] The lowest level is internal benchmarking and the highest is world-class benchmarking.
最低水平是内部标杆管理,而最高水平是世界级的标杆管理。

[5] Comparing the performance of a function or process with the best practice of the function or process by another internal department is internal benchmarking.
将某一功能或者某一过程的绩效与另一个内部部门的功能或过程的最佳实践相比较,就是内部标杆管理。

[6] A comparison of the same against the process of a world-class company is world-class benchmarking.
与一个世界级公司的流程中同一内容相比较就是世界级标杆管理。

Unit 24

Passage A Reverse Logistics

1. Introduction

Reverse logistics systems move products from customers backward through the supply chain. It refers to logistics activities and management skills used to reduce, manage, and dispose of waste from packaging and products. This passage addresses several common types of reverse logistics systems.

(1) **Recycle.**

The primary goal of the reverse system is to move the goods backward through the distribution network. The logistics system must take the empty package from the customer and return it to the party responsible for the actual recycling process. The recycling process cannot be successfully completed without an effective reverse logistics system.

(2) **Custom Returns of New Products.**

Reverse logistics systems also allow customers to return unwanted or defective products. Customers often buy an item, only to return it later. If retail stores compete more and more on service, then reverse logistics systems must quickly restock returned items. Such reverse logistics systems may be short, since the product only travels from the customer back to the retail outlet.

(3) **Customer Returns of Used Products.**

Occasionally customers are encouraged to return used products to their retail outlet and obtain a financial credit. This logistics system starts with incentives to return the used product to the retail outlet. The most common incentive is a discount on a remanufacturer replacement part. To receive the discount the customer must return the used part ("core") at the time of purchase. Failure to provide the used part will result in a "core" charge that will increase the cost of remanufacturer part.

(4) **Custom Returns of Reused Products.**

Many returned products must undergo some sort of remanufacturing or alteration process. However, some products can be reused with minimal effort. With sterilization and cleaning, some glass bottles can be reused several times.

2. Outsourcing Reverse Logistics Requirements

Environmental concerns prompt many firms to outsource some or all of their reverse logistics functions. Logistics outsourcing is "the decision to use independent, external organizations as the means of accomplishing some, or all, of the logistics related functions within the firm."[1]

Recently, as demand for reverse logistics increases, as more customers demand both traditional and reverse logistics functions, many businesses have asked third-party providers to augment traditional service offerings to include reverse logistics functions.

3. Green Marketing and Life-cycle Analysis

The impact of consumer behavior on the environment has become so important, and companies are increasingly being held accountable for actions that adversely affect the environment. Several firms have responded by creating "green" alliances to improve their environmental performance and public reputation. In green alliances, businesses and environmental groups work jointly to integrate corporate environmental responsibilities with market goals. Some U.S. firms elected to enter into alliances to improve their environmental practice, while others focused on implementing internal environmental programs.

4. Designing an Effective Reverse Logistics System

Reverse logistics systems are necessary for a complete environmental program.[2] Government agencies, suppliers, buyers, and competitors can affect the reverse logistics activities of a firm.[3]

Typically, firms evolve through three phases in implementing an environmentally conscious program.

(1) Phase 1 is reactive. Cost savings or newly enacted environmental standards usually force reactive companies to meet environment standards.

(2) Phase 2 is proactive. Companies often implement recycling and reuse programs voluntarily and attempt to develop a competitive advantage by designing superior environmental programs.

(3) Phase 3 is value-seeking. Firms actively engage in a strategic planning process that addresses environmental concerns. They also incorporate environmental standards into daily operations.[4] Most companies in this phase have highly advanced environmental programs with extremely efficient reverse logistics systems.[5]

Governmental regulations, customer demands and the existence of a policy entrepreneur within the organization determine which phase a firm will seek. Other factors may constrain the implementation of a reverse logistics system. Key constrains include the quality of inputs, vertical coordination, incentive system, top management support, and stakeholder commitment.

5. Determining Transportation and Location for a Reverse Logistics System

If the total cost associated with recycling or reuse efforts exceeds the total cost of purchasing new materials, firms have no profit motive for implementing a reverse logistics system.[6] Therefore, transportation decisions become crucial to recycling or reuse programs.

Cost usually drives the transportation decision for reverse logistics. Extreme pressure to minimize costs affects not only transportation mode choice but also facility location. Location analysis considers the potential impact transportation costs can have on the resale value of recycled products. Often, locations are chosen specifically to minimize future transportation outlays.

6. Handling of Environmentally Sensitive Materials

Many hazardous materials with unique properties require special handling. In response to the variety of hazardous materials available in the marketplace, the U.S. Department of Transportation (DOT) has enacted several new regulations to help users deal with the unique properties associated with different compounds.[7]

New Words and Expressions

1. sterilization [ˌsterəlaiˈzeiʃn]   n. 灭菌,杀菌,绝育
2. enact [iˈnækt]   v. 制定法律,规定,颁布,颁布,担任……角色
3. compound [ˈkɒmpaʊnd]   n. 复合物,场地,(筑有围墙的)院子
4. DOT (Department of Transportation)   交通运输部(美国)

Notes

[1] Logistics outsourcing is "the decision to use independent, external organizations as the means of accomplishing some, or all, of the logistics related functions within the firm."
物流外包是指"决定采用独立的外部组织机构完成公司内部一些或所有物流相关功能的方式。"

[2] Reverse logistics systems are necessary for a complete environmental program.
对于一个完整的环境规划来讲,逆向物流系统是必要的。

[3] Government agencies, suppliers, buyers, and competitors can affect the reverse logistics activities of a firm.
政府部门、供应商、买方以及竞争者都会影响一个公司的逆向物流活动。

[4] They also incorporate environmental standards into daily operations.
它们(they 指前句中的 firms)还将环境标准并入日常运营中。

[5] Most companies in this phase have highly advanced environmental programs with extremely efficient reverse logistics systems.
大多数公司在这一阶段都有非常先进的且具有极为有效的逆向物流系统的环保计划。

[6] If the total cost associated with recycling or reuse efforts exceeds the total cost of purchasing new materials, firms have no profit motive for implementing a reverse logistics system.
如果与回收或再利用的努力结果相关联的总成本超过了购买新材料的总成本,公司就没有了实施逆向物流系统的利润动机。

[7] In response to the variety of hazardous materials available in the marketplace, the U.S. Department of Transportation (DOT) has enacted several new regulations to help users deal with the unique properties associated with different compounds.

根据市场上可获得的各种危险物料,美国交通运输部颁布了一些新法规以帮助用户处理与不同化合物相关联的独特性能。

Passage B Global Integrated Logistics

1. Introduction

Global logistics offers the integrated logistics manager a difficult challenge. Domestic integrated logistics is hard enough to coordinate, but global logistics frustrates at a whole new level. All integrated logistics activities are more involved and more complex. Packaging requirements vary, labeling differs, lead times lengthen, inventory management becomes more complex, intermediaries multiply, carrier selection and pricing increase in difficulty, and the list goes on.[1] But almost every company in the world is involved in international trade to some extent. This means that it must coordinate the movement of products across national boundaries.

This unit surveys global integrated logistics to familiarize students with basic concepts and practices. Topics covered include global integrated logistic strategic options, global integrated logistic activities, intermediaries, and terms of sale (INCOTERMS).

After completing this Passage, the reader should be able to:

(1) identify strategic options in integrated logistics;

(2) discuss the correct use of INCOTERMS;

(3) discuss the types of carriers used in global logistics;

(4) discuss the types of intermediaries used in global logistics.

2. Global Integrated Logistics Management

Global integrated logistics activities differ from domestic integrated logistics. The following deserve special attention: (1) transportation, (2) warehouse management, (3) packaging, (4) inventory management, and (5) material handling.

3. Global Transportation

Global transportation is defined as exporting and importing products or services beyond the boundaries of a country. Ocean and airfreight move goods between the United States, Europe, South America, Asia and then Pacific Region. For North America, ocean, air, rail, and motor carriage may be used. There is a limited amount of transborder pipeline transportation. Also important are motor, pipe, and railroad services to and from the seaports and airports.

4. Warehouse Management

Global warehouse serves the same purposes as its domestic counterparts; that is, receiving, transferring, picking, and shipping. However, rapid movement of products through the warehouse receives more emphasis than in domestic warehousing. The global warehouse mirrors a distribution center, with little long-term storage. Third-party warehousing is also quite common globally.

5. Packaging

Protective packaging takes on special importance in global logistics. The product is in transit longer, is handled more, and is more susceptible to adverse weather. Packaging requirements add substantial costs to global integrated logistics. Packing adds material and labor costs, but other factors may add still more. Labeling and marking requirements vary from country to country. Labeling informs the parties involved in the movement of exactly the nature and quantity of the package contents. Labeling regulations generally attempt to (1) force shippers to adhere to the existing product standards, (2) restrict and control the use of additives, (3) prohibit the use of misleading information, and (4) establish standard descriptions of products.

6. Inventory Management

Inventory is the life of integrated logistics. Without it, there is nothing to do in physical supply—nothing to store, nothing to carry, and nothing to package. Inventory management on a global scale becomes even more difficult and more important. Distance, port delays, custom delays, and transit times encourage higher inventories. This, of course, increases the costs of inventory. Political decisions such as closing borders to trade or instituting or increasing tariffs and duties only add to the inventory problems.[2] Companies may be forced to carry additional inventory to offset stockouts. Stockouts are much more common globally than would be acceptable domestically.[3] Superior customer service sometimes becomes irrelevant because the company has little or no control over the timing and availability of the product.[4]

7. Material Handling

Material handling systems vary globally. In countries like the United States, Canada, Australia, New Zealand, Singapore, and most of Western Europe, these systems will be among the world's best, usually highly mechanized or automated. In developing countries, the majority of systems are manual.[5] Product throughout in warehouses and plants tends to be much slower in manual systems. Also, some products require more sophisticated handling equipment, so some countries or ports may not be able to receive them.[6] For example, some ports can handle only twenty-foot containers, while others cannot handle containers at all.[7]

New Words and Expressions

1. frustrate[frʌ'streit]　　　　　　*vt.* 挫败,阻挠,使受挫折
　　　　　　　　　　　　　　　　adj. 无益的,无效的
2. familiarize[fə'miliəraiz]　　　　 *v.* 使(某人)熟悉,使通晓

3. adhere [əd'hiə]　　　　　　　　　*vi.* 坚持,依附,黏着,追随
　　　　　　　　　　　　　　　　　　vt. 使粘附
4. prohibit [prə(ʊ)'hibit]　　　　　*vt.* 阻止,禁止
5. tariffs ['tærif]　　　　　　　　　*n.* 关税,关税表,价格表
　　　　　　　　　　　　　　　　　　v. 征收关税,定税率,定收费标准

Notes

[1] Packaging requirements vary, labeling differs, lead times lengthen, inventory management becomes more complex, intermediaries multiply, carrier selection and pricing increase in difficulty, and the list goes on.
包装要求变化,标签不同,前置时间延长,库存管理变得更加复杂,中介机构倍增,承运人选择和定价困难增加,并且这样的列举持续不断。

[2] Political decisions such as closing borders to trade or instituting or increasing tariffs and duties only add to the inventory problems.
诸如关闭贸易边界、制订关税或增加关税之类的政治决定只会加大库存问题。

[3] Stockouts are much more common globally than would be acceptable domestically.
全球性缺货比国内应该能够接受的缺货更为常见。

[4] Superior customer service sometimes becomes irrelevant because the company has little or no control over the timing and availability of the product.
高端客户服务有时变得无关紧要,因为公司对产品的时效性和可用性很难控制或者无法控制。

[5] In developing countries, the majority of systems are manual.
在发展中国家,大部分系统是人工的。

[6] Also, some products require more sophisticated handling equipment, so some countries or ports may not be able to receive them.
同样,一些产品需要更加复杂的搬运设备,因此一些国家或港口可能无法接收这些产品。

[7] For example, some ports can handle only twenty-foot containers, while others cannot handle containers at all.
例如,一些港口只能搬运20英尺的集装箱,而有些港口根本就不能搬运集装箱。

Vocabulary

Note:

1. There are some signs in the end of the following words, the number and the letter represents unit number and the relative passage, for example:

abate[ə'beit]v. 减少,减轻 11A

11 means Unit 11 and A means Passage A of Unit 11.

2. Signs-page is listed as Table1.

Signs-page   Table 1

Signs	Page	Signs	Page	Signs	Page	Signs	Page
1A	4	7A	55	13A	107	19A	163
1B	8	7B	60	13B	111	19B	167
2A	11	8A	66	14A	116	20A	172
2B	14	8B	71	14B	121	20B	176
3A	17	9A	78	15A	126	21A	182
3B	20	9B	81	15B	130	21B	184
4A	23	10A	85	16A	134	22A	187
4B	26	10B	88	16B	137	22B	189
5A	34	11A	92	17A	144	23A	192
5B	39	11B	95	17B	149	23B	195
6A	45	12A	98	18A	154	24A	199
6B	49	12B	101	18B	159	24B	201

A

abate[ə'beit]　　　　　　　　　　　　v. 减少,减轻 11A

absolute['æbsəluːt]　　　　　　　　　adj. 绝对的,完全的,专制的

　　　　　　　　　　　　　　　　　　n. 绝对,绝对事物 3A

access['ækses]　　　　　　　　　　　v. 使用,存取,接近

　　　　　　　　　　　　　　　　　　n. 进入,使用权,通路 4A

accumulation[əˌkjuːmju'leiʃən]　　　n. 积聚,累积,堆积物 1B

acquisition[ˌækwɪ'zɪʃ(ə)n]　　　　　n. 获得物,获得,收购 2A

adept['ædept,ə'dept]　　　　　　　　n. 老手,擅长者

　　　　　　　　　　　　　　　　　　adj. 熟练的,拿手的 19A

英文	音标	释义
adequate	[ˈædikwit]	adj. 充足的,适当的,胜任的 2B
adhere	[ədˈhiə]	vi. 坚持,依附,黏着,追随
		vt. 使粘附 24B
adjacent	[əˈdʒeisənt]	adj. 邻近的,接近的 8B
administrative	[ədˈministrətiv]	adj. 管理的,行政的,行政勤务的 3A
aggregate	[ˈægrigət]	vt. 集合,聚集,使积聚,合计
		n. 合计,聚集体,骨料,集料(可成混凝土或修路等用的)
		adj. 总数的,总计的,聚合的,[地]聚成岩的 4B
aggressively	[əˈgresivli]	adv. 积极地,大胆地,侵略地,攻击地 3B
AGV (Automated Guided Vehicle)		自动导引车 13B
aisle	[aɪl]	n. 过道,通道,侧廊 13B
albeit	[ɔːlˈbiːit]	conj. 尽管,假使 11A
algorithm	[ˈælgəriðəm]	n. 算法,运算法则 4B
alliance	[əˈlaiəns]	n. 联盟,联合,(国家、政党等的)结盟,同盟,联盟,联合,联姻,同盟条约,同盟者 5A
alternative	[ɔːlˈtəːnətiv]	adj. 供选择的,选择性的,交替的,替代的,备选的,其他的,另类的
		n. 二中择一,供替代的选择 1B
aluminium	[æljəˈminiəm]	n. 铝 21B
amortize	[ˈæmətaiz]	vt. 摊销(等于 amortise),分期偿还 16A
amplification	[ˌæmplifiˈkeiʃən]	n. [电子]放大(率),扩大,详述 22A
anchor	[ˈæŋkə]	v. 抛锚,锚定
		n. 锚 18A
antenna	[ænˈtenə]	n. [电讯]天线 8A
anticipate	[ænˈtisipeit]	vt. 预见,预料,先于……行动,预测 5A
apparel	[əˈpærəl]	v. 给……穿衣服(尤指华丽或特殊的服装)
		n. (商店出售的)衣服,外观,外表,覆盖物 22B
appear to be		看来像是 19B
application-oriented modules		面向应用模块 6A
appropriate	[əˈprəupriət]	adj. 适当的,恰当的,合适的
		v. 占用,拨出 3B
approximation	[əˌprɔksiˈmeiʃən]	n. 接近,近似值,粗略估计 4B
apron	[ˈeiprən]	n. 挡板,护栏 19B
APS (Advanced Planning and Scheduling)		高级计划与排程 6B
arbitrary	[ˈɑːrbətreri]	adj. 随意的,任性的 14A
articulated	[ɑːˈtikjulitid]	adj. 铰接(的),枢接(的),有关节的 13B
as opposed to		与……相反,与……相对(比) 19B

Vocabulary

ASRS (automated storage and retrieval systems)	自动存储与分拣系统 2B
assembly line	装配作业线,流水作业装配线 14B
asset [ˈæset]	n. 资产,财产 2A
assist [əˈsɪst]	n. 帮助,助攻
	v. 参加,出席,帮助,促进 5A
assumption [əˈsʌm(p)ʃ(ə)n]	n. 假定,设想,担任,采取 21A
at first sight	乍看起来,初看起来 19B
attachment [əˈtætʃmənt]	n. 附件,附加装置,配属 18A
attenuate [ətenjueit]	v. 变(稀)薄,变细(小),减弱 9B
auction [ˈɔːkʃ(ə)n]	n. 拍卖
	v. 拍卖,竞卖 8B
audible [ˈɔːdɪb(ə)l]	adj. 听得见的 8A
audit [ˈɔːdit]	n. 会计检查,查账
	v. 检查,查账 5A
automated [ˈɔːtoumeɪtɪd]	adj. 自动化的,
	v. 自动化(过去分词) 13B
a variety of	各种各样的,种种 20A

B

backbone [ˈbækbəun]	n. 支柱,主干网,决心,毅力,脊椎 6A
backhaul [ˈbækhɔːl]	n. 回程,载货反航 7A
backward [ˈbækwəd]	adj. 向后的,反向的,发展迟缓的
	adv. 向后地,相反地 1A
bar-code [ˈbɑːkəud]	n. 条形码
	vt. 给……印(或标)上条形码 22B
barometer [bəˈrɔmitə]	n. 晴雨表,气压计,显示变化的事物,标记 3A
batch [bætʃ]	n. 一批,一次所制之量
	v. 分批处理 7A
be a match for	和……匹敌,敌得过 19A
be attached to	把……放(系/连)在……上 18A
be compatible with	与……不矛盾,与……兼容 20A
be in a position to	能够 10B
benchmarking [ˈbentʃˌmɑːkiŋ]	n. 基准,定位,标杆管理 5A
berth [bəːθ]	n. (车、船、飞机等的)铺位,停泊处,泊位 12A
berthing place	泊位 12B
be responsible for	负责 3B
be instrumental in	有助于,助长 11A
bill of lading	提单 19B

bill-of-materials file		物料清单文档 6A
bonanza [bəuˈnænzə]		n.(突然的)财,意想不到的幸运,富矿脉 1A
bottleneck [ˈbɒt(ə)lnek]		n. 瓶颈,障碍物 7B
bracket [ˈbrækɪt]		n. 支架,括号
		v. 括在一起,把……归入同一类,排除 8B
breadth [bredθ]		n. 宽度,幅度,宽宏 7B
break down		分解,发生故障,失败,毁掉,制服 21A
buffer [ˈbʌfə(r)]		n. 缓冲器,起缓冲作用的人(或物),缓冲剂 14A
bulk [bʌlk]		n. 体积,容量,大多数,大部分,大块
		vt. 使扩大,使形成大量,使显得重要 9A
bullwhip effect		牛鞭效应 1A

C

cable car(美)		缆车 10A
candidate [ˈkændədet]		n. 候选人,申请者,应征人员 16A
carousels [kærəˈselz]		n.pl 回转机构,旋转木马 13B
carton [ˈkɑːtən]		n. 硬纸盒,纸板箱 8A
cascade [kæˈskeid]		v. 流注,大量落下
		n. 串联,倾泻,小瀑布,瀑布状物 21A
case fill rate		供应比率(质量衡量) 5A
cases per labor hour		每工时生产量(生产率衡量) 5A
caster [ˈkɑːstə]		n. 投手,(家具的)脚轮,调味瓶 18B
category [ˈkætəgɔːri]		n. 类型,种类,部门,类别,类目[逻]范畴 3A
cater for		供应伙食;迎合;为……提供必要条件 11A
central database		中央(心)数据库 6A
centralised purchasing		集中采购 15B
centre [sɛntə]		vi 以……为中心
		vt. 集中,将……放在中央
		n. 中心
		adj. 中央的 13A
chain [tʃen]		n. 链,束缚,枷锁
		vt. 束缚,囚禁,用铁链锁住 1A
changeover [ˈtʃeindʒˌəuvə]		n. 转换,逆转,(方针的)转变 3B
chip [tʃɪp]		n.[电子] 芯片,筹码,碎片
		v. 削,凿,削成碎片 8A
circuit [ˈsɜːkɪt]		n.[电子] 电路,回路,巡回,一圈,环道
		v. 环行,绕回……环行 8A

circumstance [ˈsɜːkəmstənsɪz]	n. 境遇,境况(由其指经济情况) 10B
clamp [klæmp]	n. 夹子,夹具,夹钳
	vt. 夹住,夹紧 20B
clamshell [ˈklæmʃəl]	n. 蛤壳式挖泥机 20B
clog 英 [klɒg]	n. 木底鞋,障碍
美 [klɑg]	v. 阻碍,堵塞 11B
CMR Notes (Convention relating to the International Road Consignment Note)	国际道路托运票据协定 9B
COFC (container on flatcar)	集装箱平车 9A
cog railway	齿轮铁路 10A
collaborate [kəˈlæbəreɪt]	v. 合作 8A
commodity [kəˈmɒdɪtɪ]	n. 商品,货物,日用品 8B
compatibility [kəmpætəˈbilitɪ]	n. [计]兼容性,相容性,适用性 5B
compatible [kəmˈpætəbl]	adj. 兼容的,相容的 5B
compete [kəmˈpiːt]	vi. 竞争,比赛,对抗 1B
compliant [kəmˈplaɪənt]	adj. 顺从的,适应的 20B
component [kəmˈpəunənt]	adj. 组成的,构成的
	n. 成分,组件,电子元件,[数]要素,组分,零件 3B
comprehensive [ˌkɔmpriˈhensiv]	adj. 综合的,广泛的,有理解力的 5A
comprise [kəmˈpraiz]	v. 包含,由……组成 4B
conceive [kənˈsiːv]	v. 构思,以为,持有 21A
configuration [kənˌfigəˈreiʃn]	n. 配置,布局,构造,结构,外形 9A
configure [kənˈfɪgə]	v. 安装,使成形 7A
confined [kənˈfaɪnd]	adj. 有限的,受限制的 13B
confusion [kənˈfjuːʒən]	n. 混乱,混淆,困惑 2A
congestion [kənˈdʒestʃən]	n. 拥挤,堵车,阻塞 8B
conjunction [kənˈdʒʌŋ(k)ʃ(ə)n]	n. 结合,连接词,同时发生 6B
connote [kɔˈnəut]	v. 意味着 19B
consecutive [kənˈsekjutiv]	adj. 连续的,连贯的 5B
consignee [kənsaiˈniː]	n. 受托者,收件人,代销人 7A
consignment [kənˈsainmənt]	n. 交货,托运物,送货 9B
consignor [kənˈsainə]	n. 委托者,发货人,货主 9B
consistency [kənˈsɪst(ə)nsɪ]	n. 一致性 7B
consistent [kənˈsɪstənt]	adj. 一致的,连续的,不矛盾的,坚持的 4B
consolidate [kənˈsɑːlɪdeɪt]	v. 统一,把……合成一体,合并,巩固,加强 9A
consolidated [kən ˈsɔlideitid]	adj. 加固的,整理过的,统一的 19B
consolidation [kənsɔliˈdeiʃn]	n. 巩固,合并,团结 1B
constituent [kənˈstitjuənt]	n. 选民,成分,构成部分,委托人

		adj. 构成的,组成的,选举的,有选举权的 21B
consumable	[kənˈsuməbl]	*n.* 消费品,消耗品
		adj. 可消耗的,可消费的 13A
containerized	[kənˈteɪnəraɪzd]	*v.* 用集装箱装运(货物),使……集装箱化 11B
context	[ˈkɔntekst]	*n.* 语境,上下文,背景,环境 2A
contour	[ˈkɔntuə]	*n.* 轮廓,周线,等高线 18A
conveyor	[kənˈveɪə(r)]	*n.* 运送者,传送者,传达者,(财产)转让人,输送机,运输机 2B
coordinate	[kəˈɔːdneɪt]	*v.* 协调,整合 1B
coordination	[kəʊˌɔːdiˈneɪʃən]	*n.* 协调,调和,对等,同等 1B
corrugated	[ˈkɔrəgeitid]	*adj.* 波纹的,波纹状的,波纹面的 2B
cost-effective		有成本效益的,合算的,划算的 20B
counterfeit	[ˈkaʊntəfɪt]	*n.* 赝品,冒牌货,伪造品
		v. 伪造,仿造,假装,伪装
		adj. 假冒的,伪造的,虚伪的 8A
counterweight	[ˈkaʊntəweit]	*n.* 平衡物,秤锤,平衡力 18B
couple	[ˈkʌp(ə)l]	*n.* 对,夫妇,数个
		vt. 连接,连合 3A
coverage	[ˈkʌvərɪdʒ]	*n.* 保险总额,承保范围 2B
CPFR (collaborative planning, forecasting, and replenishment)		协作性计划、预测和补给(是一种软件,也是一种战略) 5B
crane	[kreɪn]	*n.* 鹤,吊车,起重机
		vt. 伸长,探头
		vi. 迟疑,踌躇 2B
criteria	[kraɪˈtiəriə]	*n.* 标准 12B
CRM (customer relationship management)		客户关系管理 6B
CRP (capacity requirement planning)		能力需求计划 7A
cushion	[ˈkuʃən]	*n.* 垫子,起保护作用的东西
		v. 起缓冲作用 10B
customer perception		顾客的满意度(客户服务衡量) 5A
cut across		打断,冲破,穿过,跨越,贯穿,与……相抵触 3B
CY (container yard)		集装箱货柜堆场 19B

D

dampen	[ˈdæmpən]	*v.* 弄湿,消沉,抑制 10B
database maintenance		数据库维护 5A
deck	[dek]	*n.* 甲板,行李仓,露天平台 12A
dedicated	[ˈdedəˌketɪd]	*adj.* 专用的,专注的,献身的

	v. 以……奉献,把……用于 16A
dedicated trucks	专用卡车 16A
delay [dilei]	vi. 延期,耽搁
	vt. 延期,耽搁
	n. 延期,耽搁,被耽搁或推迟的时间 9B
delivery [di'livəri]	n. 递送,交付,分娩,交货,引渡 1B
delivery scheduling	日程安排 23B
departure [dɪ'pɑrtʃə]	n. 离开,出发,违背 9B
deployment [diːˈplɔimənt]	n. 调度,部署 1B
deposit [dɪ'pɒzɪt]	n. 存款,押金,订金,保证金,沉淀物,堆积物,存放物
	vt. 使沉积,存放,堆积 16B
depreciation [diˌpriːʃiˈeiʃən]	n. 折旧,货币贬值,跌价 3A
derivation [deri'veiʃən]	n. 引出,来历,出处 19A
derrick ['derik]	n. [机]起重机,[矿]井口上的铁架塔,悬臂式起重机 18A
deterministic [diˌtəːmiˈnistik]	adj. 确定性的,决定性的,命中注定的 4B
deviation [diːviˈeiʃ(ə)n]	n. 偏差,偏离,离经叛道的行为,误差,背离 14B
dictate [dik'teit]	v. 命令,支配,指定 8A
diesel train	柴油机车 10A
differentiator [difəˈrenʃieitə]	n. [自]微分器,微分电路,区分者 8B
dilute [daɪ'lut]	adj. 稀释的,淡的
	vt. 稀释,冲淡,削弱
	vi. 变稀薄,变淡 16A
dimension [di'menʃən]	n. 尺寸,尺度,维度 2B
discharge [dis'tʃɑːdʒ]	vt. 解雇,卸下,放出,免除,放出
	vi. 排放,卸货,流出,流注
	n. 排放,卸货,解雇 12B
dispatch [di'spætʃ]	n. 派遣,急件
	v. 分派,派遣 10B
dispatcher [dɪs'pætʃə]	n. 调度员,[计]调度程序,[计]分配器 8B
disrupt [dis'rʌpt]	v. 使中断,使分裂,使瓦解,使陷于混乱,破坏 9A
disruption 英 [dɪs'rʌpʃn] 美 [dɪs'rʌpʃn]	n. 分裂,瓦解;破裂,毁坏;中断 1B
distillery [dɪ'stɪləri]	n. 酿酒厂,蒸馏间 14A
DRP (distribution requirements planning)	配送需求计划 15A
dock 英 [dɒk] 美 [dɒk]	n. 船坞,码头,(供汽车或火车装卸货物的)月台,港区
	v. (使)船停靠码头 (dock 的第三人称单数),

dock bumper	（使宇宙飞船在外层空间）对接,减少,扣除 9B
	月台缓冲器,船坞缓冲器 17A
DOT(Department of Transportation)	交通运输部(美国)24A
downtime [ˈdauntaim]	n.(工厂等由于检修,待料等的)停工期,[电子]故障停机时间 21B
draught [drɑːft]	n. 吃水 12A
drawback [ˈdrɔːbæk]	n. 缺点,障碍 14B
dumbwaiter	小件升降机,（楼上下之间）送饭菜的小升降机 18B
duplicate [ˈdjuːplikət]	vt. 重复,复制,复印
	adj. 复制的,副本的,完全一样的 1B
dynamic [daiˈnæmik]	n. 动态,动力
	adj. 动态的,动力的,动力学的,有活力的 1B

E

economic order quantity	经济订货批量 14B
ECR(efficient consumer response)	有效客户响应 22B
EDI(electronic data interchange)	电子数据交换 1A
effective [iˈfektiv]	adj. 有效的,被实施的 1A
efficient [iˈfiʃənt]	adj.（直接）生效的,有效率的,能干的 1A
elaborate [英][iˈlæbəreit]	vi. 详尽说明,变得复杂
[美][ɪˈlæbəret]	vt. 详细制定,详尽阐述,[生理学]加工,尽心竭力地做
	adj. 复杂的,精心制作的,（结构）复杂的,精巧的 17A
elevating machine	举升机械,提升机械 18A
elimination [ɪˈlɪmɪˈneɪʃn]	n. 排除,除去,根除,淘汰 15A
elusive [iˈljuːsiv]	adj. 难懂的,难捉摸的 5A
embedded [emˈbedid]	n. 装入的,压入的,嵌入的 20A
emerge [iˈmɜːdʒ]	vi. 浮现,摆脱,暴露 22B
empower [imˈpauə]	vt. 授权,允许,使能够 4A
enact [iˈnækt]	v. 制定法律,规定,颁布,颁布,担任……角色 24A
encompass [inˈkʌmpəs]	vt. 围绕,包围,包含或包括某事物,完成 2A
EOQ (economic order quantity)	经济起订量;经济订货批量 14B
EPC (electronic product code)	电子产品码 8A
equivalent [ɪˈkwɪvələnt]	adj. 相等的,对等的,相当的
	n. 对等物,当量 6A
ergonomics [əːgəuˈnɔmiks]	n. 人类工程学,生物工程学,工效学 19A

ERP (Enterprise Resource Planning)	企业资源计划 6A
estate [ɪˈstet]	n. 房地产,财产,身份 16B
estimate [ˈestɪmət]	n. 估计,报价
	v. 评估,估计,预算 14A
evolve [iˈvɔlv]	vt. 发展,进化,制订出,发出,散发 11B
except…that	除了……之外 6A
execution [eksɪˈkjuːʃ(ə)n]	n. 执行,实行,完成 6A
expenditure [iksˈpendɪtʃə]	n. 花费,支出,费用,经费,(金钱的)支出额,(精力、时间、材料等的)耗费 3A
expense [ikˈspens]	n. 损失,代价,消费,开支
	vt. 向……收取费用 3A
expensive [ikˈspensiv]	adj. 昂贵的,花钱的 4B
external [ɪkˈstɜːnl]	adj. 外部的,表面的,[药]外用的,外国的,外面的
	n. 外部,外观,外面 1B

F

fabricated [ˈfæbrɪˈket]	adj. 焊接的,组合的装配式的(fabricate的过去分词)
	v. 制造,组装,伪造,捏造,装配 15A
facilitate [fəˈsiliteit]	vt. 促进,帮助,使容易 5A
facilitator [fəˈsiliteitə]	n. 服务商,促进者,帮助者 1B
facility [fəˈsɪləti]	n. 设施,设备,容易,灵巧 4B
facsimile [fækˈsɪmɪlɪ]	n. 传真,复写
	adj. 复制的
	v. 传真,临摹 8B
familiarize [fəˈmiliəraiz]	v. 使(某人)熟悉,使通晓 24B
FCL (full container load)	整箱货 19B
feedback [ˈfiːdbæk]	n. 反馈,反应 5A
financial [faɪˈnænʃl]	adj. 金融的,财政的,财务的 1A
financing [fɪˈnænsɪŋ]	n. 筹措资金,理财,筹集资金,融资 14A
finished goods	产成品 6B
finished goods warehouse	产成品库 13A
FIFO (first-in first-out)	先进先出 14B
flange [flændʒ]	n. 边缘,轮缘,[机]凸缘,法兰 19A
flexibility [fleksəˈbiliti]	n. 弹性,适应性,机动性,灵活性 4B
floor space (设备的)	占地面积 20B
FOB (Free On Board)	离岸价 10B
forecast [ˈfɔːkɑːst]	vi. 进行预报,作预测

	vt. 预报,预测,预示
	n. 预测,预报,预想;forecasting 是动名词或现在分词 2A
fork truck	叉车,叉式运货车 20A
forklift ['fɔːklɪft]	*n.* 叉车,铲车,堆高机,叉式升降机
	v. 用铲车搬运 2B
formulae ['fɔːmjəliː]	*n.* 配方,公式(formula 的名词复数),分子式,方案 23A
fragment ['frægmənt]	*n.* 碎片,断片,片段,未完成的部分,将文件内容)分段
	vt. (使)碎裂,破裂,分裂
	vi. 破碎,碎裂 5B
fragmentary ['frægməntəri]	*adj.* 由碎片组成的,断断续续的,零散的,支离破碎的 5B
freight elevator	货运电梯 18B
freight-handling	货物搬运 18B
frustrate [frʌ'streit]	*vt.* 挫败,阻挠,使受挫折
	adj. 无益的,无效的 24B
fulfillment [ful'filmənt]	*n.* 实现,完成,满足,实施过程 2B
full-ranged	全方位的,完全的 5B
funicular [fju'nikjulə]	*n.* 索道 10A

G

gantry ['gæntri]	*n.* [机]构台,桶架,门式起重机 12B
gateway ['geɪtweɪ]	*n.* 门,网关,方法,通道,途径 8A
gauge [geidʒ]	*n.* 铁路轨距,标准尺,规格,评估,测量的标准或范围,尺度,标准,测量仪器
	vt. (用仪器)测量,评估,判断,采用 3A
GDP (gross domestic product)	国内生产总值 3A
geographical [dʒɪə'græfɪkl]	*adj.* 地理的,地理学的 15B
gigantic [dʒai'gæntik]	*adj.* 巨大的 19B
girder ['gəːdə]	*n.* 梁,钢桁的支架 18A
godown ['gəudaun]	*n.* 仓库 19B
grinding ['graindɪŋ]	*adj.* 磨的,摩擦的,碾的
	v. 磨碎,旋转开动,压迫 21B
groove [gruːv]	*n.* (唱片等的)凹槽,惯例,最佳状态
	vt. 开槽于 18A
guarantee [gærən'tiː]	*n.* 保证,保证书,担保,抵押品

	vt. 保证,担保 4A
guideline ['gaɪdˌlaɪn]	*n.* 指导方针,指导原则 14B

H

handler ['hændlə]	*n.* 处理者,管理者,训练者 7A
hardware ['hɑːdweə]	*n.* 计算机硬件,五金器具 5A
haulage ['hɔːlidʒ]	*n.* 拖运,运输 9B
hazardous ['hæzədəs]	*adj.* 危险的,冒险的,危害的 10B
headquarter ['hedkwɔːtə]	*v.* 设立总部,在……设总部 8B
helpdesk ['helpdesk]	*n.* 帮助台,技术支持中心,售后服务部门 4A
heuristics [hjuə'ristik]	*n.* 启发(法),启发式算法,探索法 4B
hierarchy ['haɪərɑːki]	*n.* 层级,等级制度 16B
hinterland ['hɪntəlænd]	*n.* 内地,穷乡僻壤,靠港口供应的内地贸易区 12A
hoist [hɔɪst]	*n.* 提升间,升起 17B
holistic [həʊ'listik]	*adj.* 全盘的,整体的,功能整体性的 22B
hook [huk]	*n.* 钩,吊钩 *v.* 钩住,沉迷,上瘾 18A
horizontal [ˌhɔri'zɔntəl]	*n.* 水平线,水平面,水平位置,水平的物体 *adj.* 横向的,水平的,卧式的,地平线的 1B
hydraulic 英 [haɪ'drɔːlɪk] 美 [haɪ'drɔlɪk]	*adj.* 水力的,水压的,用水发动的;[建]水硬的;水力学的 18A
hypothetical [ˌhaɪpəʊ'θetɪkəl]	*adj.* 假想,假设的,假定的,有前提的,猜想的 1A

I

I-beam	工字梁 18A
ID (identification)	*n.* 鉴定,识别;验明;身份证明;认同 8A
imperative [im'perətiv]	*adj.* 紧急的,必要的 10A
implement ['ɪmpləmənt]	*n.* 实施,执行 1B
implementation [implimen'teiʃ(ə)n]	*n.* [计] 实现,履行,安装启用 5A
implication ['ɪmplɪ'keʃən]	*n.* 含义,暗示,牵连,卷入,可能的结果,影响 21A
inbound ['inbaund]	*adj.* 入境的,回内地的,内部的,入厂的,文中指原料采购物流 1A
in a timely manner	及时地 2A
incentive [in'sentivz]	*n.* 动机,诱因,刺激,鼓励 7B
inception [in'cepʃən]	*n.* 起初,获得学位 5A
incur [ɪn'kɜː(r)]	*v.* 遭受,招致,引起 14A
indicate ['indikeit]	*vt.* 表明,指出,预示,象征 1A
indication [indi'keiʃən]	*n.* 指出,指示,迹象,暗示 5B

indispensable 英 [ˌɪndɪˈspensəbl] 美 [ˌɪndɪˈspɛnsəbəl]	*adj.* 不可缺少的,绝对必要的,责无旁贷的,不可避开的
	n. 不可缺少的人或物, 10B
inevitably [ɪnˈevɪtəbli]	*adv.* 不可避免地,自然而然地;必然地,无疑;难免;终于只好 14B
infinite [ˈɪnfɪnət]	*adj.* 无限的,无穷的,无数的,极大的
	n. 无限,[数]无穷大,无限的东西(如空间,时间) 16B
inflation [ɪnˈfleʃən]	*n.* 膨胀,通货膨胀 14A
inflexibility [ɪnfleksəˈbiliti]	*n.* 不屈性,顽固,不变性 13B
infrastructure [ˈɪnfrəstrʌktʃə]	*n.* 基础设施,公共建设,下部构造 6B
infrequent [ɪnˈfrikwənt]	*n.* 罕见的,稀少的 3B
infusion [ɪnˈfjuʒn]	*n.* 灌输,浸泡,注入物,激励 16A
ingredient [ɪŋˈriːdɪrnts]	*n.* 组成成分,原料,要素 14A
inherent [ɪnˈhɪərənt]	*adj.* 固有的,内在的,与生俱来的 4A
in-house	*adj. & adv.* 内部的(地),室内的(地) 9B
in-line	在线,串联 20B
install [ɪnˈstɔːl]	*v.* 安装,任命,安顿 5B
instruction [ɪnˈstrʌkʃ(ə)n]	*n.* 指令,命令,指示,教导,用法说明 6A
in such a way as to	以这样的方式,通过下述方式 20A
insulate [ˈɪnsjʊleit]	*v.* 使绝缘,隔离 23B
intangible [ɪnˈtændʒəbəl]	*adj.* 触摸不到的,难以理解的,无法确定的 14A
integrate [ˈɪntigreit]	*vt.* 使成整体,使一体化
	v. 结合 1A
integrated logistics	一体化物流 1A
integration [ˌɪntɪˈgreɪʃ(ə)n]	*n.* 集成,综合,整合,一体化,结合,(不同、种族、宗教信仰等的人的)混合 1B
interchange [ˌɪntəˈtʃeɪn(d)ʒ]	*n.* 互换,立体交叉道
	v. 交换,互换 6B
interchangeable [ɪntəˈtʃeindʒəbl]	*adj.* 可互换的 18A
interface [ˈɪntəfeɪs]	*n.* 界面,[计算机]接口,交界面
	vi. 接合,连接,[计算机]使联系,相互作用,交流,交谈 3B
intermediary [ˌɪntəˈmiːdiəri]	*n.* 媒介,中间人,调解人,仲裁者,中间阶段
	adj. 中间的,调解的,居间的,媒介的,中途的 4B
intermittent motion	间歇运动 18A
intermodal [ˈɪntəˌməʊdl]	*adj.* 联合运输的,多式联运 9A
internally [ɪnˈtəːnəli]	*adv.* 内部地,国内地,内在地 5A

interpretable [ɪnˈtə:prətəbl]	*adj.* 可说明的,可判断的,可翻译的 8B
interruption [ɪntəˈrʌpʃən]	*n.* 中断,打断,障碍物,打岔的事 1B
interval [ˈɪntevl]	*n.* 间隔时间,间隔 14B
in the form of	用……的形式 18A
inventory [ˈɪnvəntɔ:ri]	*n.* 库存,存货清单 1A
inventory turnover	库存周转(资产衡量) 5A
investigation [ɪnˌvestɪˈgeʃən]	*n.* 调查,调查研究 16B
investment [ɪnˈvestmənt]	*n.* 投资,投资额,(时间、精力的)投入,封锁 3A

J

jack [dʒæk]	*n.* 千斤顶 17B
JIT (just-in-time)	准时制,准时送货 2B
JMI (joint-managed inventory)	联合管理库存 22A
justification [dʒʌstifɪˈkeiʃən]	*n.* 认为有理,认为正当,理由,辩护 5A

K

knuckle [ˈnʌkl]	*n.* 指节,关节 20B

L

layout [leiˈaut]	*n.* 规划,设计,(书刊等)编排,版面,配线,企划,设计图案 5B
LCL (less than the full container load)	拼箱货 19B
lead time	前置时间,提前期(即订货至交货的时间) 2B
lean thinking	精益生产 21B
legacy [ˈlegəsɪ]	*n.* 遗赠,遗产 6A
leveller [ˈlevələ]	*n.* 使平等(或平均)者,校平机 18B
LIFO (last-in first-out)	后进先出 14B
light load vehicle	轻载运货车,轻便式小车 20A
likelihood [ˈlaɪklɪhʊd]	*n.* 可能性,可能,似然 7A
linear programming	线性规划 4B
literature [ˈlɪtərətʃə]	*n.* 文学,文献,著作 2A
loading and unloading	装载和卸载 18A
location [loˈkeʃən]	*n.* 位置,地址,地点,外景拍摄场地 1B
locomotive [ləukəˈməutiv]	*n.* 机车,火车头 10A
logistics management	物流管理 1A
LTL (less-than-truckload)	零担货 9A

M

maglev [ˈmæglev]	*n. & adj.* 磁力悬浮火车(的);磁浮列车 10A

malfunction [ˌmælˈfʌŋkʃn]		n. 失灵,故障,功能障碍 17A
manoeuvrable [məˈnuvərəblː]		adj. 可调动的,可移动的 13B
manufacturing [ˌmænjuˈfæktʃəriŋ]		adj. 制造的,制造业的
		n. 制造业,工业
		v. 制造,生产(manufacture 的 ing 形式)1B
marketplace [ˈmɑːkɪtpleɪs]		n. 市场,商场,市集 1B
markup [ˈmɑːkʌp]		n. 涨价,利润,审定 8A
marshalling [ˈmɑːʃəliŋ]		adj. 编组的,集结待发的
		n. 信号编集 13A
marshalling yard		铁路货运编组站 19B
material [məˈtɪəriəl]		n. 材料,物料,原料,素材,布,织物,适当人选 1A
material handling		物料搬运,原材料处理 7A
mechanism [ˈmɛkənɪzəm]		n. 机制,原理,途径,进程,机械装置,技巧 15B
merchandise [ˈmɜːtʃəndais]		n. 商品,货物
		v. 销售,买卖,经商 22B
merchandiser [ˈmɜːtʃənˌdaɪzə]		n. 商人 8A
military [ˈmilitəri]		n. 军队,军人,军事
		adj. 军事的,军人的,战争的 2A
mirror [ˈmirə(r)]		v. 反射,反映
		n. 镜子,反光镜,真实的写照,反映,借鉴,榜样 4A
mismatch [mɪsˈmætʃ]		v. 使配错,失配,使配合不当 14A
modeling analysis		建模分析 5A
modification [ˌmɔdifiˈkeiʃən]		n. 更改,修改,修正 7A
modular [ˈmɔdjuːlə]		adj. 模块化的,模数的,有标准组件的 6A
monitoring [ˈmɔnɪtəriŋ]		n. 监视,控制,监测,追踪 5A
monopolistic [məˌnɔpəˈlɪstɪk]		adj. 垄断的,独占性的,专利的 8B
monorail [ˈmɔnəureil]		n. 单轨铁路 10A
motivation [ˌməutəˈveʃən]		n. 动机,积极性,推动 16A
mount [maunt]		vt. 装上,设置,安放 8B
mounting [ˈmauntiŋ]		n. 装备,衬托纸,登上,乘骑
		adj. 上升的,增长的
		v. 登上,骑上(mount 的现在分词);增加,上升;上演;准备 18A
MPS(master production schedule)		主生产计划 7A
MRO(Maintenance, Repair, and Operating)		维护修理及操作 6A
MRP(material requirements planning)		物料需求计划 2B
MRP II(manufacturing resources planning)		制造资源计划 15A
MS SQL		大型分布式数据库系统 5B

multi-placed		多个地点的,多点的 5B

N

necessitate [nɪˈsesɪteɪt]		vt. 使……成为必要,需要,强迫,迫使 1B
negotiating [nɪˈɡəʊʃɪeɪtɪŋ]		n. 谈判 15B
noncounterbalance [ˌnɒnkaʊntəˈbæləns]		vt. 使不平均,使不平衡
		n. 不平衡量,不平衡力,非势均力敌 18B
notification [ˌnəʊtɪfɪˈkeɪʃn]		n. 通知,通告,[法] 告示 7A
notwithstanding [英] [ˌnɒtwɪθˈstændɪŋ]		prep. 尽管,还是,虽然
[美] [ˌnɑtwɪθˈstændɪŋ,-wɪð-]		adv. 尽管如此,仍然,还是
		conj. 虽然,尽管,10B

O

obsolescence [ˌɒbsəˈlesns]		n. 废弃,陈旧,过时,[生物] 退化,荒废 3A
obsolete [ˌɑːbsəˈliːt]		adj. 过时的,老式的,废弃的 1A
obviate [ˈɒbvieɪt]		vt. 消除,排除(危险、障碍等),预防,避免 18B
offset [ˈɒfset]		n. 抵消,补偿,平版印刷,支管
		vt. 抵消,弥补,用平版印刷术印刷
		vi. 装支管 11B
offshore [ˈɒfˈʃɔː]		adj. 离岸的,海外的,近海的,吹向海面的 3B
oil hydraulic plunger electric elevator		油压柱塞式电力升降机/油压柱塞式电梯 18B
oligopolistic		市场供应垄断者 9A
oligopoly [ˌɒliˈɡɒpəli]		n. 求大于供的市场情况 9A
on account of		由于 10B
on the job education		在职培训 10A
operational cost		经营成本,营业成本 19B
optical [ˈɒptɪkəl]		adj. 光学的;视觉的;视力的;眼睛的 8B
optimal [ˈɑːptɪməl]		adj. 最佳的,最优的,最理想的 8A
optimize [ˈɒptɪmaɪz]		vt. 使最优化 5B
ORACLE system		大型分布式数据库系统 5B
order fill rate		订单完成率,订单交付率 4A
order filling		订单填充,订单填补 23B
ore [ɔː(r)]		n. 矿,矿石,矿砂 9A
outbound [ˈaʊtbaʊnd]		adj. 开往外地的,开往外国的,出厂的 1A
outlet [ˈaʊtlet]		n. 出口,批发商店,排水口,通风口,发泄(情感)的方法 22B
outperform [ˌaʊtpəˈfɔːm]		vt. 做得比……好,胜过 9A

outsource [autˈsɔːs]		v. [商]外部采办,外购(指从外国供应商等处获得货物),业务外包 5B
outsourcing [ˈautˈsɔːsɪŋ]		n. 外包,外购,外部采办 15B
over time		随着时间的过去 6A
overhead crane		桥式起重机 2B
overheight 英 [ˌəuvəhaɪt] 美 [ˌəuvəˈhaɪt]		adj. 超高的 12A
overload [ˌəuvəˈləud]		v. 使负担太重(overload 的现在分词),使超载,使过载,给……增加负荷,超过负荷
		n. 超载,负荷过多,过载,过负载 7B
overwhelming [ˌəuvəˈwelmɪŋ]		adj. 势不可挡的,压倒一切的,巨大的 1B
overwidth [英] [ˌəuvəwɪdθ] [美] [ˌəuvəwɪdθ, ˌəuvəwɪtθ, ˌəuvəwɪθ]		adj. 超宽的,超广的 12A

P

pallet [ˈpælɪt]		n. 托盘,平台,运货板,扁平工具,[机]棘爪,货盘 8A
pallet truck		码垛车,托盘式小车 20A
palletize [ˈpælɪtaɪz]		vt. 把……放在货盘上,码垛堆集,用货盘装运 20B
palletizer [ˈpælɪtaɪzə]		n. 堆积机,堆码机 20B
paradoxically [ˌpærəˈdɒksɪkli]		adv. 自相矛盾,荒谬,反论,似非而可能是 23A
parallel [ˈpærəlel]		n. 平行线,平行面
		adj. 平行的
		vt. 用手推车运 19A
parameter [pəˈræmɪtə]		n. 参数,参量,限制因素,决定因素 3B
participate [pɑːˈtɪsɪpeɪt]		vi. 参与,参加,分享
		vt. 分享,分担 22B
part-to-picker system		货到人前系统 17B
pawl [pɔːl]		n. [机]棘爪,制转杆
		vt. 用制转杆使停转 18A
peak [piːk]		n. 山顶,顶点,帽舌,(记录的)最高峰 5B
perforce [pəˈfɔːs]		adv. 必然,一定 11A
periphery [pəˈrɪfəri]		n. 外围,四周,边缘,周边 18A
perishable [ˈperɪʃəbl]		adj. 容易腐烂的 9A
perceive…as		把……视为 5A
perspective [pəˈspektɪv]		n. 观点,远景,透视图
		adj. 透视的 1A
pertinent [ˈpɜːtɪnənt]		adj. 有关的,相干的,恰当的,中肯的,切题的 4B
philosophy [fɪˈlɒsəfi]		n. 哲学,哲理 21A

picker-to-part system	人到货前系统 17B
piggy-back	背驮式 11B
pilferage ['pilfəridʒ]	n. 小偷小摸,赃物 10B
pipeline ['paiplain]	n. 管道,输油管道,渠道,传递途径
	v. (通过管道)运输,传递,为……安装管道 1A
pivot ['pivət]	n. 枢轴,支点 19A
place reliance on	依靠 19B
play an important role in	在……起着非常重要的作用 3B
pneumatic [nju(:)'mætik]	adj. 装满空气的,气动的,风力的
	n. 气胎 18A
POD (proof of delivery receipts)	交货收据证明 8B
point to	对准,瞄准,指向 10A
polystyrene [pɔli'staiəri:n]	n. 聚苯乙烯 10B
POS (point-of-sale)	零售点 1A
postponement [pə'spəunmənt]	n. 延期,推迟,延缓,延期的事 1B
pre-commitment [kə'mitmənt]	n. 预先承诺(/许诺/委任/委托/致力/献身),承担义务 15B
precision [pri'siʒən]	n. 精确,精密度,精度 8A
predetermine ['pri:di'tə:min]	vt. 预先确定,预先决定,预先查明 2B
predominantly [pri'ɔmineit]	vt. 掌握,控制,支配
	vi. 统治,成为主流,支配,占优势 9A
premise ['premis]	n. 前提,[复数]房屋,[复数][合同、契约用语]上述各点
	v. 预述(条件等),提出……为前提,假设,做出前提 23A
premium ['pri:miəm]	n. 额外费用,奖金,保险费,溢价
	adj. 高价的,优质的 4A
prerequisite 英 [ˌpri:'rekwəzit] 美 [pri'rɛkwɪzɪt]	n. 先决条件,前提,必要条件
	adj. 必须先具备的,必要的,先决条件的 11A
pressing ['presiŋ]	adj. 紧迫的 5B
presumption [pri'zʌmpʃən]	n. 假定 9B
prevail [pri'vel]	vi. 盛行,流行,战胜,获胜,占优势,说服,劝说 15A
proactive [prə'æktiv]	adj. 前摄的;积极主动的;主动出击;先发制人的 5A
procurement [prəu'kjuəmənt]	n. 采购,获得,取得 2B
prohibit [prə(u)'hibit]	vt. 阻止,禁止 24B
proprietary [prə'praɪət(ə)rɪ]	n. 所有权,所有人

	adj. 所有的,专利的,私人拥有的 8A
prosperity [prɔs'periti]	*n.* 繁荣 5B
protocol ['prəutəkɒl]	*n.* 礼仪,(外交条约的)草案,(数据传递的)协议,科学实验报告(或计划)
	v. 把……写入议定书,在议定书中拟定(或颁布),拟定议定书,拟定草案 22A
prototype ['prəutətaip]	*n.* 原型 18B
provoke [prə'vəuk]	*vt.* 驱使,激怒,煽动,惹起 12B
pulley ['puli]	*n.* 滑车,滑轮,辘轳,皮带轮,滚筒 18A
pump [pʌmp]	*n.* 泵
	v. 用泵抽 11B
PO (purchase order)	采购订单 6A
pyramid ['pirəmid]	*n.* 角锥,棱锥,金字塔,叠罗汉
	v. (使)成金字塔状,(使)渐增,(使)上涨 5A
quotation [kwoʊ'teɪʃn]	*n.* 引用,引证,[商业]行情 14A

R

railcar [reil'kɑː]	*n.* (单节)机动有轨车 9A
ramification 英 [ˌræmɪfɪ'keɪʃn] 美 [ˌræməfɪ'keʃən]	*n.* 衍生物,结果,分叉,分支,支流 11A
ramp [ræmp]	*n.* 斜坡,斜道,匝道 17A
range from	分布在……范围,从……延伸到 18B
ratchet ['rætʃit]	*n.* [机](防倒转的)棘齿 18A
rate of throughput	物料通过速率 20B
rationale [ræʃə'nɑːli]	*n.* 基本理论 8B
rationalize ['ræʃnəlaiz]	*v.* 使合理化,据理解释,使消根,文饰 22B
raw materials warehouse	原料库 13A
real time	实时 5A
receipt timing	收货时间 15A
reciprocating [ri'siprəkeitiŋ]	*adj.* 往复的,交替的,互换的摆动的 18A
recommend [rekə'mend]	*vt.* 推荐,介绍,劝告,使受欢迎,托付 18A
redundancy [rɪ'dʌnd(ə)nsɪ]	*n.* [计数]冗余,裁员 6A
reefer ['riːfə(r)]	*n.* 冷藏车,收帆的人,双排扣水手上衣 12A
refrigeration [rɪˌfrɪdʒə'reɪʃn]	*n.* 冷藏,冷冻 10B
reliable [ri'laiəbl]	*adj.* 可靠的,可信赖的 1B
remote control	遥控,遥控装置,遥控操作 18B
replenishment [ri'pleniʃmənt]	*n.* 补充,补给,补货,库存补充 2B
replication [ˌrepli'keiʃən]	*n.* 复制,折叠,重复,回答,反响 4B

reroute [ˌriˈraʊt]	vt. 变更旅程,按新的特定路线运送 16A
reservation [ˌrezəˈveiʃ(ə)n]	n. 预约,预订,保留 12B
reshuffle [ˌriːˈʃʌfl]	n. 重新洗牌,改组(尤指政治组织),倒垛
	vt. 改组,重新洗牌,重作安排 12B
responsive [rɪˈspɑːnsɪv]	adj. 响应的,反应灵敏的,共鸣的,易反应的 7A
responsiveness [risˈpɔnsivnis]	n. 响应,响应性,响应能力 5A
resultant [riˈzʌltənt]	adj. 作为结果而发生的,合成的 9B
retrieval [rɪˈtriːvəl]	v. 检索,收回,挽回 2B
retrieve [riˈtriːv]	v. 重新得到
	n. 找回 7A
revenue [ˈrevinjuː]	n. 收入,国家的收入,税收 3B
reverse [riˈvəːs]	n. 背面,相反,倒退,失败
	vt. (使)反转;(使)颠倒;调换,交换;[法]撤销,推翻
	vi. 倒退,[桥牌]逆叫
	adj. 反面的,颠倒的,反身的 1A
reverse logistics	逆向物流 1A
RFDC(radio-frequency data communication)	无线电频数据通信技术 8A
RFID(radio frequency identification)	无线射频识别 8A
ROA(Return on Assets)	资产回报率 3B
ROI(Return on Investment)	投资回报率 3B
RO–RO(roll-on-roll-off)	滚上滚下(滚装)11B
routing [ˈruːtiŋ]	n. 发送,程序安排,路线选择,轨迹 5A
rubber-tired underground	胶轮地下轨道列车 10A
rudimentary [ˌruːdiˈmentəri]	adj. 初步的,未发展完善的 11A
ruggedness [ˈrʌgidnis]	n. 险峻,粗野/强度,耐久性,坚固性,坚固度 18B

S

S&OP(sales and operations planning)	销售和运作计划 6B
scenario [siˈnɑːriəu]	n. 方案,情节,剧本,设想 1A
schedule [ˈskedʒuːl]	vt. 安排,计划,编制目录,将……列入计划表
	n. 时间表,计划表,一览表 2A
scheduling [ˈʃedjuːəliŋ]	n. 行程安排,时序安排,排时间表,调度 2A
SCIS(supply chain information systems)	供应链信息系统 5A
scrutiny [ˈskruːtini]	n. 详细审查,详尽的研究,推敲,细看 19A
S.D.R.(Special Drawing Right)	特别提取权 9B
seagoing 英 [ˈsiːgəuiŋ] 美 [ˈsiːgoiŋ]	adj. 适于远航的 19B

seamless ['siːmlis]	adj. 无缝合线的,无伤痕的 5B
sector ['sektə]	n. 部分,部门,环节,扇形 2A
SCARA (selective compliant articulated robot arm)	有选择适应的铰接机器手 20B
self-propelled	adj. 自力推进的,自行驱动的 10A
sensible ['sensib(ə)l]	adj. 明智的,通情达理的,意识到的
	n. 可感觉到的东西,敏感的人 21A
shed [ʃed]	vt. 流出,摆脱,散发,倾吐
	vi. 流出,脱落,散布
	n. 小屋,棚,分水岭 12A
shipside ['ʃipsaid]	n. 码头 18A
shortage ['ʃɔːtidʒ]	n. 缺少,不足,缺点,缺少量 5A
shovel ['ʃʌvl]	n. 铲,铁铲,挖斗机,铁锹
	v. 铲,挖,舀,翻动 18A
shutdown ['ʃʌtdaʊn]	n. 关机,停工,关门,停播 1B
sidewalk ['saidwɔːk]	n. 人行道 18B
SKU (stock keeping unit)	货物储存单元 8A
sling [sliŋ]	n. 投掷器,弹弓,悬带,吊索[绳,环,链,具],吊重装置
	v. 投掷,用悬带吊挂 18A
smack [smæk]	v. 拍,打,捆
	n. 掌掴(声),海洛因,(打的)一拳,打巴掌
	adv. 直接地,准确地,猛烈地,急剧地 23A
sophisticated [sə'fistikeitid]	adj. 复杂的,精致的,完善的,久经世故的,富有经验的,深奥微妙的 13A
sophistication [səˌfistɪ'keɪʃn]	n. 复杂,诡辩,老于世故,有教养 7A
sort [sɔːt]	n. 分类,类别;品质,本性;方法;一群
	vt. & vi. 分类;整顿,整理;适合
	vt. 挑选;把……分类;将……排顺序
	vi. 拣选;交往;协调 5B
sorting ['sɔːtiŋ]	n. 资料排架
	v. 分类,整理(sort 的现在分词);挑选;[计算机](根据指令的模式)把……分类;把……归类(常与 with,together 连用) 5B
sortation [sɔː'teiʃən]	n. 分类 8A
spatial ['speiʃl]	adj. 空间的,存在于空间的,受空间条件限制的,占大篇幅的 7B
spawn [spɔːn]	v. 大量生产 21A

specialty ['speʃəlti]	n. 专业 20B
specification [spesɪfɪ'keɪʃ(ə)n]	n. 规格,说明书,详述 6A
sprocket ['sprɔkit]	n. 链轮齿 18A
spur-gear	直齿轮提升机 18A
S/R (storage and retrieval)	存储和拣货 17B
stack [stæk]	n. 堆,一堆,堆栈
	v. 堆叠 20B
stacker ['stækə]	n. 堆码机,堆码工,叠式存储器 17B
stationery ['steɪʃəneri]	n. 文具,办公用品,信封,文房四宝 14B
sterilization [sterəlai'zeiʃn]	n. 灭菌,杀菌,绝育 24A
stochastic [stə'kæstik]	adj. [数] 随机的,猜测的 12B
stockout [s'tɒkaʊt]	n. 无存货,缺货,存售完 15A
storage ['stɔːrɪdʒ]	n. 存储,贮存,储存处 1B
storage planning	存储计划 12B
stow [stəu]	v. 装载 12A
stowage ['stəʊidʒ]	n. 堆装物,积载,装载,装载物,装载方法 12B
straddle ['strædl]	n. 跨坐,观望
	v. 跨坐,叉开腿,不表明态度 12B
straddle carrier	集装箱吊车,轮胎吊 12B
stretch wrap	拉伸膜,收缩膜 2B
strides [straid]	adj. 步幅,大步,阔步,进展,一跨(的宽度)
	v. 跨过,大踏步走,跨 22B
strip [strip]	vt. 剥夺,剥去,脱去衣服
	n. 带,条状,脱衣舞
	vi. 脱去衣服 12A
stripper ['stripə]	n. 剥离器,卸料器,拆卸机,刨煤机 20B
stuffed [stʌft]	n. 东西,材料,填充物,素材资料
	vt. 塞满,填塞,让吃饱
	vi. 吃得过多 12A
subdivision [ˌsʌbdi'viʒən]	n. 分支,细分,一部 2A
subjective [səb'dʒektɪv]	adj. 主观上的,个人的,自觉的
	n. 主观事物 15B
subjunctive [səb'dʒʌŋktiv]	adj. 虚拟的,持续的,完善的 5B
subsequent ['sʌbsɪkwənt]	adj. 后来的,随后的 9B
subsidy ['sʌbsidi]	n. 津贴,补助金 9B
substantial [səb'stænʃ(ə)l]	adj. 大量的,实质的,内容充实的
	n. 本质,重要材料 3A
substitute ['sʌbstitjuːt]	n. 代用品,代替者
	vi. 替代,代替 1B

suction ['sʌkʃən]	n. 吸入,吸力,吸引 20B
supersede [ˌsjuːpəˈsiːd]	v. 代替,接替 10A
supplier [səˈplaɪə(r)]	n. 供应商,供应国,供应者,供给者,补充者 1A
susceptible [səˈseptəbl]	adj. 易受影响的,易受感染的 9A
swivel hook	转钩 18A
synchronization [ˌsɪŋkrənaɪˈzeɪʃn]	n. 同步,同一时刻,使时间互相一致,同时 1A
synchronize [ˈsɪŋkrənaɪz]	vi. 使……合拍,使……同步,同步,同时发生 4A
synergy [ˈsɪnədʒi]	n. 协同,配合,企业合并后的协力优势或协同作用 10A
synonym [ˈsɪnənɪm]	n. 同义词 1A
synthesis [ˈsɪnθɪsɪs]	n. 综合,[化学] 合成,综合体 7A
synthesize [ˈsɪnθɪsaɪz]	v. 综合,合成 5A

T

tactical [ˈtæktɪkəl]	adj. 战术的,策略上的,巧妙设计的,有谋略的,策略(高明)的,善于机变的 4A
tandem [ˈtædəm]	n. 前后双座自行车 9B
tandem trailer	串列拖车 9B
tariffs [ˈtærɪf]	n. 关税,关税表,价格表 v. 征收关税,定税率,定收费标准 24B
temporarily [ˈtempərerɪli]	adj. 暂时地 18B
TEU (twenty foot equivalent unit)	标准箱(系集装箱运量统计单位,以长20英尺的集装箱为标准)11B
the agile supply chain	敏捷供应链 23A
throughput [ˈθruːput]	n. 生产量,生产率,生产能力,吞吐量,容许量 13B
tier [tɪə]	n. 等级,阶梯座位等的一排,一行,一层,捆扎装置 vt. 层层排列,使层叠,堆积成层,堆叠,堆垛(货) 4A
TL (truckload)	整车货 9A
TMS (transportation management system)	运输管理软件 7A
TOFC (trailer on flatcar)	(铁路)平板车装运载有集装箱的拖车 9A
towing vehicle	拖曳车,牵引车 20A
towline [ˈtəʊlaɪn]	n. 拖链,拖绳 13B
trackage [ˈtrækɪdʒ]	n. 轨道,轨长,铁路轨道线路,线路使用权 18A
tradeoff [ˈtreɪdˌɔːf]	n. 交换,(公平)交易,折衷,权衡,协定 1A
trailer [ˈtreɪlə(r)]	n. 拖车 v. 用拖车运 7A
tramper [ˈtræmpə]	n. 不定期货船 11A

transaction [træn'zækʃən]	n. 交易,事务,办理,会报,学报 3B
transaxle [trænz'sæksəl]	n. 变速驱动桥,变速差速器 6A
transmit [trænz'mɪt]	vt. 传输,传播,发射,传达,发射信号
	vi. 传输,发射信号 8A
transshipment [træns'ʃipmənt]	n. 转运,转载 12A
trigger ['trigə]	v. 引发,引起,触发
	vi. 松开扳柄
	n. 扳机,[电子]触发器 21A
trolley ['trɑːli]	n. 小车,手推车,触轮,(有轨)电车 18A
truck [trʌk]	n. 载货汽车,手推车,(铁路)无盖货车,滚轮,转向轮 19A
turnover [tə:nəuvə]	n. 营业额,成交量,证券交易额,周转 5A

U

underhung ['ʌndə'hʌŋ]	adj. 支承在(下方的)轨上的 19A
underpin [ʌndə'pin]	v. 用砖石结构等从下面支撑(墙等),加强……的基础 21B
unfixed ['ʌn'fiksd]	adj. 解脱的,放松了的,不固定的,没确定的 5B
unit load	成组运输 20A
unit load vehicle	组合运货车 20A
upsell ['ʌpsel]	vi. 向上促销,增销 4A
upstream ['ʌp'striːm]	adv. 逆流地,向上游
	adj. 向上游的,逆流而上的
	n. 上游部门 2A
utilization [juːtɪlaɪ'zeɪʃən]	n. 利用,使用 5A
utilize ['juːtilaiz]	vt. 利用,适用,运用 2A

V

vacuum ['vækjuəm]	n. 真空,空间,真空吸尘器
	adj. 真空的,产生真空的,利用真空的 20B
validation [ˌvæli'deiʃən]	n. 确认,批准,生效 22B
variability [veəriə'biləti]	n. 可变性,变化性,[生物][数]变异性 9A
variation ['vɛrɪ'eʃən]	n. 变化,[生物]变异,变种 13A
vendor ['vɛndə]	n. 卖主,小贩,供应商,[贸易]自动售货机 1A
VMI (vendor managed inventory)	供应商管理库存 22A
versatile ['vəːsətail]	adj. 通用的,万能的,多才多艺的 20A
versatility [ˌvɜːsə'tɪləti]	n. 多用途,多功能,多才多艺 17A
versus ['vəːsəs]	prep. 对,与……相对,对抗 3B

vertical [ˈvəːtikəl]	n. 垂直线,垂直面,竖杆,垂直位置
	adj. 垂直的,竖立的,头顶的,顶点的 1B
viability [ˌvaiəˈbiləti]	n. 生存(存活)能力,发育能力,生活力 1A
visibility [ˌviziˈbiliti]	n. 可见度,可见性,显著,明显度,能见度,能见距离,明显性 5B
vogue [vəug]	n. 时尚,流行,时髦
	adj. 时髦的,流行的 1A
vulnerability [ˌvʌlnərəˈbiləti]	n. 易损性,弱点 1A

W

warehouse [ˈweəhaus]	n. 仓库,货栈,大商店,批发商店,福利库
	vt. 储入仓库,以他人名义购进(股票) 2B
WMS (Warehouse Management Systems)	仓库管理系统 5B
warehousing cost per pound	每磅仓储成本(成本衡量) 5A
weight [weit]	n. 重量,体重,重担,重任,重要,[统]权,加重值,权重
	vt. 加重于,使变重,使负重,使负担或压迫,[统]使加权 3B
wharf [wɔːf]	vt. 使靠码头,为……建码头,把货卸在码头上
	vi. 靠码头
	n. 码头,停泊处 12A
whereby [英][hwɛəˈbai] [美][hwɛrˈbaɪ, wɛr-]	adv. 凭借,通过,借以, 与……一致 21A
whilst [wailst]	conj. 同时 10A
winch [wintʃ]	n. 绞盘,卷扬机,曲柄 18A
witness [ˈwitnis]	vt. 目击,为……作证,证明,表明 5B
worm gear	蜗轮 18A
worthwhile [ˌwəːθˈwail]	adj. 有价值的,值得的,值得花时间的 2B
4PL (fourth-party logistics)	第四方物流 5B

Y

yield sign	让路标志 20A

References

［1］（加）唐纳德.沃特斯著.高咏玲译注.供应链管理概论物流视角（第二版）［M］.电子工业出版社.2011.

［2］（英）艾伦·哈里森（荷）雷姆克·范赫科著.张杰审校.物流管理（第二版）［M］.机械工业出版社.2005

［3］Alan Rushton. The Handbook of Logistics and Distribution Management［M］, The Institute of Logistics and Transport，KOGAN PAGE，2000.

［4］Coyle. Langley. Gibson. Novack. Bardi. Supply Chain Management-A Logistics Perspective［M］. South-western Cengage Learning. 2008.

［5］David J. Bloomberg, Stephen LeMay &Joe B. Hanna. 物流学［M］. 清华大学出版社. 2004.

［6］David J. Bloomberg. Logistics［M］. 北京：清华大学出版社,2004.

［7］RajaG.. Kasilingam, Logistics and Transportation — Design and planning［M］. Kluwer Academic Publishers，1998

［8］Satish C. Ailawadi, Rakesh P. Singh. Logistics Management（Second Edition）［M］. PHI Learing Private Limited. Delhi 2013.

［9］乐美龙.现代物流英语［M］,上海：上海交通大学出版社,2005.

［10］唐纳德·J·鲍儿索克斯，戴维·J·克劳斯,M 比克斯比·库珀著.马士华译注.供应链物流管理（第三版）［M］.机械工业出版社.2009.

［11］张庆英.物流工程英语［M］.北京：化学工业出版社,2005.

［12］李晓霞,胡大伟. 物流工程专业英语［M］.北京：人民交通出版社. 2007.

人民交通出版社汽车类本科教材部分书目

1. "十二五"普通高等教育本科国家级规划教材

书号	书名	作者	定价	出版时间	课件
978-7-114-10437-4	汽车构造（第六版）上册	史文库、姚为民	48.00	2016.7	配光盘
978-7-114-10435-0	汽车构造（第六版）下册	史文库、姚为民	58.00	2016.8	配光盘
978-7-114-13444-9	汽车发动机原理（第四版）	张志沛	38.00	2017.04	有
978-7-114-11616-2	汽车运用工程（第五版）	许洪国	39.00	2016.7	有

2. "十一五"普通高等教育本科国家级规划教材

书号	书名	作者	定价	出版时间	课件
978-7-114-09527-6	汽车排放及控制技术（第二版）	龚金科	28.00	2016.7	有
978-7-114-09749-2	汽车检测技术与设备（第三版）	方锡邦	25.00	2015.4	有
978-7-114-09545-0	汽车电子控制技术（第二版）	冯崇毅、鲁植雄、何丹娅	35.00	2016.7	有
978-7-114-11612-4	汽车理论（第二版）	吴光强	46.00	2014.8	有
978-7-114-10652-1	汽车设计（第二版）	过学迅、黄妙华、邓亚东	38.00	2013.9	有
978-7-114-09994-6	汽车制造工艺学（第三版）	韩英淳	38.00	2016.2	有
978-7-114-11157-0	汽车振动与噪声控制（第二版）	陈南	28.00	2015.7	有
978-7-114-05467-9	汽车节能技术	陈礼璠、杜爱民、陈明	19.00	2013.8	
978-7-114-09884-0	专用汽车设计（第二版）	冯晋祥	42.00	2013.7	有
978-7-114-07419-6	汽车营销学	张国方	41.00	2016.7	
978-7-114-11522-6	汽车发动机原理（第二版）	颜伏伍	42.00	2014.9	有
978-7-114-11672-8	汽车事故工程（第三版）	许洪国	36.00	2015.11	
978-7-114-10630-9	汽车再生工程（第二版）	储江伟	35.00	2013.8	有
978-7-114-13643-6	汽车电子控制技术（第四版）	舒华	48.00	2017.3	有
978-7-114-09561-0	汽车运行材料（第二版）	孙凤英	16.00	2016.5	有
978-7-114-06226-1	专用汽车设计	冯晋祥	36.00	2010.12	
978-7-114-07875-0	汽车理论	许洪国	20.00	2009.8	
978-7-114-06742-6	汽车排放与噪声控制（第二版）	李岳林	28.00	2017.4	有
978-7-114-06651-1	汽车运行材料	孙凤英	15.00	2011.7	

3. 应用技术型高校汽车类专业规划教材

书号	书名	作者	定价	出版时间	课件
978-7-114-13075-5	汽车构造·上册（第二版）	陈德阳、王林超	33.00	2016.08	有
978-7-114-13314-5	汽车构造·下册（第二版）	王林超、陈德阳	45.00	2016.12	有
978-7-114-11412-0	汽车液压与气压传动	柳波	38.00	2014.07	有
978-7-114-11411-3	汽车营销	谢金法、赵伟	35.00	2014.07	有
978-7-114-12846-2	汽车电器设备	吴刚	39.00	2016.04	有
978-7-114-11281-2	汽车电气设备	王慧君、于明进	32.00	2015.07	有
978-7-114-11280-5	发动机原理	訾琨、邓宝清	40.00	2014.07	有
978-7-114-11279-9	汽车维修工程	徐立友	43.00	2014.07	有
978-7-114-11508-0	汽车电子控制技术	吴刚	45.00	2014.08	有
978-7-114-13147-9	汽车试验技术	门玉琢	33.00	2016.08	有
978-7-114-11446-5	汽车试验学	付百学、慈勤蓬	35.00	2014.07	有
978-7-114-11710-7	汽车评估	李耀平	29.00	2014.10	有
978-7-114-11874-6	汽车专业英语	周靖	22.00	2015.03	有
978-7-114-11904-0	新能源汽车	徐斌	29.00	2015.03	有
978-7-114-11677-3	汽车制造工艺学	石美玉	39.00	2014.10	有
978-7-114-11707-7	汽车CAD/CAM	王良模、杨敏	45.00	2014.10	有
978-7-114-11693-3	汽车服务工程导论	王林超	25.00	2016.05	
978-7-114-11897-5	汽车保险与理赔	谭金会	29.00	2015.01	有
978-7-114-11905-7	汽车诊断与检测技术（第四版）	张建俊	45.00	2016.05	有

咨询电话：010-85285253；010-85285977. 咨询QQ：64612535；99735898